# The Catholic Ethic
# in American Society

John E. Tropman

Foreword by
Rembert G. Weakland, O.S.B.
Archbishop of Milwaukee

# The Catholic Ethic in American Society

**An Exploration of Values**

Jossey-Bass Publishers · San Francisco

Substantial discounts on bulk quantities of Jossey-Bass books are available to corporations, professional associations, and other organizations. For details and discount information, contact the special sales department at Jossey-Bass Inc., Publishers. (415) 433-1740; Fax (800) 605-2665.

For sales outside the United States, please contact your local Paramount Publishing International Office.

**TCF** Manufactured in the United States of America on Lyons Falls Pathfinder Tradebook. This paper is acid-free and 100 percent totally chlorine-free.

The passages in Chapter Seven on the social encyclicals from Gerhard J. Schwab's unpublished manuscript (1991) are reprinted with permission.

Gregory Baum's unpublished commentary on the issue of theology and sharing quoted in Chapter Seven is reprinted with permission.

The quotation on Catholic Charities USA in Chapter Six is from a personal letter to the author from the Reverend Thomas J. Harvey. It is reprinted with permission.

**Library of Congress Cataloging-in-Publication Data**

Tropman, John E.
  The Catholic ethic in American society : an exploration of values / John E. Tropman. — 1st ed.
    p.    cm. — (The Jossey-Bass nonprofit sector series)
  Includes bibliographical references and index.
  ISBN 0-7879-0123-7
  1. Catholics—United States—Attitudes.  2. Values—United States.
3. Sociology, Christian (Catholic)—United States.  4. United
States—Church history—20th century.  5. Catholic ethic.
I. Title.  II. Series.
BX1406.2.T765    1995
241'.04273—dc20                                                    95-12644
                                                                   CIP

*HB Printing*    10 9 8 7 6 5 4 3 2 1                    FIRST EDITION

# Contents

# Foreword

Ever since Max Weber, at the beginning of this century, published his influential book *The Protestant Ethic and the Spirit of Capitalism*, the question has arisen whether there is also a distinctive Catholic ethic and how it relates to capitalism. Many have seen the importance of this question, especially in seeking a historical explanation for the differences between the manifestations of capitalism in the northern part of this continent and those in Latin America. It has often been repeated that the Protestant ethic dominated here and the Catholic ethic there, this latter ethic prohibiting capitalism from flourishing there as it should have.

Somehow, however, no one has taken the time to explain what the differences are between these two ethics, to describe them more accurately, at least in their most extreme positions. In particular, no one has tried to explain the Catholic ethic, its sources, and its origin.

Professor Tropman rightly says there is indeed a Catholic ethic and then goes on to show how it can be described and what its origins are, seeking its roots in the whole of the Catholic tradition. Although he prudently gives many cautions to avoid exaggerations and wants to make it clear that neither ethic is found in its pure and unaltered state, he works out in detail what that Catholic ethic is all about. The final result is convincing. He has put into words what so many of us feel instinctively.

For this reason, this study is a pioneer one and most useful.

From the beginning, Catholicism was ill at ease with the capitalist agenda and many of its categories. In Catholic ethical thinking, the term *self-interest* has always been found to be troubling. Self-interest cannot stand alone in Catholic thought. It cannot be dissociated from love of God and love of neighbor. In fact, love of neighbor becomes the criterion for love of God. In this perspective, cooperation becomes as strong a motive as competition. Professor Tropman uses the term *sharing* to express that Catholic nuance.

In Catholic social teaching, these concepts have found expression in the use of terms that were not common to the capitalist theoreticians. So, for example, the bishops of the United States in their pastoral letter *Economic Justice for All*,\* in their search for new terms, seemed to have a preference for the word *participation*. That concept marks the whole economic vision of the bishops. They characterized any economy that fulfills the Catholic ethic as one in which all can participate. Participation becomes a key concept for judging any economy. This concept is similar to Professor Tropman's use of *sharing*.

The bishops were so captivated by that concept of participation that they wrote a separate chapter to spell it out even more clearly. That chapter was entitled "A New American Experiment: Partnership for the Public Good." Just the listing of the subtitles in that chapter shows the thrust that Professor Tropman has rightly called the Catholic ethic: A. Cooperation Within Firms and Industries; B. Local and Regional Cooperation; C. Partnership in the Development of National Policies; and D. Cooperation at the International Level. The following passage from that chapter shows the depth at which this ethic was working in the minds of Catholic bishops in 1986:

> Completing the unfinished business of the American experiment will call for new forms of cooperation and partnership among those whose daily work is the source of the prosperity and justice of the nation.

---

\*For one source of complete text of Economic Justice for All (the Bishops' Letter), see Gannon, 1987.

*Two different errors*
*a) ~~an that proctor~~ make "ethic" too strongly*
*determinateness — i.e. if you hold CE you will*
*of Effect                cooperate.*
*b) make ethic only source of an effect*  *emphasize*

The United States prides itself on both its competitive sense of initiative and its spirit of teamwork. Today a greater spirit of partnership and teamwork is needed; competition alone will not do the job. . . . Only a renewed commitment by all to the common good can deal creatively with the realities of international interdependence and economic dislocations in the domestic economy. The virtues of good citizenship require a lively sense of participation in the commonwealth and of having obligations as well as rights within it [¶296].

*BS*   Such a view could only come out of those steeped in the Catholic ethic!

Pope John Paul II has preferred to use the word *solidarity* to express this same ethic. It was not by chance that the word became so popular in Poland in the last decades, as it has a long and venerable history in the Catholic tradition. The following commentary from Pope John Paul II sums up the Catholic ethic: "Solidarity helps us to see the 'other'—whether a person, people or nation—not just as some kind of instrument, with a work capacity and physical strength to be exploited at low cost and then discarded when no longer useful, but as our 'neighbor,' a 'helper' (cf. Gen. 2:18–20), to be made a sharer, on par with ourselves, in the banquet of life to which all are equally invited by God" (*On Social Concern (Sollicitudo rei socialis)*, 1987, ¶39).

This Catholic ethic is also the reason why there is so much talk in official Catholic documents of the common good. Searching for that common good is another manifestation of the Catholic ethic.

As Catholics take a more active role in U.S. society, Professor Tropman's book will be a help to our understanding of where that Catholic tradition is coming from. No one Catholic will embody that ethic perfectly, but it will continue to color how the question is discussed by Catholics who have absorbed, even if unconsciously, the Catholic tradition.

The book will also be of help to Catholics seeking to understand better what their own tradition is all about. It is helpful to have that tradition in this area of social ethics so well articulated and described. It will not be a problem for them that the label "Catholic" is dropped in an attempt to give objectivity to the book's contents.

How the future of that ethic will develop, especially in its relationship to the Protestant ethic pointed out by Weber, as the world moves into an interdependent and global economy and—perforce—culture, remains to be seen. It is helpful to have it so ably described now since it remains a valid, alternative way of looking at human relations as the global culture continues to emerge.

*July 1995*                           Rembert G. Weakland, O.S.B.
                                      *Archbishop of Milwaukee, Wisconsin*

# Preface

*The Catholic Ethic in American Society* deals with a number of inter-related ideas. To begin with, I argue simply that there is a Catholic ethic, a parallel to the more famous Protestant ethic. The fact of its existence may seem obvious, but it is only recently that a Catholic ethic has been acknowledged and then articulated in some depth by those studying our society (Tropman, 1986; Novak, 1993). I also identify the core values specific to each ethic. Broadly speaking, the Protestant ethic is oriented heavily to work, wealth, and achievement (Weber, [1904–1905] 1956), while the Catholic ethic is oriented to sharing.

The primary conclusion that arises from an examination of these core values is that people find it easier to provide help to others—and especially to the poor and the disadvantaged—from within the Catholic ethic, where providing help to the poor is part of the larger ethos of sharing. The Protestant ethic, with its emphasis on work, achievement, and self-reliance, makes offers of help fraught with worry and hesitancy. The poor, especially, become problematic, pushing those who would assist them to distinguish between the worthy and the unworthy poor as an essential step in the helping activity.

However, the Protestant ethic and Catholic ethic are not completely separated from each other by their core values. Instead, they exist in a dynamic tension with each other. Not only do they *abut* one another, but elements of each exist *inside* the other. The dominant and subdominant relationships in each, however, are reversed. So, on the one hand, Protestant ethic values do support concern for others, but that concern is subdominant to the core value of work, wealth, and achievement. While on the other hand, Catholic ethic values do support achievement, but that support is subdominant to the core value of sharing. As a result, there is not only tension *between* the Catholic ethic and the Protestant ethic but *within* each ethic as well.

Nowhere is this intermixing more clear than in the "conservative" response to *Economic Justice for All,* the Catholic bishops' 1986 pastoral letter to U.S. Catholics (Gannon, 1987). The contents of this letter were drawn largely from the broad Catholic ethic tradition. However, a number of those in its intended audience felt that it insufficiently recognized other and, for them, American, principles, such as liberty and individual responsibility and the importance of political "rights" before economic "rights" (Finn, 1990; Simon and Novak, 1990; Novak, 1993). The conservatives believe that their view draws on the same Catholic ethic as the letter, that the issue is one of interpretation. However, another way to see their reaction is that the ethic itself is variegated, containing ideas that are more often associated with the Protestant than the Catholic ethic.

Although the ethics are complex and overlap to some extent, they are not to be confused with each other. They are essentially different, and those differences are my focus. Therefore, I explore how the two religious traditions think about salvation—its availability and the ease of our access to it—because it is possible that our ideas about the supply of *salvation resources,* about heaven as a Garden of Eden or an exclusive club, may model our views of earthly resources as plentiful or scarce.

Finally, I generalize the Protestant and Catholic ethics beyond their religious linkages and expressions into their core, or deep structure, value systems, which I call the Alpha and Omega orientations. And I suggest that each of us could rely on some of each value system, a notion at odds with the tradition of religious exclusivity. In many ways, a person may actually be a little Catholic and a little Protestant.

When we think about an *ethic* as a core set of religiously derived ideas (whether drawn from the Protestant, Catholic, or any other religious view), it must be distinguished from religious theologies, practices, and people. Throughout, I have emphasized the perspective that the Catholic ethic, like the Protestant ethic, is an ideal type, an archetype. The varieties of Protestant and Catholic doctrine, their historical evolution, and actual church teachings are issues here only insofar as they show us the roots of our ethics. My object is not to define and label doctrines and teachings. It is to explore their *consequences* as they have shaped our society and our culture.

Individuals' values and actions also need to be seen in this context. There are few "pure" Protestant ethic Protestants and "pure" Catholic ethic Catholics. We are all a mixture, and one of my aims in this book is to show how such a mixture is possible. To take the most general view of this phenomenon, one would never expect any set of beliefs to be so complete, so full of upsides and so lacking in downsides, that there would be no need for any kind of balancing or alternative emphases, whatever their source. Each and every action has a compensating reaction. Each thesis spawns an antithesis. (They eventually come together in a synthesis. Then, in time, the synthesis becomes a fresh thesis, and so on.) Value systems are thus structured in juxtaposed sets.

For years, sociologists have picked up on the duality or competitive nature of belief systems and operating codes. (I have pulled together a lot of the thinking in this area in my book *American Values and Social Welfare*, 1989.) For just a few instances, think of Émile Durkheim's view (1960a) that *mechanical solidarity* competes with *organic solidarity* as a method of group bonding; Ferdinand Tönnies' contrast ([1887] 1957) of *gemeinschaft* values (small community attachments) and *gesellschaft* values (society-citizen attachments);

Talcott Parsons's ideas (Parsons and Bales, 1955) about "pattern variables" as *instrumental* and *expressive* orientations; Seymour Martin Lipset's concept (1963) that views of *achievement* and *equality* form competing value sets; and Kai Erikson's analysis (1976) of the competing values that made assistance to Appalachian Mountain dwellers so difficult in the wake of a flood. Psychologists, too, have long seen competing values in individuals. The psychologist Erik Erikson's list of life conflicts (1950) is a case in point, as are Milton Rokeach's ideas (1968) about the psychological dualism surrounding the values of freedom and equality. Some approaches to organizational and business analysis are also based on human dualism. For example, Robert Quinn (1989) has developed a competing values theory of leadership.

In short, the idea of values competition is a productive tool in social science. The fact that it has not been applied to religion (except in the sense of seeing the sacred opposed to the secular, or, more historically, God opposed to the devil and good opposed to evil) suggests that it is the way we think about religion that is the inhibiting agent, not the theoretical approach itself.

In sum, *The Catholic Ethic in American Society* is an exploration into the development of ideas, their possible antecedents, structure, and consequences, and their likely connections to other ideas. It is not intended to "prove" the existence of the Catholic ethic or to be a history of what Catholics or Protestants uniformly think, or a religious history, or a theological study. The References, of course, contain only works actually cited in this book; however, the Suggested Readings list additional materials for those who wish to pursue the ideas further. In addition, I have used a number of popular and contemporary sources with the intention of showing how widespread and current the ideas embedded in Protestant and Catholic ethics are.

## Audience

This book is intended for those who have an interest in the effect of religious views on our nation's social and political culture, those who are trying to help the poor and disadvantaged in our society and who must deal with the values that govern others' willingness to offer assistance, and all those who are seekers after understanding in the field of human beliefs and behavior. After all, if we wish to do "the right thing" by all in our society, we must first understand why people define the right thing as variously as they do. It is becoming clear that religiously based values are a strong influence on our social thought. We can no longer ignore them.

## Acknowledgments

Books are collective products. I want to recognize the influences of those who helped me think through this idea.

First, of course, there is my family. My wife, Penny, went over the ideas and the text many times, and each discussion with her brought new insights, each reading new improvements. Our children, Sarah, Jessica, and Matthew, also provided insights and material that appear throughout the book. My parents, Elmer and Elizabeth Tropman, made helpful comments along the way. My father, in particular, took a deep interest in the project, commenting on many drafts, and it is a source of great sadness that he died before he could see the book come to fruition.

Other influences also were important. Five professors at Oberlin College in the early 1960s made a big difference to me. Bernard Silberman, professor of history, first introduced me to Max Weber and to ideas concerning the flow of history. Joseph Elder, professor of sociology, stimulated my interest in religion as culture, an interest that has remained to this day. Milton Yinger's work in religion inspired me, especially as I developed an early project of researching first-year students' religious preferences. The late Robert Holbrook, professor of religion, accelerated my interest in religion. And finally, the late Aaron Wildavsky, professor of government, honed my appetite for the policy development and crafting process, especially in regard to policies surrounding the disadvantaged.

The work of professors at the University of Chicago, especially that of Edward Shils, Morris Janowitz, and Alan Wade, supported my interest in a new cultural way of looking at things.

My colleagues at the University of Michigan, especially Jesse Gordon and Armand Lauffer, have been immensely helpful. Henry J. Meyer claims to remain unconvinced about the Catholic ethic concept, and addressing his concerns was always a challenge. James Davidson of Purdue University was also helpful at every stage, responding to and challenging my ideas throughout. Gerhard Schwab, who is completing his doctorate at the University of Michigan, and Gregory Baum of McGill University each made important contributions as well. Reverend Tom Harvey, former CEO of Catholic Charities USA, also read and commented on many sections. Schwab, Baum, and Harvey also contributed written material, portions of which appear in this book.

Two other individuals were immensely helpful. The first I have met; the second I have not. Robert Wuthnow, of Princeton University, read an early draft of these ideas and commented most helpfully, and we have had several occasions to talk about the Catholic ethic concept. Beyond that, Wuthnow's work is a constant source of thought. The other individual is Andrew Greeley, whose work is immensely interesting and thoughtful. His exploration of Catholics and Catholicism has been an important stimulus as I developed the concept of the Catholic ethic.

An idea needs resources to develop. For these, I express appreciation to the Lilly Endowment and to Jean Knoerle and her colleagues at the endowment, who could see merit in the idea of a Catholic ethic and who provided the essential support that allowed me to devote time to researching, thinking, and writing.

An idea is one thing; a book is another. I was fortunate to have one of the most supportive and thoughtful editors I have ever worked with—Alan Shrader of Jossey-Bass. Alan was more than an editor; he was an intellectual colleague. In the best spirit of colleagueship, he offered detailed reactions, thoughts, and observations, but never insisted on his way. Alan believed in the project, invested in it, and deserves a deep expression of appreciation and thanks. I should also mention my copyeditor, Elspeth MacHattie, who helped me to hone the argument and avoid pitfalls. Her work improved the book hugely.

Finally, there were the technical elements of producing the manuscript. This book simply would not exist without Dan Madaj. A writer himself, he seamlessly handled the many drafts, the countless reorganizations, the dozens of computer glitches. His flair for the proper expression, the right touch, helped everywhere.

*July 1995*                                                    John E. Tropman
                                                              *Glen Arbor, Michigan*

# The Author

John E. Tropman is a professor of social policy and nonprofit management at the School of Social Work at the University of Michigan. He is head of the Catholic Ethic Project and the Meeting Masters Research Project and also teaches in the Organizational Behavior and Human Resources Management Program of the Michigan Business School. He earned his A.B. degree (1961) in sociology at Oberlin College, his A.M. degree (1963) in social service administration at the University of Chicago, and his Ph.D. degree (1967) in social work and sociology at the University of Michigan.

Tropman's research has focused on values: conflict between values and the translation of values into policy and action. The Catholic Ethic Project, supported by the Lilly Endowment, is an outgrowth of his work in value conflicts, first discussed in his book *American Values and Social Welfare* (1989). He also explores how individuals and, especially, groups of people make decisions when conflicting values are involved. Meeting Masters Research Project, funded in part by the 3M Meeting Management Institute, explores this and other decision-making questions.

# The Catholic Ethic
# in American Society

*Introduction*

# Conflicting Values
# in American Society

American society has always reached out to help others. Communal barn raising and mutual assistance in rural communities have become legendary. Town neighbors have always been ready to lend "a cup of sugar" if you were a bit low. The tendency for neighbor to help neighbor in the daily tasks of living is a historical part of the American experience.

We also help those in serious need. Generous foreign aid is one case in point. And though the United States moved into the welfare state era (providing the use of state power and state resources to those in need) later than other developed countries, for all practical purposes, it now is a welfare state in that it makes substantial public expenditures at federal and state levels for programs like social security, unemployment compensation, and child welfare.

Much help is also provided through private charity. Billions are given in voluntary contributions for those in need—an average of $649 for each of our 93.5 million households in 1991 (Hodgkinson and Weitzman, 1992, p. 1). Nor do gifts of money tell the whole story. Millions of Americans devote untold hours in volunteer work—20.5 billion hours in 1991 (Hodgkinson and Weitzman, 1992, p. 1). For example, in a program called Choice, "recent college graduates work . . . 70-hour weeks for a year for a pittance." They are assigned a small number of juvenile delinquents, the "cream of the crap," and seek to help them (Klein, 1994b, p. 28).

## Self-Help

But there is another, careful side to our society's generosity. "Help" often is first thought of as "self-help." Americans have the urge to assist, but they have a hesitancy about assistance as well. Part of the American character celebrates "Yankee ingenuity," doing it yourself and being self-reliant. You can dip into the community pot too often, it seems. As Vidich and Bensman point out in *Small Town in Mass Society* (1968), when neighbors provided that cup of sugar, *they remembered it and had an expectation that the borrower would repay it.* The help was not a gift but a loan.

Moreover, as open as the United States is overall, in smaller groups, its citizens have favored exclusion rather than inclusion of "others." The recent development of the PLUs (*people like us*) group is not new but rather represents an extension of the historical American approaches of isolationism and nativism. "People like us" depicts those who select residences in tight enclave communities, usually with a guard at the community entrance. Communities ("plantations") on Hilton Head Island, South Carolina, for example, have been this way for many years. The guards are a formal and public expression of a deeper set of policies, practices, and values designed to keep people of similar social and ethnic status within an enclave.

Sometimes the enclave concept gets pushed right into the home. Faith Popcorn (1991) talks about modern *cocooning*, a withdrawal into one's own house with everything one needs to do organized around that dwelling: one shops by phone, has food delivered, goes to the movies by watching videos, and so on. Cocooning is "the impulse to get *inside* when everything *outside* gets too scary" (p. 27).

This withdrawal into family or self can be associated with a desire for personal ownership, often quite independent of "need." Attitudes abound that express the sense of "It's mine! You can't have it, even if I don't need it or can't use it." Everyone has "my" snowblower, "my" lawn mower, and "my" car (or, more likely, cars).

This focus on ourselves and what is ours leads to a diminished focus on others and on assisting them in meeting their needs. In today's world, we see many examples of social concern for those in need, but we also see examples of self-absorption, of a narcissism that seems to define the current population as a "me" generation as opposed to an "us" generation.

## Suspicion of the Poor

Ambivalence about helping often shifts to suspicion when those Americans called the "poor," the "underclass," the "needy," and the "homeless" are discussed. On the one hand, Americans want to help out. On the other hand, they ask whether the needy person is worthy of help. Adding to their concern is their uncertainty about the process of helping itself. Too much help, they often feel, may sap the recipient's independence and ability to do things for herself or himself.

This concern is often heavily involved with moral disparagement of the poor. People in need are frequently referred to as "them," a fact Joyce Carol Oates acknowledged when she called her novel about the Detroit poor *Them* (1969). "Them," of course, implies an "us," and it is only a half a step or less from "them" and "us" to "we're okay" and "they're not okay" (compare Katz's study of "the undeserving poor," 1989).

When we do help out, we often do so with skepticism and concern about why the recipients are so needy and what they might do with the resources provided. We continue to suspect what Rauschenbusch thought in 1907: "To accept charity is at first one of the most bitter experiences of the self-respecting workingman. Some abandon families, go insane, or commit suicide rather than surrender the virginity of their independence. But when they have once learned to depend on gifts, the parasitic habit of mind grows upon them, and it becomes hard to wake them back to self-support" (p. 238).

We have a sense that the needy will "rip us off." Here is a common example of the attitudes in the daily press and elsewhere. A 1992 column in the *Detroit News* was headlined: "City Merchants' Anti-Panhandling Campaign Raises an Issue of Morality," In that column, Kate DeSmet wrote:

> The Central Business District Association recently handed out 1,200 flyers in Detroit asking people to stop giving money to panhandlers. "Avoid supporting what in most cases is an alcoholic and destructive lifestyle," the posters say. "You need not feel guilty when saying no." Many business owners applauded, but others question the morality of such a move. In a conversation overheard among several Metro Detroit businessmen, one said, "You know, it's never bothered me to give money to someone who walks up to me on the street. If it's because he wants to go and get drunk, I figure that's his problem, but if the guy is hungry and I don't give him anything, then that's what bothers me" [p. 3B].

In Berkeley, California, merchants tried a different tack. They gave out chits you could carry around in your pocket. If you felt like giving to a street person, you could give a chit, redeemable only for food and essential items. This approach seemed to solve a problem for those who wanted to be helpful but were doubtful about the uses to which cash might be put.

For people in the helping professions, experiencing hostile attitudes toward the disadvantaged are a common part of everyday work life. Indeed, many helping professions practitioners feel that the problematic status of those they help somehow rubs off on them. It may be overstating the case to say that Americans *dislike* the poor—but not by a great deal.

Linda Gordon has observed that racism and sexism have played a part in making welfare a "dirty word." And she is surely correct. However, she also says that "no one likes welfare," and she points out that "the poorer and more maligned welfare recipients are, the more difficult it is for them to build political support for improving welfare" (1994, p. B1). Her observations imply that Americans do not like the poor *whoever* they are. Indeed, dislike of the poor antedates what we call welfare today (Aid to Families with Dependent Children, a program of the Social Security Act). While the American people do not withhold basic material support for those in need, we do withhold approval, sympathy, empathy, and understanding.

## Conflicting Values

How do we account for conflicting attitudes and actions about providing help to others? And what explains our lurking or open negative orientation to helping the most disadvantaged, the poor. We are clearly looking at what a social scientist would call "the dependent variable." On what does it depend and why does it vary?

In this book, I suggest that it depends on *values*, and *religious values* in particular. I make the argument that much of the way we think about the poor and our attitudes toward the poor are driven by our value systems and that understanding these value systems helps us understand better why we think what we think and why we do what we do.

Our values conflict with each other, however. On the one hand, we seek to be compassionate; on the other hand, we encourage people to "stand on their own two feet." On the one hand, we seek to help those who have been injured and need assistance. On the other hand, we applaud the blind making and selling brooms and support the Association of Foot and Mouth Artists (which encourages disabled artists to master painting with a brush held with the toes or in the mouth.) How did we acquire these competing values?

### The Protestant Ethic

Many important values of U.S. society seem embodied in the Protestant ethic. It has been a capturing vision, and most of the attention and thinking devoted to it has emphasized its upside—its support of work, especially hard work, achievement and getting ahead, and a healthy self-reliance. But it is reasonable to think that it must have a downside as well. An ethic that emphasizes achievements in work and status may well have both direct and indirect implications for the way we think about those who are poor in achievement and even for the way we define "the poor." Exploring the Protestant ethic and its implications for helping behavior is one part of this book, and the hypothesis I present is this: the Protestant ethic is based on valuing work, money, individualism, and self-reliance, and it celebrates these values as indicators of their owners' sacred status. On the upward slope, these values support individual attainment and the importance of the individual person. Helping others is important but should be mixed with self-help and be occasional. It is best if it occurs, like the borrowed cup of sugar, within a framework of exchange. On the downward slope, the Protestant ethic raises explicit and implicit questions about those who are not working, have no or little money, and are "dependent" on others. It is from this "dark side" of the Protestant ethic that hostility toward and suspicion of the poor derives. An ethic that is based on "getting ahead" has trouble with those who "fall behind." They seem to fall into a morally unfavorable category.

## The Catholic Ethic

Over the years, the values of the Protestant ethic have stood alone in discussions of U.S. values. There are other religions and therefore must be other religion-based ethics, but exploring the Catholic ethic, the Jewish ethic, the Muslim ethic, and so on, has not been a priority for social analysts. In this book, I explore the Catholic ethic, showing how it differs from the Protestant ethic and probing the ways in which both ethics affect our views of helping in general and providing aid to the disadvantaged in particular.

Ambivalence, worry, and negativity about helping and about

those helped are not the only attitudes we can take. Other outlooks exist in which help is simply part of human exchange. In
such a view, little difference exists between "them" and "us." Material poverty is a temporary condition rather than a proxy for inner,
even spiritual, failure. It is even possible to see poverty as a desirable, spiritually enhancing condition. The Catholic ethic contains
these views.

Like the Protestant ethic, the Catholic ethic has attitudes
toward work, money, and the nature of the human individual, but
they tend to reverse the Protestant ethic attitudes. The Catholic
ethic is suspicious of those who have much and supportive of those
who have little. It is more willing to provide for those who have
needs. It is interested in why problems occur, but it is first and foremost interested in ameliorating need and eschews distinguishing
between the worthy and the unworthy poor.

My purpose here is to articulate this Catholic ethic and demonstrate that the value of *sharing* is one of its core elements, that it
supports interdependence and communalistic orientations, and that
it views work and money simply as tools through which the needs
of life are met.

I have chosen the word *sharing* with considerable care. Its pre-
cise meaning as a central element in the Catholic ethic is important. Sharing is not exactly the same as an attitude of helping and
supporting the disadvantaged and of being pro-poor. That attitude
tends to focus only on those at the bottom of the status/financial
ladder, whereas the Catholic ethic focuses on all those who might
be in need of assistance of some sort or other. Sharing is not exactly
the same as welfarism or the welfare state. In the Catholic ethic,
the welfare state is only one of a number of means; it is not an end
in itself. Sharing is not exactly the same as charity. Charity puts the
focus on the method, not the recipient. Moreover, especially in this
country, it suggests private sector as opposed to governmental mechanism) and, even worse, has a bit of an unctuous turn to it. Givers
seem to be saying, "These resources really are mine. I've earned

them. I'll let you have some of them, out of my surplus. But I expect gratitude and appreciation in return." The receivers in this asymmetrical relationship are in the "one down" position. Perhaps that is why those in need may say, "I don't want to accept charity." Or why President Bush once remarked that the United States did not want to give other countries "charity." Recipients of charity are viewed as somehow diminished by receiving it, a diminishment both they and the giver may feel.

What *sharing* means is not only the willingness to help others but the obligation to do so. It conveys a sense of equality between sharers. As a culture of sharing, the Catholic ethic contains a sense that sharing is part of a natural and expected exchange. That natural obligation to share is as central to the Catholic ethic as achievement and work are to the Protestant ethic.

As a value system that supports sharing thoughts and actions, the Catholic ethic takes a sympathetic, helpful, and understanding position toward the human condition. It expects that individuals will progress toward a state of grace, even if that progress is halting at times—two steps forward, one step back. The Catholic ethic does not separate the affluent and the financially deprived. Since it does not support the belief that having money and property make you a better person, not having these things will not make you a worse person. When you need help, it does not ask if you are worthy of assistance; it just helps you out. *gimme a break*

## The Structure of Value Systems

In this book, I have viewed the Protestant ethic and the Catholic ethic as ideal-typical constructs, pure types (or ideal types, as Weber would have called them), an approach that allows us to look carefully at each, contrast them, and explore their properties. Of course, as types, they do not predict individual behavior. A simple comparison is a recipe on the printed page. It is an ideal-typical rendering of a dish. If it is for spaghetti, you will not wind up with fried eggs, but each individual instance of the prepared dish will vary, sometimes resembling the recipe closely and sometimes not so closely. Similarly, Protestant and Catholic individuals will vary around the central tendencies of each ethic a great deal while still feeling its influence. We would not find all Protestants responding in one direction to a questionnaire about attitudes toward poverty nor all Catholics responding in the other direction, but we would find different tendencies and patterns for each group.

We often define ideal types in pairs, as opposites of each other. The "ideal" male and the "quintessential" female often are presented as polar opposites. But sociological thinking today suggests that rather than inhabiting opposite ends of a scale as antitheses, ideal types are better seen as juxtaposed to each other. They are more usefully thought of as standing at right angles rather than opposite ends. Thus, if one had a Protestant ethic scale (there are some; Heaven, 1980, for example) and a Catholic ethic scale (there are none, as yet), one could score individuals from 0 to 9 on each scale. While the "purer" individuals would be high on one scale and low on the other, others would be low on both, and yet others high on both.

The latter two results are possible because the ethics are not either/or propositions. Each has a prominent perspective on certain dimensions (work and money, for example). These perspectives differ, so in that sense, each ethic has a dominant orientation. But at the same time, some ideas dominant in the Protestant ethic are subdominant in the Catholic ethic and vice versa. Moreover, some Protestant denominations, for example, the Quakers, the Mormons, the Salvation Army, and the social gospel movement, make prominent what is typically subdominant in Protestantism. And not only are there different manifestations, or crystallizations, of the Protestant ethic, but different policies and practices result. Therefore, individual Protestant policies and practices are related to, but not identical to, the archetypal Protestant ethic.

The structural idea of juxtaposition makes sense in discussing many concept pairs, because the sharpness of difference is reduced but a tension remains (see Tropman, 1989). Compare the relationship of two other current cultures in our society: the culture of competition and the culture of cooperation. Rarely does anyone completely ignore one of these cultures; so in practice, neither culture is completely devoid of the other emphasis. The culture of cooperation has competition in it, though in a subdominant mode; the culture of competition has cooperation in it, though in a subdominant mode. The fact that the value systems I discuss are religiously linked does not make them different on the practical level from such cultural, social, or nonreligious value systems. It will be important to keep this web of relationships in mind as we look at the two ethics, remembering that their differences are abutting, not opposite, and that what is dominant for one might well be subdominant for the other.

As I shall argue, when we take away the religious buttresses from certain ways of thinking, it is easier to see that most of us hold competing values, which we apply at different times under different conditions. It sounds strange to us to say that we could be both Catholic and Protestant, but it is possible for us to hold both Protestant and Catholic values and, later investigations may show, Jewish and Muslim values, too.

When we find ourselves asking new questions, it frequently means that old answers do not suffice. For a long time, the discourse about the importance of "getting ahead" in U.S. society used a Protestant ethic text. We have talked about those who do not get ahead, those who "fall from grace" and experience downward mobility over the course of their lives or between generations largely through this same Protestant ethic rhetoric. It is important to explore the results of that way of talking and thinking and hence about the Protestant ethic itself. It is time for us to consider and possibly learn from alternatives that are already present in our society, if we choose to recognize them.

# Part One

---

# *The Protestant and Catholic Ethics in Context*

This book is an exploration. Part One begins the journey of discovery by examining the issue of religion as culture and the Protestant ethic in particular.

In Chapter One, I explore the idea that religion can be thought of as a basis for diversity, similar to other elements or characteristics on which diversity analysis is based. From the birth of our country, religious differences have been important; sects split off, and people argued and disagreed over doctrine, but the differences were seen as "religious" rather than "cultural" or "social." Cultural differences have seemed to go deeper: keeping races, ethnicities, and even North and South apart in ways that affected everyday life. Religious differences, though also an everyday fact of life, have seemed less basic.

Yet, I suggest, it is the Protestant ethic itself that has become the dominant ethic in the United States, even though there are other religions, other belief systems. One of these other ethics is the Catholic ethic.

Historically, the Catholic ethic is older. After all, Catholicism—

Christianity—was around for 1,500 years before the Protestant Reformation came on the scene. However, it is the Protestant ethic that has had our attention for many years. Therefore, I have chosen to summarize the Protestant ethic and its ambivalence toward the poor first, in Chapter Two, before moving on to the more detailed discussion of the Catholic ethic in Part Two.

*Chapter One*

# Religion as a Basis of Cultural Values

### The Protestant and Catholic Ethics

In the United States, we have many bases for both unity and difference. Common aspirations and hopes continue to be a magnet drawing people to American shores, in spite of our national problems and in spite of the difficulties many illegal immigrants and "boat people" encounter in getting here. In the marketplace of nations, the United States has long been the country of choice.

The very heterogeneity of our populace has perhaps led us to emphasize common themes and common properties rather than differences in our public discussions. But at the same time there *are* differences among us.

## Religious Difference: The Quiet Undercurrent

The Kerner Commission Report on the U.S. riots of the 1960s described our society as dividing into two societies, one black and one white. Other divisions have also been offered as important cleavages in the U.S. body politic: North versus South, East versus West, urban versus rural, men versus women, straights versus gays and lesbians, and of course, haves versus have-nots. Yet we have been, especially in the period from 1850 to 1990, relatively quiet about whether religious difference is as fundamental and important as race or class in shaping and defining our subcultures. While Jews have always been concerned about the fatefulness of religious and ethnic identification and have paid attention to the perils of anti-Semitism, and while escape from religious persecution brought many of this country's early settlers to its shores, religious differences have been secondary in our serious discussions. We are much more likely to talk about ethnic food, ethnic dress, and ethnic culture than religious food, religious dress, and religious culture.

Religion was once a recognized basis of divisions in U.S. society. In the early years of our country, religious differences were a source of great rancor. But they were essentially differences within Anglo, or "white," Protestantism. When large groups of Catholics and Jews began to flow into the country, emphasis on uniformity, rather than difference, became the norm. Most popular was the idea of America as a melting pot.

### The Melting Pot

The title of Israel Zangwill's play *The Melting Pot* (produced in 1915–1916) reflects what was then coming to be the ideal U.S. cultural script (though the reality was often the very opposite). All expectations and hopes were to be blended. Differences, in one of the coinages of former Vice President Spiro Agnew, were to be "blanded out." All immigrants were to jump into the pool, and all were to come out with the same culture and values. The media reflected this view. I recall, for example, a radio program called "Life with Luigi," about an Italian immigrant and his struggles to become "U.S." Language was presented as Luigi's greatest problem as he struggled with phrases like "Howza ita gon?" and tried to master pronunciation that would hide his background. Not only were accents smoothed and values homogenized, people's very names were Anglicized, simplified, and attenuated, thus disguising ethnic origin. "Mike" might once have been Mikhail, Michael, Mikola, or any of a number of ethnic originals.

But the single melting pot idea began to dissolve almost as quickly as it had begun. Perhaps the theme of unity had been a first response to the waves of immigrants or to the differences that surfaced so violently in the Civil War. Perhaps it had always been just talk and pretense. Whatever the reason for the idea of cultural homogenization in the first place, a new, tentative overall exploration of division and diversity in U.S. society had begun by the 1940s. Gunnar Myrdal completed his *An American Dilemma* in 1944, for example, pointing to and predicting the deep divisions that race embodied in America. He argued that the United States recognized but could not come to grips with the issue of race and that people of color were not part of the melting pot. The door was opening to discussions of diversity, and religious divisions began to be examined also. Ruby Jo Reeves Kennedy's classic work, *Single or Triple Melting Pot* (1944), pointed out that there were at least three melting points, one for each of the major religious groups—Catholic, Protestant, and Jewish. When it came to marriage, in particular, one stayed in one's own kettle, whatever differences there might be within it. Kennedy's article, written only thirty years after Zangwill's play, helped make religious differences once again a topic for public conversation. Now though, it was the three major religions in the United States that were the crux of the discussion, rather than differences among Protestant groups.

### Protestant, Catholic, Jew

Investigations of religious differences continued. Will Herberg's *Protestant, Catholic, Jew* was published in 1960, exploring differences and divisions as well as commonalities and constancies. (Herberg viewed himself as an exemplar of both the melding of perspectives and the retention of identity. I once heard him comment, "I am a Jewish scholar teaching Protestant theology at a Catholic school!") Researchers began to use public surveys to look seriously at religious differences. In the early 1960s, Gerhart Lenski (1963), a professor of sociology at the University of Michigan, used Detroit-area study data to call attention to differences between Catholics and Protestants. Expecting from his data that the

Catholic population would increase in the city of Detroit, he specifically predicted that "behavior patterns linked with the Catholic group are likely to become somewhat more prevalent while patterns linked with the white Protestant group become less common." Most importantly, he was able to pick out specific religiously linked cultural changes that he thought would occur:

1. Rising rates of church attendance in U.S. society

2. Strengthening of religious group communalism

3. Strengthening of both the nuclear and extended family systems

4. Declining emphasis on intellectual independence

5. Increasing support for welfare state policies

6. Increasing support for the Democratic Party

7. Shifting focus from work group to kin group

8. Slowing rate of material progress and perhaps also of scientific advance

9. Rising birth rates

10. Narrowing latitude for the exercise of the right of free speech

11. Increasing restraints on Sunday business, and divorce, and possibly birth control

12. Declining restraints on gambling and drinking [p. 361]

Lenski's overall conclusion was that his study "provided striking support for Weber's basic assumption—at least as it applies to major religious groups in contemporary [that is, 1963] U.S. society. As the findings . . . make clear, the four major socioreligious groups ['White Catholics,' 'Jews,' 'White Protestants,' 'Negro Protestants'] differ from one another with respect to a wide range of phenomena affecting economic, political, kinship, and scientific institutions. Furthermore, these differences cannot be accounted for in terms of the economic position of either the individuals involved or the groups" (p. 357). While not all of Lenski's expectations came to pass, what is important for our purposes is that Lenski did find attitudinal differences among religious groups.

In the late 1960s, sociologist Howard Schuman (1971), using the same Detroit-area study mechanism and methodology, replicated Lenski's analysis. Schuman was not able to find as many differences among religious groups (that is, not all of Lenski's ideas were supported), but he did find a few, and his most interesting conclusion, to us, was that "in particular, under a variety of controls, Protestants significantly more than Catholics rank as most important their attitude 'that work is important and gives a feeling of accomplishment'" (pp. 45–46).

In short, there are important cultural (as distinct from theological) differences between religions, and it is not likely that these differences are reducible to (or the product of) something other than religion, such as economic position.

Many studies of religion are limited in focus, looking as they do at a single period of time, but some have looked at effects of religious affiliation over time. Catholic priest, sociologist, and popular author Andrew Greeley (1977, 1990), concerned about the historical economic disadvantage felt by Catholics in the United States, has shown that today Catholics are as well educated and/or doing as well financially as Protestants. He sees Catholics as once excluded and disadvantaged but overcoming that position as time went on. (Glenn and Hyland, 1967, make the same point. See also Kosmin and Lachman, 1993.) These findings, too, suggest that cultural differences between Protestants and Catholics are not economically based. In addition, they show that people are now considering religion as an important dividing line in society, like race and gender. Religion is seen as a way to define people's specific orientation toward the world and what things they expect from it. It is seen as a cultural system that emphasizes alternative social and personal elements in relation to other religions.

## Defining Culture

A *culture* is a set of interrelated beliefs, norms, values, and attitudes that exist over time and that influence other beliefs, norms, values, and attitudes. Even though no simplistic connection between a culture and a specific set of behaviors can be drawn, a culture is relevant to behavior in that it provides guides for behavior. *too vague*

Early students of values, like Robin Williams (1960) and Milton Rokeach (1968, 1969a, 1969b), produced "lists" of values—dictionaries of sorts—that they felt people "used" or drew upon all the time. It seemed as if each value guided a specific set of actions. However, actions often did not follow values' dictates. When behavior differed from values, there was inconsistency and "dissonance."

It is certainly correct to say that no specific value is likely to guide us each and every time something happens. Different values pertain as situations differ. Different values demand our attention and create or construct different situations in which they might be used. But to say that in many decisions specific values are used and other values set aside does not mean that those set aside are not important. Values do make a difference—it is just that the relationship between values and action is more complex and multifaceted than most of us think. Specific surrounding conditions as well as values influence any action we might take. And of course, conflict occurs between values and behavior, producing the disparity between values and behaviors that social psychology often calls the attitude/behavior gap.

It now seems reasonable to think that there is a *grammar of values*. Not only do most of us have lots of values but they conflict with each other. Different, ever opposed, values may be available to us to guide and legitimize action. Deciding which value or values should govern which action in which instance and how much weight conflicting values should be given with respect to any particular action is a complex task for any individual or society, and numerous authors have dealt with such value conflicts (for a review, see Tropman, 1987, 1989).

The approach of seeing values in a structure of contention and conflict is a step forward in social psychology because it allows both scholars and the person on the street to more adequately explain and understand the complexity we know exists when we choose our actions. It also helps us understand that there may well be gaps between values and behavior because behavior might have to satisfy two or more values claiming jurisdiction in a particular case. And it is likely that value-behavior dissonance has two possible outcomes. Sometimes values will change to conform to behavior, and sometimes behavior will change to conform to values.

Consider the intricacy in this simple example: walking along a street, we find a fat wallet. The first thing that most of us would do is look around, furtively perhaps, to see if anyone saw us find it. We are assessing how much wiggle room we have as a part of our decision-making process about what to do with the wallet.

We pick up the wallet and look inside. It is stuffed with cash. Our heart leaps! But then what are we to do? What does our faith require? For the purposes of this example, we can say that if the stereotypes in an old joke are any guide, the Catholic will consult a priest, the Jew will consult tradition, and the Protestant will make up her or his own mind. But our religious values are not all we will consult. We will also look at the "facts" of the case to help us select which among many values should be operative. If the wallet has a note in it that says "drug dealer's money," we may be less inclined to return it than if there is a note that says "senior citizen's surgery money." Thus, aspects of the specific situation come into play and different values guide us (senior citizen's money versus drug dealer's money; who saw us and how much they saw).

Cultural systems are much more complex than this example, and thus the determinants of what we do are very complex. However, we do have *systems*; our specific values are likely to connect, to mesh in some way at some level even when they appear to represent different and perhaps conflicting ideas, as in the case of competition versus cooperation or adequacy of resources versus equity of resources. Although values can be in contention in a cultural system, they can also coexist. Religious systems, too, are cultural systems, with similar complexities of conflict and connection.

## Religion as Culture

There are many ways to look at religions, but seeing them as cultural systems is a particularly important approach. Some existing studies of religions as cultural systems are Max Weber's famous *The Protestant Ethic and the Spirit of Capitalism* ([1904–1905], 1956) and Herberg's *Protestant, Catholic, Jew* (1960). These works sought the value matrix within the deep structure of religion. Both Weber and Herberg's books achieved some level of intellectual success at a wider level than simply sociology of religion.

Andrew Greeley's *The Catholic Myth* (1990) also goes well beyond narrow parochial interests and introduces an idea, a Catholic worldview, that is a useful advance in scope and sophistication. It expands the view of religion from a narrow definition of beliefs and practices to a definition in which religious differences are essentially seen as cultural ones. This search for a larger scope for religion also underlies Michael Novak's *The Catholic Ethic and the Spirit of Capitalism* (1993).

It is important for us to acknowledge, as Greeley, Herberg, Novak, and Weber have, that an individual's beliefs, values, and cultural orientation are influenced and shaped by religion, even when the individual is not devoutly religious in the doctrinal or narrowly sectarian sense of the term. Religiously derived values thus influence both a religion's practitioners and its former believers, those who may have left the faith but are still touched by its core values. It is in this sense that one can speak of "cultural Jews" or "cultural Catholics."

To the extent that there are broader manifestations of religious values—like the Protestant ethic and, as I shall argue, the Catholic ethic—they extend beyond individuals to the country and society. And as the core ethos of a religion extends to become part of a nationwide culture, it affects believers and nonbelievers alike.

Baltzell (1979), for example, describes finding this cultural effect on a limited scale when he examined Puritan and Quaker cultures in specific geographical areas.

> Just as our whole post-Christian and secular world today is still living, as a kind of cultural rentier, on the spiritual and moral capital built up in the more religious periods of the Judeo-Christian tradition, so the citizens of modern Massachusetts and Pennsylvania, whether they are professing Jews, Catholics, Presbyterians, Episcopalians, or just plain agnostics or atheists, are still marked, to greater or lesser degrees, by the original ethics of Puritanism and Quakerism. There is, for instance, a great difference between the Puritan Catholicism of Boston and the much milder Quaker Catholicism of Philadelphia. If immigrants absorb some of the values of the host society, one would predict that the Irish Catholics of Boston would be more driven to leadership and excellence than their countrymen who settled into the milder and more egalitarian climate of Philadelphia [p. 7].

And Baltzell concludes that "Bostonians, whether Puritans, Unitarians, Episcopalians, Catholics, Jews, agnostics or atheists have continued to be influenced by the hierarchical communalism of Puritanism, just as their counterparts in Philadelphia are still influenced by the egalitarian individualism of the Quaker founders of the holy experiment on the Delaware" (pp. 433–444).

In this book, we will look at similar cultural effects of religion on a national scale, comparing the Protestant ethic and the Catholic ethic.

## Where Has This Idea Been?

The idea that there is a Catholic ethic organized around Catholic culture, beliefs, and organizational forms and that it competes with a similarly organized Protestant ethic strikes most people as obvious once it is mentioned to them. There are a number of reasons why this obvious idea has taken some time to be articulated.

The United States was Protestant first and Catholic second. The United States was founded by Protestant thinkers and believers. While from the very start there were a few Catholic and Jewish citizens, "Protestantism had," in Hudson's words, "established undisputed sway over almost all aspects of national life" (1961a, p. 109) for the nearly three hundred years from the time the Pilgrims landed in 1620 until the end of the nineteenth century, when the effect of the great Catholic and Jewish migrations that began in 1830 began to be felt. During this two-hundred-plus-year span, the Protestant ethos was firmly established. And indeed, when Catholics came to this country, they experienced hostility and resentment (see Billington, [1938] 1964). Anti-Semitism was present in good measure as well.

Baltzell (1979) observes that the original thirteen Colonies "formed a mosaic of Protestant ethics" and that "America gave the members of the various denominations and sects an opportunity to put their ideas into practice in virgin sociological situations" (p. 6). He goes on to quote H. R. Niebuhr's point that "there were no settled institutions defining the privileges of the religiously, politically, or economically powerful, and by the same token, there were no social organizations of any kind to provide for orderly procedure in the contact of men with men. Whatever else . . . America came to be, it was also an experiment in constructive Protestantism" (Baltzell, p. 7).

Although this Protestantism was not all of a piece, in the larger view it is possible to say, as Baltzell (p. 453) and Ernst Troeltsch ([1911] 1960) do, that, in Troeltsch's words, "Calvinism . . . has *assumes that anyone who has ever used the term "Prot" or "Protestant" means the same Weberian thing by it —*

merged with and to some extent produced that political and social way of life which may be described as 'Americanism.' It is obvious that today this 'Americanism' has an independent existence, which is almost entirely divorced from a religious basis" (vol. 2, p. 511).

The Protestant ethic, then, was a founding ethic for U.S. society and, as such, continued to be unthinkingly accepted and unchallenged by most people. Moreover, because of its early influence on the country and its pervasiveness, Protestantism seemed to embody U.S. values in their essence. Religion, nationalism, and patriotism merged into a single value, embodied in such phrases as "one nation, under God" (see Williams, 1960, for further discussion of the "nationalism/patriotism" value complex). In such a cultural context, the articulation of competing religion-based ethics could well have been thought of as anti-American if those ethics put, for example, a greater emphasis on sharing and less emphasis on individualism than the Protestant ethic.

Catholicism was not only a late arrival and different, it was in some sense considered by many to be inferior to Protestantism. Gusfield (1963), in considering the history of Prohibition, even speculates that the turning against the use of liquor and other alcoholic spirits was an attempt on the part of native Protestants to gain the moral upper hand over immigrant Catholics, since up until the Prohibition movement began in the 1820s and 1830s, U.S. Protestant society itself had been a liberal user of alcoholic spirits, as we know from records of taxes collected on alcohol (see Rorabaugh, 1979). More importantly, we can recall that it was not until the election of John Kennedy that a Roman Catholic succeeded in becoming president of the United States, and that Al Smith's Catholicism was probably one reason he lost the presidential election in 1928 (he was also a "wet").

In addition, there was no development in the United States of a strong Catholic religious ethic on a subgroup basis, as happened among the French-Canadian Catholics in Quebec (and, on the Protestant side, among the Mormons in the United States). Instead,

U.S. Catholics tended to identify with Catholics of similar ethnicity rather than with all Catholics. There were multiple Catholic identities, then, not just one. (This point was also made some time ago by Nathan Glazer and Senator Patrick Moynihan, 1963, who said that religious differences are expressed in an ethnic vocabulary, a vocabulary somewhat more acceptable in the United States.) The in-group emphasis among Catholics did not help to bring their values before the larger society. Catholic outreach was low. With prohibitions (mainly pre–Vatican II) abounding, Catholics stayed in their own halls, schools, and geographic areas. They emphasized working within their ethno-Catholic communities, not in articulating bridges to those who very well might reject them. An ethno-Catholic identification was thus a way to slide by some of the anti-Catholic feeling.

Because, as I intend to show, the Catholic ethic represents a set of beliefs and social foci different from mainstream U.S. values, particularly as we think of them in the last decade of the twentieth century, articulation of such differences creates a number of problems, first for the dominant culture and then for the subdominant one. This is another reason why the Catholic ethic has not received much attention—it is perceived as a threat. Articulation of it cannot help but call into question those mainstream values, generating confusion and consternation. Indeed, to the extent that Protestant values seem at one with U.S. values, such an articulation can even seem disloyal.

Moreover, Catholics in U.S. society have been not only subdominant but scorned. Targets of that scorn have included Catholic religious rituals, the use of a foreign language (Latin), ornamental vestments and dress for priests, and a celibate clergy. The way that ownership of church property winds its way to Rome itself rather than to the community that gave the money to build it has also been very troubling to Americans. The fact that the property was owned by "foreign powers" gave credence to the idea that Rome was indeed a grey eminence, interfering with U.S. ideas and practices and subverting American (read Protestant ethic) values.

Catholics, then, were seen as a potential threat due to their "strange practices" and "foreign control."

Given all this background, it becomes much less surprising that even through a Catholic ethic was growing in America, the *concept* of a Catholic ethic did not develop. The ground was not fertile for discussion of a Catholic ethic or, for that matter, any religiously based ethic other than the Protestant ethic.

In addition, the very presence of Catholics' differences from Protestants might have encouraged people to try to emphasize Catholics' similarities as a way to reduce tension. The melting pot ideology could smooth over ecumenical differences as well as ethnic ones. Scholars, thinkers, and academics may have found it more natural not to stress differences between Christian sects but rather to emphasize their commonalities and uniformities. Such a process might be mainly unconscious. One would simply be working toward exploring common ground rather than points of difference. "Why," as one bishop has observed to me, "should one develop a concept that accentuates the differences Catholicism has with Protestantism, when we spent our whole life trying for ecumenical rapprochement?"

Finally, despite socially based efforts to find commonalities, most people have a sense that it is impossible to be of two religions. One cannot be Catholic *and* Protestant; one has to be *either* Catholic *or* Protestant. Although, we understand that we can be a mixture of ethnicities, we view religious affiliation differently. I will discuss in Chapter Eight how viewing the Catholic ethic and the Protestant ethic as cultural constructs allows us to see that we can have elements of both ethics. It is only the names that make them seem mutually exclusive. However, the *belief* that a religiously based ethic cannot be shared by people of another religious persuasion has doubtless been yet one more reason why formal development of the concept of a Catholic ethic was hindered.

*Then why write a book that contributes to this?*

## Conclusion

The history of religious thinking in the United States in this century has deemphasized religious differences and highlighted uniformities, as we can see in such concepts as the society as melting pot and by the powerful fact that the Protestant ethic appeared to stand alone for many years, a hegemony that seemed to satisfy all comers.

In our new awareness of the enormous worth of diverse views, it is now time to consider a new ethic and explore its properties. Such an exploration will broaden our knowledge of both religious and cultural experience. And it will broaden our knowledge of ourselves, since values of different sorts are often mixed within each of us, if we choose to see them. When values have religious names, those names too often become fences that prevent people from recognizing the values favored by a religion different from theirs, even though they may actually hold similar values. A similar phenomenon has existed with respect to gender-related values for example. Values of aggression and caring exist in all of us, although to different degrees. However, once aggressiveness gets identified as a male value, and caring as a female one, then it is difficult for a member of one gender to acknowledge the presence of the other gender's value in himself or herself without appearing to deny his or her gender identification. The concept of androgyny allows us to free ourselves from the prison of gender labels. The concept that we can share religious ethics can free us from a similar prison of thought.

Each religious culture promotes certain kinds of actions and discourages others. The Protestant ethic is connected to the work ethic and perhaps to our ideas of capitalism itself. The Catholic ethic is oriented to support of others through sharing, emphasizing not only helping in general but a "preferential option for the poor" (*Economic Justice for All: Catholic Social Teaching and the U.S. Economy*, section 52, cited in Gannon, 1987).

In the next chapter, I will review the Protestant ethic, laying out Weber's basis conceptions in a way that will act as a springboard for a discussion of the Catholic ethic.

## Chapter Two

# A Closer Look at the Protestant Ethic

Max Weber's book *The Protestant Ethic and the Spirit of Capitalism* ([1904–1905] 1956) introduced one of the most interesting and stimulating concepts in the study of society. Weber made two major points: first, he argued that there is a "package of ideas and beliefs" that constitute a "Protestant ethic," and second, he said that this ethic was necessary for the development of capitalism. In my discussion of the Protestant ethic, I accept Weber's first proposition and withhold judgment on the second. Whether Protestantism came first and stimulated capitalism or whether a nascent capitalism was already present and stimulated Protestantism remains an open question. Many other factors, such as the development of science and technology, were present as well, and while there is little question that the Protestant ethic played some role—perhaps, for example, engendering or justifying competition—studies of causal ordering remain to be done.

Clearly, Protestantism was at least an accomplice in the "Western miracle," the transformation of the West from a collection of sleepy medieval villages into a world power. However, it is not essential for the Protestant ethic to have *caused* capitalism for that ethic to exist. Weber's description of it immediately struck a chord with his public and has been striking chords, both pro and con (Marshall, 1982), ever since. While social scientists are cautious, the public is accepting. In various forms—the Protestant ethic, the Protestant work ethic, or simply the work ethic—it has become a household term. Virtually everyone knows that it refers to a set of beliefs, values, and attitudes that involve working hard and valuing money and personal achievement. Even non-Protestant Americans who might not confess to a belief in the Protestant ethic would probably admit to having a work ethic, or an "American" work ethic, because the concept is so deeply in-grained in our culture.

In this chapter, I will review the tenets of the Protestant ethic, [*awkward*] looking at its popular positive features (especially its support of work) but exploring as well its less-considered problematic fea-tures (especially attitudes toward helping in general and the poor in particular). *is true in Weber? I don't think so —*

## A Three-Legged Cultural Stool

The Protestant ethic as Weber outlined it rests on three legs: atti-tudes and beliefs about work, about money, and about character. Each is important and requires some discussion.

### Work: The Calling

The association between work and moral value has become so ingrained in us that it is hard for us now to understand the profound revolution in the *meaning* of work that Protestantism wrought. It was a transformation ethic. The concept that work is a calling ennobled work and stigmatized activities that were not work. It established work as more than the transference of energy, the process through which one resource becomes another resource. It transformed work into a sacred ritual.

Professor Phillippe Desan of the University of Chicago states:

Everything in our physical and mental environments has a value and a price. It's a way of thinking that has its roots in the Renais-sance. . . . Renaissance society had a particular conception of work. In this age, as today, work permitted the evaluation of all produc-tion—mental as well as material—and became a dogma invoked to justify remuneration or profit. It is enough to consider the place of work—in all the forms it can take—in the literature of the Renaissance to see to what extent the idea of labor itself occupied the mind. *Work served as the keystone to a bourgeois ideology that . . . ultimately confounded [that is, mixed or entangled] work and religion* [1993, pp. 8–9; emphasis added].

The special nature of work was central in the ascetic Protestantism of John Calvin (1509–1564) and Martin Luther (1483–1546). Work as a calling was a sacred duty that had been identified by God as one's own area of effort and expertise. As work took on not just a civil but a religious status, it was considered to attract divine interest and attention. Engaging in work became a necessary ritual act, one that not only produced goods and services but also kept people out of trouble. The proverb, "Idle hands are the Devil's workshop," sums up part of the Protestant point of view toward productive activities. But there is more.

Revolutions may make the previously meaningful mundane. But they can also make the previously mundane meaningful. Ideas, concepts, processes, and artifacts may be transformed and take on special meaning. What was once only a bird comes to contain signs from the gods (the auspices). Water becomes wine; bread and wine become body and blood; the burning brand becomes a sacred flame. The idea of work went through such a change. A daily human activity became, as Desan said, entangled with religion. When work became a calling, all work became God's work. The daily routine of production to meet daily needs took on new importance and meaning. Individuals began to find in work much more than a job. Thus, if absolutely necessary, any job would do to fulfill the need to express oneself in work, through work, and by work. As well-known author and statesman Amitore Fanfani (1936) puts it, work "transformed capitalistic efforts into religious efforts which, although not meritorious, for otherwise God would be rewarding man, were the sole way in which man could burn a grain of incense to the terrible Lord of Heaven and Earth" (p. 208).

While these ideas developed several centuries ago, the continued emphasis today upon work as important, as a test of good character, as a demonstration of effort, as a source of income, and as a source of meaning (and for all these reasons, as necessary to receive welfare benefits) testifies to their continued force. Work, moreover, was not the alternative to fun but rather *became* fun. It was fun because busyness (like cleanliness) is next to Godliness.

Today, work also continues to be a source of deep personal meaning for many, quite apart from the social evaluation of work. People as individuals draw significant aspects of their own self-validation from the jobs that they do—enjoying the sense of doing a job well or of accomplished a job that helps others in some way. Individuals' sense of self-worth, of personhood, is linked to their work. For those holding the Protestant ethic, striving for or achieving "success" in work is an important way to feel good about oneself. Conversely, those who lose their jobs in our society can also lose their sense of self. After months of searching for new employment, as one writer says, "unemployed managers begin to realize with horror the stigma of having lost their jobs, and the fact that they are applying for new ones as 'unemployed persons' outweighs their many years of experience, formal credentials, and specialized expertise. Instead of being treated as experienced applicants, ready to work, they are treated as 'spoiled goods'" (Newman, 1988, p. 56). Yet, again, this is not the only possible view of things. Tom Rugh, an experienced human services agency executive, comments on different attitudes toward unemployment in the United States and Italy: "In the United States, success is equated with goodness, with a resultant alienation of poor and unemployed people from others. In Italy, a person's value is not measured in terms of economic success, and family members and friends can socially relate on a relative [sic] equal footing regardless of the employment status of the individuals" (personal communication, 1994).

When work becomes sacred, it can also become all-consuming. Fanfani quotes one early view of this result—R. Croiset's *Christian*

*Reflections of Various Moral Subjects*, published in 1752. Croiset observed that "the day is not long enough for the overwhelming occupations of the capitalists; they deny themselves the rest of which even slaves are not deprived; night rivals day in respect to their assiduous labor; meals, rest, everything is broken by business" (Fanfani, 1936, p. 132). In contemporary society, we, too, sometimes see the sacredness of work run amok in what we call the workaholic—the hard-driving businessperson at work day and night or the supermom or superdad who has to do it all. What is more, out of our belief in the value of work, we may actually respect the workaholic, seeing his or her excesses as somehow positive (see Killinger, 1992).

However, once work was conceived of as a calling and a sacred duty, there were also implications for those who, for some reason, did not work. Not working is one of the ways that the poor acquire questionable moral status. The very reason the poor often are poor, in this view, is that they do not work and thus have no income. When work is so important that some can overdo it to the admiring approval of society in general, then those who do not work have a questionable standing. Those who work become the "good guys"; those who do not become the "bad guys." It is only a short step from observing the associations to assuming cause and motive: people are poor because they are not working; therefore, they must not want to work; therefore, they must be lazy. Certainly, there are cases of laziness, but more to the point is the reality of such problems as lack of work, low pay for work (creating a class of "working poor"), and illnesses and injuries that prevent people from working. In spite of these well-known problems, the idea that poverty is caused by aversion to work remains widespread. Over the years, one of the most popular programs for poverty relief has been the work-based program, which conveys notions of earning one's keep. Perhaps more importantly, such programs provide a morally acceptable vehicle for helping the poor, one that reinforces the sense of moral virtue among the well-off. Thus, as President Clinton looks to reform welfare in the 1990s ("to end welfare as we know it"), he is seeking to link receipt of benefits to working for them, a concept as old as indentured servitude and the workhouse.

## Money: The Sacred Payoff

In the Protestant ethic, work became a divine activity. One would therefore expect that its fruits—cash, money, wealth resources—would in some sense become a sacred payoff as well. In effect, this is what Weber argues. That attitude toward money was then strengthened by its links to predestination.

At one time, most people, with the exception of the aristocracy, lived off what they produced and sold only the surplus. Production (work) resulted directly in food and clothing and shelter and money was extra. Then, as work began more and more to result directly *in money*, it was *through money* that people lived. Hard work, busyness, activity—a constant sense of one's nose to the grindstone and one's shoulder to the wheel—were likely to produce this money. Seen in terms of commercial success, money was important in its own right, but it also had accelerated or augmented meaning as a sacred product of sacred involvement—it was money *as a result* of work.

For Protestants who believed in predestination, especially, not only was money good because it was a product of approved activity but its possession also became a proxy for God's approval of those who worked to acquire it. Money, like work, became of transcendent rather than instrumental importance. It indicated one's heavenly value.

This concept came along with the Protestant Reformation of the sixteenth century and, indeed, may have been a partial driver for it, since the newly monied burghers needed a legitimacy which, till then, only the aristocracy had possessed. At the time, this concept of work and money began to take hold in people's thinking, the most powerful, prestigious people were the *leisure* classes—the aristocracy, who believed that labor lowered one's status—while the bourgeois were laboring hard, primarily in the trades, looking to improve their material lot. A new view of work was one way to rationalize this activity, to make what had been viewed with scorn acceptable and legitimate. The Protestant ethic contained a concept that so powerfully legitimized work that it blunted and ultimately made ridiculous the social concept of the leisure class. Weber puts it this way: "one thing was unquestionably new: the valuation of the fulfillment of duty in worldly affairs as the highest form which the moral activity of the individual could assume. . . . The only way of living acceptably to God was not to surpass worldly morality in monastic asceticism, but solely through the obligations imposed on the individual by his position in the world. That was his calling" (p. 80). Indeed, "the effect of the Reformation was such that, as compared to the Catholic attitude, the moral emphasis on and the religious sanction of organized worldly labor in a calling was mightily increased" (p. 83).

A number of practical results emerged from this point of view about money. On the upside, working hard tended to produce money, and money was a resource through which one could meet needs. It was hard to be too rich.

But then money's association with work softened over time. Money assumed its own, independent value. So strong has the totemic value of money become that its mere possession still bestows a sense of moral approval. Business success became and remains a synonym for success itself. (Consider what we mean when we say, "He [or she] has been so successful." We are almost always referring to money.) "Good" things seem to move ever outward. Success in business, too, seems to have a halo effect, giving its possessor wisdom, prestige, influence, and power.

Even when labor was freely given and people volunteered their time, some personally enhancing reward was and still is expected, typically in the form of special recognition and public thanks. The value of work and the status it confers must be publicly "compensated" through awards and ceremonial banquets and other honors.

On the downside, lack of money was trouble for the poor. Since having money was good and not having money was bad, the rich were somehow better, the poor somehow worse. They were thrice hobbled: first, because they did not work; second, because they did not have money; and third, because their not working and not having money indicated a low moral character.

The relationship of money to work and the nature of money itself are not, never have been, and probably never will be settled to everyone's satisfaction. Nonetheless, the recent Presbyterian report *Vocation and Work* regrets seeing a *growth* in the belief that money derives through work and is thought to be of sacred importance (Schaeffer, 1991). The report states that, "Calvin's doctrine has eroded in recent years so that wealth is sometimes viewed as a sign of God's blessing for a righteous life, and poverty associated with sin" (p. 8). However, given the strength of the historical associations among the values of work, the possession of money, and good moral character, this finding should not be surprising. Many continue to grow up believing that to be rich is to be both goodly and godly.

### Character and Predestination

According to Weber, the ascetic Protestants believed that salvation (or a state of grace) was not something earned or lost. Rather, God was infinite and His decisions were also infinite, and thus those decisions had all been made at one time. Therefore, one was either saved or damned by predetermined fiat.

Predestination is by no means a doctrine of the past. Just one small sign of its continued currency was a 1994 letter to a newspaper remarking on an article that "maintained that heaven is gained solely by the way we conduct ourselves." The letter writer stated, "For 2,000 years, the Christian religion has maintained as its central truth that 'we are saved, not by works, but by the unmerited favor of God (grace) which we receive through faith in Jesus Christ who died for our sins'" (Zehnder, 1994, p. 4).

Those who believed in predestination naturally sought proof of their salvation. Cotton Mather (1663–1728), for example, was "alternately abased with doubt and elated with conviction" that he was saved, because he was "thoroughly indoctrinated with Calvin's concept of election and the necessity of a good Christian to discover his own state of grace (justification)" (Piercy, 1967, p. vi).

The rather grim doctrine of predestination met with challenges right from the start. In a novel set partly in the Plymouth Colony of the seventeenth century, Louis Auchincloss captures the doubts and concerns that plagued people about the perspective that no matter how good or bad a person one was, he or she could not alter his or her celestial status. The speakers in the following scene are Governor John Winthrop of the Plymouth Colony and William Hutchinson.

"Are you now joining in your wife's meetings?" There was no threat in the tone, but the hush that followed was of the ominous sort that precedes tempests.

"That I am not."

"I am glad to hear it, Master Hutchinson. I am glad to hear it."

William scanned those watery eyes for a hint of the fire beneath, but he saw none. "I wanted to ask you a question about the covenant of works."

"Did you want to? Then ask it."

"There are some in the colony who believe that divers of our ministers preach such a covenant. They argue that if these ministers find evidence of salvation in godly deportment and religious demeanor, there is an implication that the cultivation of godly deportment and religious demeanor may *help* a man to salvation. Is there not such an implication, Governor?"

"No, Master Hutchinson, there is not."

"Will you allow me to say that I find this disheartening? For if there is nothing I can do to save myself—if that decision has been made, irrevocably before my birth—what does it matter what I do, or do not do, in this fleshly life—or in Boston?"

"I will tell you, Master Hutchinson," the grave voice replied. "I will tell you and ask, at the same time, that you repeat my words to your good wife. It will be especially for her good and the good of those unfortunately empty-headed women whom, I fear she is sadly deluding." Here Winthrop paused to let his interlocutor take in the sudden change in their relationship. "The reason it matters how a man behaves himself even in this remote and isolated community is that God will help him *here*" [Auchincloss, 1976, pp. 22–23; for a historical account of the theological tensions of the time and of William Hutchinson and his wife Anne, see Baltzell, 1979, pp. 134–135].

In other words, God was unlikely to let those who were destined for celestial salvation suffer an unseemly status here on earth. If, as Governor Winthrop thought, God will help you *here*, then your position here must be a reflection of that help and, perforce, God's favor. Signs were needed. Assurances were sought. How one could know whether God was providing assurances or not is a question that has troubled more than one soul. Cotton Mather could be found "lying prostrate on his study floor in the dust to obtain 'fresh Assurances from Him'" (Piercy, 1967, p. vi). But more public signs were sought, too. Doing well financially and commercially, amassing money and resources, came to be seen as a sign of heavenly favor. This approach to predestination resulted in at least two important cultural attitudes.

First, it made financial resources an indicator of moral resources. This connection buttressed the link already established for the probity of money, provided as it was through the sacred ceremony of work.

Second, it created a bifurcated, either/or status system. Unlike status systems that have a number of grades through which one might progress up or down, this system stated that you were either saved or you were not saved, elite or not elite. (It is perhaps for this reason that Katherine Newman titled her book about downward mobility in the U.S. middle class *Falling from Grace,* 1988.)

It is likely that this bifurcated view of salvation is one source of the either/or attitude that is still such a strong force in U.S. moralism and judgmentalism in many areas. An example from the U.S. conception of race relations illustrates the point. Around the world we have long seen racial and ethnic prejudice expressed in wars of "ethnic cleansing," theories that "one drop of blood" consigns a person to an "inferior" race, and pogroms and attempted genocide against people with anybody Jewish in their ancestry. In the United States, too, the typical attitude is that people are representatives of single races. This attitude does not admit of racial or ethnic mixtures. "How did this come about?" Irving Kristol asks, that "in America, with its liberal traditions, race nevertheless remains a permanent fixed and deadly problem" (1994, p. A18). He has the right question but gives the wrong answer. His explanation cites "the enduring curse of slavery that instilled a degree of race-consciousness." A more likely explanation is that the intellectual apparatus for permanent divisions, an idea of either/or, of elect or nonelect, was *already present* and that firm views of racial lines are legacies of this kind of thinking. Kristol states that the only other country in which he currently sees such a propensity is South Africa. The United States and South Africa do not often appear on the same list, but in respect to racial views they do, both for Kristol and for Talcott Parsons (1968a) the late Harvard sociologist.

However, we can look to one of our own states, Hawaii, to see that it does not have to be this way. Hawaii is one example of a place where there is a great sense of racial mixing and such either/or-ness seems less applicable.

## This World and the Next and the Question of Status

In addition to the three major areas of work, money, and character, Weber discusses the Protestant ethic's traditional orientation to *this* world, the here and now, which contrasted to the traditional Catholic orientation toward the other (next) world, the future. The difference was a question of where one wished to put one's energy.

The otherworldly focus was aimed at managing the salvation transaction to achieve salvation. The here and now was trouble ("a vale of tears"), and status and success here were not worth much ("a cup of dust"). That did not mean that this world did not count at all but rather that the other world (the salvation world) was the one that counted a great deal more. Moreover, there were things one could do in the here and now to make that other world attainable.

The Protestant ethic, however, focused on this world. That emphasis was partly by default—God helps us in this world. Given the doctrine of predestination, there was not much one could do to secure help with respect to the next world. So an emphasis on things that one could do here and now became important. (These ideas are discussed further in Chapter Five.) And that emphasis meant that worldly status became important.

## The Transformation of Status

In the matter of worldly status, in one of those paradoxical transformations so common in social change episodes, Protestantism reversed its predecessor. The here-and-now Catholic world before Protestantism was one of stationary social statuses and floating-point celestial statuses, that is, *status in this world was relatively fixed*—kings were kings and commoners were commoners—their status just was. The political economy that surrounded Catholicism was not related to anything except birth or other uncontrollable events. One did not earn it or lose it. High effort did not lead to high worldly status and low status did not result from low effort.

However, *status in the next world was open to influence*. Heavenly status was controllable, and high heavenly status achievable. The soul was mobile: its position could and did change depending upon what one did here in this world. What mattered was the celestial calculation, the heavenly calculus (see p. 106). One could, through good works—lighting candles, attending mass on the first Friday of every month for nine months, and the like—experience or earn an upwardly mobile position in the celestial hierarchy.

In the Protestant ethic, however, celestial status was fixed. And in that ethic, God's reasons for assigning a person to salvation or damnation in the next world were as unknowable as were, in the Catholic ethic, His reasons for assigning a person to aristocratic or servile status in this world. But where the Catholic could change his or her celestial status and look for God's help in doing so, the Protestant could change status in the here and now and look for God's help in doing so. That is, the Protestant ethic reflected and addressed the human need for some equity in relationships in some sense, even a loose one—*equity* meaning that one could identify some observable, positive, controllable relationship between what one did day to day and what happened to one in that day-to-day world. Hard work, for example, should bring wealth and resources. And that idea became a part of social structure and culture. Under the Protestant ethic (and during the Enlightenment generally), social rather than celestial status became the floating point. One could work oneself up the ladder just as one could fall to the bottom of the heap. The Protestant ethic and the Catholic ethic, then, have alternate applications of fixed and variable statuses. Within the tradition of the Catholic ethic, variable status is otherworldly and fixed status obtains in this world. Within the tradition of the Protestant ethic, fixed status is otherworldly and variable status obtains in this world.

There are additional implications of the distinction between this-worldly and otherworldly orientations that deserve mention. In both views, the variable status carries significant personal and social levels of value. Thus, within the Catholic ethic tradition, being in a *state of grace* (high celestial status) is thought of as clearly better than being in a lower state of grace or not being in a state of grace at all. Qualitative distinctions operate on the celestial level.

The sixteenth-century Reformation that established Protestantism simultaneously attributed personal qualities to various social levels in this world. (The celestial order was still valuable, of course, but again, there was not much a Protestant could do about it.) Worldly effort, however, was seen to be rewarded through the worldly social order. Hence, in the Protestant ethic, a person who was higher on the social scale was, and to a large extent still is, clearly better—morally better—than a person of lower status. The "best people" in town are never the poor; they are always the well-to-do.

This qualitative moral difference did not pervade the medieval hierarchy to the same extent. For example, kings were of higher social status, and in theory, blood would tell—a nobly born person would be more nobly behaved than a low-born person—but as a practical matter, everyone knew kings were at least as likely to be immoral as anyone else. The Reformation, however, changed the social structure of status.

## Social Status and the Poor

The moral characterization of here-and-now social status was bad news for the poor. If reaching higher social status was an indication of predestined celestial favor as well as a reward for hard work, then lower social status and poverty were an indication of the reverse. (This connection is the one of which the Presbyterian report *Vocation and Work* disapproves.)

This line of thinking makes it clear why there is ambivalence about helping others within societies strongly affected by Protestant ethic and why the impetus for special aid for the most disadvantaged has been muted or stunted in this country. Providing social welfare aid of any sort can be perceived as providing inappropriate aids to social mobility.

Early Protestants had found the medieval Catholic practice of buying or earning indulgences particularly objectionable. An indulgence was a sort of heavenly chit or credit that Catholics sought because it took a certain number of years off the time the buyer's soul would spend in Purgatory. Some prayer books, for example, had the number of years of indulgence a person would get for saying certain prayers printed just below each prayer. For Protestants, providing social aid for people in worldly need could be seen as roughly equivalent to the practice they despised of buying indulgences that assisted people in a sort of heavenly need. To put the case in more contemporary terms, in the Protestant ethic, providing help to the poor could be analogous to taking the Law School Admission Test (LSAT) for someone in order to get him or her into a prestigious law school.

In this view, any social assistance to the poor (like any academic assistance to the test-taking student) must be such that it does not muddle the direct relationship between effort and work and the secular results of that effort and work. She or he who does not work, does not eat. Teaching the poor how to work is acceptable and even desirable, just as educating the student in preparation for the LSAT is acceptable and desirable. In each case, though, the people who want the results of work must do the work themselves. Otherwise, the results will not be socially valid.

It is the philosophical link between effort and results that underlies the preoccupation of Western society (and particularly English and U.S. societies) with differentiating between the worthy poor and the unworthy poor. So common has this distinction been, and so much a part of the lives of most people in this country, that it may never have crossed most people's minds to ask, Why does it matter? We don't talk about the worthy sick and the unworthy sick; nor do we talk about worthy children and unworthy children. (However, we are beginning to do so in relation to scarce resources. For example, we argue whether the alcoholic should get a liver transplant. This trend makes discussion of our values and their foundations imperative.)

The issue of people's worthiness to be helped is also raised in

Simon and Novak's essay "Liberty and Justice for All" (1990). Widely thought of as a conservative response to the Catholic bishops' 1986 pastoral letter to U.S. Catholics (Gannon, 1987), "Liberty and Justice for All" emphasizes the importance of personal responsibility as a first principle. Simon and Novak point out that Pope John XXIII, in his 1963 encyclical *Pacem in Terris*, allows for welfare rights—including, in his words, "the right to security in cases of sickness, inability to work, widowhood"—when an individual is "'deprived of the means of subsistence *through no fault of his own*' [*Pacem in Terris*, no. 11, italics added]. . . . In other words, the individual has the duty to be self-reliant" (Simon and Novak, 1990, p. 12). It is thus Simon and Novak's view that "one measure of a good society is how well it cares for the weakest and most vulnerable of its members." However, their perspective is a circumscribed idea of rights to welfare: one that "carefully places welfare 'rights' in the context of duties of self-reliance and ascribes them only to those persons unable *through no fault of their own* to fulfill these duties" (p. 13).

One can sense the struggle here—on the one hand, wanting to help and feeling the imperative to offer help; on the other hand, worrying that helping can hurt, can sap initiative and creativity, can reward the laggard along with the hurricane victim. And this idea of self-reliance is where worthiness comes from. You may *need* help for many reasons; you are only *worthy* of help if the need occurs through no fault of your own. "The moral dimension of welfare is crucial" (Simon and Novak, 1990, p. 24).

Why should the establishment of worthiness be so important? The answer to this question lies in understanding that the moral classification of the needy comes prior to the provision of assistance. If somebody is worthy, then there is limited danger in providing help to him or her. It will not erode his or her character (by destroying motivation, for example). It will not inappropriately elevate the person vis-à-vis others, giving him or her a status he or she does not truly "deserve."

## Conclusion

The conceptual frame that is the Protestant ethic is powerful and pervasive. In its emphasis on achievement and accomplishment, the ethic tends to be positive. It allows people to feel comfortable about enjoying the fruits of their labor. However, at the same time, it allows people to feel morally superior about their successes as well. Though it is always problematic to have more when others have less, if one "deserves" that six-figure salary while others deserve their four- or five-figure salaries, one need not worry too much. We are taught this connection in school. You deserve the A, and somebody else deserves the D–. You feel bad for a moment for the person who got the D–, but then you conclude, and perhaps are told by the teacher, that the grades are "fair." Fair in this context means that the differential allocation of rewards matches the distribution of ability and/or effort. And there is no such thing as a person's having too many A grades.

With this perspective, people are less likely to experience what the popular press has called "affluence guilt," described as the feeling that "we earn more than we ever imagined we would, spending too much on things we never thought we'd want, owning far more than we need. One friend apologizes in the middle of the tour of her new home: 'This is really too much'" (Ager, 1993, p. 3F). In America, it is said, we seem to equate "good" with "plenty"; people have multiples of things, "more than they really need" (Ager, 1994, p. 3A). A journalist, viewing a "show home," is bothered by the attitude toward the $2.6 million, 13,000-square-foot structure: "Why is it that only the *biggest* and *most expensive* homes are held up as models for us to strive for? Why is something so far beyond the reach of the average citizen held up as our ideal?" (Gallagher, 1993, p. 6F).

In sum, despite the controversy surrounding it, Weber's identification of a Protestant ethic opens up an important perspective on the human condition. However, such feelings as affluence guilt, a subdominant theme in the Protestant ethic, reflect the awareness of some people that the Protestant ethic cannot be the only perspective from which to view work and money and character. Moreover, certain Protestant denominations and Protestant-based groups—the Quakers, the Mormons, the Salvation Army, the social gospel movement, and some denominations with largely African American congregations—have a more sharing attitude about wealth and toward the poor than the attitude depicted here.

This view that sharing is important, subdominant in the Protestant ethic, is a dominant view in the Catholic ethic. Weber did not address the Catholic ethic (probably because he took it for granted), but it is time now for us to study this alternative religion-centered set of beliefs and practices.

why not study ethic of selfishness (achievement) v. ethic of sharing? what is gained by labeling one 'Prot.' + the other 'Cath'?

This book offers no evidence or argument for these connections, it just asserts that they exist.

# Part Two

---

# *Facets of the Catholic Ethic*

The concept that there is a coherent and important body of Catholic social thought is not new. Recent explorations include Coleman's *One Hundred Years of Catholic Social Thought* (1991), Finn's *Private Virtue and Public Policy* (1990), and Gannon's *The Catholic Challenge to the American Economy* (1987). Misner's *Social Catholicism in Europe from the Onset of Industrialization to the First World War* (1991) covers continental ground and especially French thought. In North America, the Catholic bishops' pastoral letter *Economic Justice for All: Catholic Social Teaching and the U.S. Economy* (Gannon, 1987) has attracted national discussion. In South America, liberation theology has become a political force that is influencing the Catholic Church as a whole as well as political regimes.

However, today, this interest in Catholic social thought is expanding to encompass the concept of a Catholic ethic. Until recently, U.S. society overall seemed to be assured that homogeneity in values was essential, even in the midst of ethnic, religious, and racial heterogeneity. But times are changing. The new emphasis on diversity and the intellectual freedom that attends this emphasis encourages a focus on cultural difference rather than on uniformity. Not only are some cultural groups newly ascending but others are under eclipse, as Peter Schrag points out in *The Decline of the Wasp* (1970).

In particular, attention is being paid to the culture that reflects the Catholic ethic. The work of Kennedy (1944), Herberg (1960), Lenski (1963), and Schuman (1971), among others, set the stage for looking at Catholics in distinction to others. Baltzell (1979) introduced the idea of multiple ethics. Out of these works came the idea of a Catholic ethic. (In addition, the term itself has been mentioned by Mack, Murphy, and Yellin, 1956, who did not, however, develop the idea. Gustafson, 1978, uses it in the context of a comparative analysis of moral systems, but his approach is philosophical, not sociological. Mueller, too, used the concept in a 1978 paper.)

My 1986 paper, "The 'Catholic Ethic' versus the 'Protestant Ethic': Catholic Social Service and the Welfare State," was the first systematic attempt to articulate the concept of a sociological Catholic ethic as a values package that addressed some of the same facets of life as the Protestant ethic but that had a different orientation, one that emphasized sharing. Michael Novak's *The Catholic Ethic and the Spirit of Capitalism* (1993) continues this approach, arguing for a Catholic ethic and suggesting that it has a sharing focus that tempers the excesses of capitalism. Novak sees the Catholic ethic as broader and more inclusive than, and a replacement for, the Protestant ethic. (Another guide to his view is that he considered calling the values he discusses the Christian ethic rather than the Catholic ethic.) However, he seems to see the Catholic ethic as rather recent, as a reaction to soften the effects of capitalism. He does not position it as a predecessor to and a contestant with the Protestant ethic.

Andrew Greeley (1990, p. 43) presented a similar general idea, describing "the Catholic myth" and "cultural Catholics" in a discussion of Catholic behavior and attitudes. To evaluate these attitudes, Greeley devised a GRACE Scale, to measure the extent to which an individual sees God as mother, spouse, and friend as opposed to father, master, judge. This scale deals with some views found in the Catholic ethic, even though Greeley did not use that term.

Finally, Lester Thurow (1992) has discussed the idea of different capitalistic orientations. He identifies "individualistic capitalism" as characteristic of the United States and "communalistic capitalism" as characteristic of Europe. The first is primarily both individualistic and acquisitive in focus. The second is also acquisitive, but an important part of its ethos is sharing with the community. These two views fit reasonably well with the views inherent in the Protestant ethic (individualistic capitalism) and the Catholic ethic (communalistic capitalism).

Therefore, the cultural climate is right for further discussion of the Catholic ethic. And this discussion is more than the introduction of a new term. It articulates a set of archetypal core values that are reflective of and expressive of Catholic doctrine, practice, and day-to-day activity while at the same time supporting and generating Catholic thought and action. The Catholic ethic is more than a religious idea; I suggest that, like the Protestant ethic and juxtaposed to it, the Catholic ethic is a sociological, anthropological, and social psychological concept. Beneath Catholicism as popularly conceived by many non-Catholics (who associate it with sets of saints, hushes of nuns, prides of priests, problematic popes, masses, eating fish on Friday, and St. Christopher medals), there is a deep structure of core values. Understanding these core values will allow us to see the common patterns in the medieval church, the Sisters Hospital in Buffalo, New York, in the late nineteenth century, liberation theology, Catholic Charities USA, and the Catholic bishop's pastoral letter on the U.S. economy, among other events and institutions. It will allow us to recognize the "cultural Catholic." And perhaps it will give us some fresh approaches to some of our most intense national and community debates.

The Catholic ethic rests on five conceptual foundations. One contains ideas about work. A second contains ideas about money.

These two foundations are discussed in Chapter Three. A third conceptual foundation consists of views of family and community. A fourth foundation treats of forgiveness and mercy. Chapter Four explores these two foundations. Finally, Chapter Five explores the implications of the fifth conceptual foundation, ideas about the relative importance of this world and the next.

Two of these foundations, work and money, are directly parallel to two legs of the three-legged stool that Weber used to construct the Protestant ethic. I used the term *character* for the third leg of the stool. In the Catholic ethic, the ideas about this world in relation to the next world and about mercy cover issues of character. And while Weber does not comment specifically on family, the individualistic as opposed to communalistic focus of the Protestant ethic is well known. Thus, the two ethics address the same set of elemental human concerns, and when compared, they show us much that is important about ourselves and our society.

# Chapter Three

# Attitudes Toward
# Work and Money

In contemporary U.S. society, the Protestant work ethic is virtually synonymous with work itself. Yet in the medieval Catholic world before the Protestant Reformation, work was simply work. You did it. It provided resources for you to eat and live. After the Reformation, work was sacred and the money that work produced was a sign of moral worth.

Looking at that bald historical outline, one might conclude that work is not valued within the Catholic tradition. But that would be incorrect. It has been suggested that *culture* is what makes you want to do what you have to do anyway. Similarly, we can say that the ideas about work in the Catholic and Protestant ethics make you want to do what you have to do anyway. What is different about the ethics is the nature of the value bestowed on work that makes you want to do it. The Protestant and Catholic ethics think differently about the *purposes* of work, the *processes* of work, the *workers*, the *use of the products of work*, and *the motivation for work*. The Reformation took the old values for these elements and gave them each a twist, developing from the old values the new ones that Weber came to call the Protestant ethic.

In pre-Reformation (which is to say Catholic) times, the purpose of work was to accomplish activities that provided goods and services, transformed materials, and gleaned resources for oneself, one's community, and one's society. The work process was instrumental, not transcendental. There was less sense than there would be later of self-validation through work. As McCarthy and McGaughey (1989) point out, "Work, by which material is converted to the use of mankind, is, therefore, seen in Christian terms [historically speaking, Catholic terms] not as an absolute value, but as subordinate to people's lives and spirits" (p. 187). Thus, in the Catholic ethic, work is a less powerful cradle of self-esteem than it is in the Protestant ethic. It is important, but one has no sense of being "spoiled goods" if one does not have a job.

Furthermore, the process of work, the actual working at work, has no magical, mutating properties. Work is an activity with a result, in much the same way as bowling is an activity with a result. The process of work is like many other human processes, no more, no less. It does not tell anything about your inner self, is no test of good intentions, and neither determines nor demonstrates inner character. Work is ceremony. It might also be fun. But it does not change you. In the Protestant ethic, on the other hand, work is ritual and, thus, has transforming properties.

The third area of difference has to do with the worker. Work is good, but it is good *because*, as Pope John II suggests, the basis for determining the value of human work is not primarily the kind of work being done but the fact that *the one who is doing it is a person.* "In fact, in the final analysis it is always man who is the purpose of the work, whatever is the work that is done by man—even if the common scale of values rates it as the merest 'service,' as the most monotonous, even the most alienating work" (McCarthy and McGaughey, 1989, p. 186). Work, then, is positive because human beings do it. The worker is special, not the work qua work. Work is not only subordinate to the worker but cannot be considered independently from the worker. Joe Holland, a writer on theology and social theory, and Peter Henriot, S.J., former director of the Center of Concern and a writer on social justice issues, make the same point: "Industrial capitalism is clearly wrong, for it has put capital over labor and thus inverted the basic structure of human dignity, leaving labor as an economic victim" (Holland and Henriot, 1983, p. xviii).

The fourth area of difference between the views of work in the

Protestant and Catholic ethics has to do with the ownership and control of products of work. In the Catholic tradition, the products of work are only partially the property of the worker. There is a community claim as well as a personal one. Since goods are created for the community, of which the worker is a part, the worker cannot completely own the products of labor. To put the difference in the broadest possible terms, in the Protestant tradition, whatever you can make is yours to keep. Decisions about it are entirely yours. Within the Catholic tradition, there are legitimate family and community claimants.

When Karl Marx talked about the alienation of the worker, he meant, in part, alienation from the sense of wholeness that participation in a complete work effort can provide. Kurt Lang (1964) puts it this way: "In Marxian theory, some men are alienated from their labor objectively by the relations of economic production and the system of class domination. This separation from their work and the products of their work also results in their being alienated from nature and from themselves" (p. 19). It's a question of motivation.

Most of us today want meaningful work, tasks with which we feel we can make a contribution and in which we have a chance to express ourselves and our creativity, to learn and develop. It is difficult for us to extract meaning from tasks that are trivial, broken up into small pieces so that we only do one repetitive piece over and over again. Meaningful work, then, requires a workplace that allows us some credit for the development of the product or service and lets us see ourselves involved in the result.

However, tangible items like swords and widgets, food and supplies, are not the only product of work. There is also the production of meaning constructed in a social setting. Workers, individually and collectively, are entitled to their share of the meaning as well as of the goods and services. In the Catholic ethic, meaningful work is seen as social, not individual. Conversely, the Protestant ethic encourages a view of meaningful work as a solo activity, done at one's office, workbench, or other location designed for individual effort. A symptom of this view is the common complaint, "I didn't get any work done today; I had to spend the entire day in meetings." That is, any collective process, such as a meeting, is defined as nonwork. Yet this view of work as something a person does alone separates the worker from the community of workers in the social workplace. Holland saw that when capital was "put over" labor, it inverted "the basic structure of human dignity." His discussion of "open, participatory model(s)" and "worker self-management" suggests that work should be meaningful through its social context. Workers are entitled to the social products of work.

Work, then, produces results (products, self-actualization, and meaningful social interaction and contact) that should be shared to some extent. The community is involved, not just the individual worker. In this view, appropriation of socially constructed products or socially constructed meaning is theft, as in Proudhon's famous epigram in his 1840 work, *What Is Property*, "Property is theft."

In large measure, the Catholic ethic view of work is a practical, matter-of-fact perspective. Work does not even rate an entry among the "over 400,000 updated articles that clarify Catholic beliefs" in the 1987 edition of *The Catholic Encyclopedia*. Yet work is a focus of Catholic discussion and thought on an ongoing basis.

And U.S. Catholic bishops, in their proposals for economic justice for all, developed ideas about work that had three of the foci we have examined here: "First, [work] is a principle way that people exercise the distinctive human capacity for self-expression and self-realization. Second, it is the ordinary way for human beings to fulfill their material needs. Finally, work enables people to contribute to the well-being of the larger community" ("Economic Justice for All," no. 97, in Gannon, 1987).

Work in its many aspects is, therefore, definitely good within the Catholic ethic tradition. Holland (1984–1985a, p. 1) refers to work as the "co-creation" of ecological, social, and spiritual elements. It provides resources, and a worker should always do the best possible job because self and others are depending on it—but one should not confuse work with more important things in life. One does not draw one's fundamental sense of meaning from work. That meaning comes from home, family, and community, including the community of other workers. McCarthy and McGaughey state that the traditional, Catholic ethic view, "called for work to find its place as an assistant to mankind, not a master" (p. 189).

From a Catholic ethic perspective, no one would be considered a better person because he or she is a hard worker or a worse person if a less efficient worker. Moral distinctions may be important differentiations that can be and are made about people. However, from the perspective of the Catholic ethic, judgment about moral character does not flow along with what kind of work one does or how hard one works, as it tends to do from the Protestant ethic perspective.

Thus, a major source of contention between the two ethics becomes clear. In the traditional Catholic view, work was a productive activity and even a community effort. The process was straightforward, and it was important because people were doing it. The resulting products were available to the whole community. You produced what you needed, consumed it, and shared the rest if others needed it.

The Protestant view inverted the Catholic view. The purpose of work was sacred, the process a cleansing one. Work became separated from the worker: work achieved predominance, and the worker was subordinated. The results of work—its products and meaning—became independent as well. The application of these ideas through industrialization and the capitalistic system became what we think of today as the Protestant work ethic.

## Work as Ceremony or Ritual

Work may be *ritual*, taking that word in its anthropological sense to mean an activity that transforms the enactor, or work may be ceremony, in the sense that one goes through it and mostly enjoys it but is not changed by it. Whether it is ritual or ceremony reflects on who is seen to control or "own" resources and who (or what) needs them. The resulting definition of ownership is central to the way people think about helping others in general and the poor in particular. Whether work is ritual or ceremony also reflects on who will work well beyond any relationship of products to need and who has a set of resources in mind that he or she needs and will rest upon reaching.

What are the daily processes that reflect attitudes about work? Work-related activity extends far beyond the work itself, into the preparation time for work, nonwork activities associated with work, and the decompressing process of returning home from work.

While many of the activities in work as ritual and work as ceremony are the same, the purpose is different. In the ceremonial case, doing the job is the goal. One thinks of the views of others, the work one needs to do, the logistics of the job itself, whom one needs to provide assistance, and so on. In the ritual case, work is a "rat race" that needs to be won. Victory over adversaries (people, processes, impediments, and ideas) becomes a goal.

Work as both ceremony and ritual has the same series of stages—preparatory, active, decompressing, and rest. The difference is that ceremonies and rituals differ in their power to alter the participant. Ceremony celebrates, recognizes, and enhances. When the Catholic ethic sees work as ceremony it sees it as a religious celebration—a liturgy as it were (Holland, 1984–1985a, 1984–1985b, 1984–1985c)—in which people are the center, the work is secondary. Rituals transform so that the work is the center and people are secondary. The difference is not so much *what* one does, but the *meaning and value associated with the activity*. What Spikard (1991) recounts about Navajo ritual applies here: "For the person cured in Navajo ritual, the content of the ritual message is less important than its experience. Just *believing* that the natural and supernatural are joined would not cure. *Living* their conjuncture does. Unlike dreams or scientific theorizing, but like music, the point of these rituals is to shape the participants' inner time, and thereby reorient them to the world" (p. 202). This is exactly true of the Protestant ethic orientation toward work. ! (

## Social Products of Work

Who "owns" the results (outputs or products) of work, and what are these results for? I touched on this topic briefly above, but it deserves more attention. Work results can include concrete products like money, cars, groceries, or clothes, and intangible products like meaning and social status, and the Catholic ethic and the Protestant ethic have different perspectives on who owns these products of labor, who besides you has a *legitimate* claim on "your" work products.

In the Catholic ethic the products of one's work are for oneself and others, and the part for others may be the more important. Work is a social product ("for man," McCarthy and McGaughey, 1989, p. 186). Fanfani (1936) comments that "the rules of religious and social morality accepted by the European pre-capitalist gave him the idea of wealth as a means for the attainment of the natural and supernatural ends both of him who had and him who *had not*. . . . This idea is of first importance for it leads directly to a social conception of the use of wealth, that is, to a satisfaction of a man's own needs with those of his neighbor" (p. 37). Novak (1993) quotes Pope John Paul II's document *Centesimus Annus* as it makes a similar point about work: "It is becoming clearer how a person's work is naturally interrelated with the work of others. More than ever, work is work with others and for others: It is a matter of doing something for someone else" (p. 130).

The corollary to this view is that work should provide a just wage—a living wage, a fair day's wage for a fair day's work—and when possible, should share some of the profits or excess created in part by the workers and their efforts that the firm enjoys. Whether or not the firm has a large profit is a secondary consideration.

The Catholic ethic perspective may already be modifying the historical U.S. view of work as *your* business, as people begin to contest some corporate practices. Vincent Paul Donnelly, for example, is a Detroit attorney who began life as a seminarian and now, seeing corporations "become more immoral every day," sues companies for wrongful discharge (Bray, 1993, p. 4F). Robert Bellah and others (1991) comment about the *emerging* work ethic that they see in the United States: "In a democratized economy it should be much clearer that the work we do is something we do *together* and *for each other* as much as by and for ourselves" (p. 105.) This perspective sounds like an emerging Catholic ethic perspective.

In the tradition of the Protestant ethic (which in this context can be thought of as the existing U.S. concept of capitalism as well), each business, whether a one-person operation or a giant corporation, owns the product it produces, negotiates, or somehow secures. As an ad for a popular business training program proclaims, "You only get what you negotiate." The implication is that you and you alone have your interest at heart. No one can be expected to look out for you or advance you. It is, after all, up to you.

The concept of "excess" is not relevant either in the Protestant work ethic, since excess is what remains after a set standard has been exceeded. If work is sacred, then one cannot have too much of its results or too many of its products. What some would call excess translates into a good year in this view. In fact, while some would call profit itself excess, from this view, it is return on investment (or return on risk). Individuals ought to accumulate as much as they can. Firms ought to make as much profit as they can. Thus, a "fair" wage is not a legitimate concept; rather wages as low as possible or as low as the market will allow is the operative concept. The idea that workers should share in any "excess" is usually out of the question (although there have always been some firms that have). The lack of a concept of excess may lie at the heart of our capitalism. Contrast this orientation with the orientation of the premiere Catholic organization, the Catholic Church. Many Catholic religious orders have a vow of poverty. Catholic schools and Catholic social services organizations have never been known for their plump paychecks. One could see this low pay as consistent with the capitalist goal of paying as little as possible. However, the Catholic motivation is different. Low pay here does not make employers rich. Rather, it enables service to the community. (There is something of a values clash here, however. Obviously, there can be, and has been, exploitation within the Catholic Church. The cui bono question ["Who benefits?"] does extend here to the community as well as to the organizations.)

## Aspects of Motivation

There are different ways to motivate workers to work. Each way makes different assumptions about the nature of work and the relationship of people to work. The Protestant and Catholic ethics tend to adopt different sides of these sets of assumptions, reflecting the differences in their approach to and thinking about human behavior, human motivation, and what finally keeps our noses to the grindstones.

The first set of assumptions distinguishes between motivation that comes from within a person (that is, the amount of self-actualization, self-supervision, and empowerment people experience) and motivation produced by outside pressure. Douglas McGregor in his famous book *The Human Side of Enterprise* (1960) identifies these assumptions with what he calls Theory X and Theory Y management. In Theory X, the general idea is that people do not want to work and that they need constant supervision, checking, and attention if they are going to get anything done. The old rules about managerial span of control embody this approach. Before organizations began the current bout of downsizing, it was thought that each worker needed so much direct supervision that a supervisor could only check on about 5 subordinates. Run forward, that means that an organization with 1,000 workers needs 200 first-line supervisors, 40 second-line supervisors, 8 third-line supervisors, 2 fourth-line supervisors, and 1 boss of all bosses, for a total of 251 supervisors per 1,000 employees.

Conversely, Theory Y assumes that people want to work and can generally supervise themselves in a task if they know what goals are to be achieved. Here, work is felt to be a natural human activity, in which people willingly join for part of their day. The "boss" becomes a "guide," talking with people as they feel they need his or her coaching or advice. Span of control is replaced with span of communication.

Because of its deep enmeshment with issues of personal meaning and the idea of work as a calling, the Protestant ethic focuses on motivation for work that is largely internal and intrinsic. One works because one wants to. The Catholic ethic pays more attention to extrinsic motivation. One works for community and to meet personal needs, and as those pressures and capacities vary, so may effort and work. Therefore, the Protestant ethic supports a self-supervising perspective. The Catholic ethic tends to emphasize supervision by authorities.

Distinguishing between work and money, one of the products of work, reveals further motivational differences. I suggest that while the Protestant ethic sees work as driven by internal motivation, external motivation is important when it comes to money. People with this ethic are driven by feelings about needing *more* ("I *need* more money, a bigger salary, more things"), because the extent to which they are seen by others as successful and as good depends on their having more. The Catholic ethic, on the other hand, sees work as guided by external motivation, but internal motivation is important when it comes to money ("I decide how much I need"). More is not in and of itself better.

A second set of assumptions relates to people's needs or desires for work's products. People can optimize or "satisfice" (March and

Simon's 1958 term for accepting something as "good enough"). If need is a bottomless pit (as in the view that "one can never be too rich or too thin"), then one will keep working day and night, rarely stopping, optimizing one's gains. But if one has some personal, family, or community needs in mind, then one can become a goal-directed earner, tapering off effort and involvement as one satisfies the goal and shifting one's time and energy to other arenas of interest and commitment. The Catholic ethic encourages satisficing in both work and money but with a sense of balance (a full day's work for a full day's pay), while the Protestant ethic encourages optimizing (business is business).

Yet a third set of assumptions about motivation posits a continuum that runs from fear-based to love-based motivation. One can do something because one has to or because one wants to. One may feel obliged to pay attention to family and community, or one may wish to do so. In either case, the results may look similar, but the motivation will be different, and the person will view his or her activities differently. In the Protestant ethic, love of work drives the urge to work and work well, but fear of losing the job and its money are also motivators for performance of the work. In the Catholic ethic, while there is fear of the loss of work's products and meaning and, of course, fear of job and pay loss as well, motivation also comes from love of the human interaction surrounding products and meaning. The sense of work as production for oneself and also for one's family and community produces an affectional, commitment-based motivation, a positive wish to work and contribute. Moreover, love-based motivation is a conscious part of the Catholic ethic today. Holland and Henriot (1983), for example, comment that "new energies are emerging to create a fresh civilization. The pope does not refer to this in traditional Catholic terms as a 'Christian civilization' but rather as a broader 'civilization of love'" (p. xvii).

The concept of love-based motivation brings us back to external motivation. External motivation in the Catholic ethic comes from this sense of family and community as affectionally important. Needs and wants in the family and community world beyond oneself play an important part in thinking about how much time to invest in the job. Externally set goals materialize in part from needs and wants in the community. Thus, external motivation is positive. It is not a question of force; rather, the interests of others are part of people's basic ethical view.

Finally, I must point out that motivation springing from the Protestant and Catholic ethics has been somewhat obscured in the U.S. by several circumstances. Until recently, Protestants were, overall, of higher social status in America. They were more likely to have professional occupations, and they earned more. Their urge to work can look like a result of their having better jobs rather than their work ethic. Catholics, typically more recent immigrants and of lower socioeconomic status, appeared to have little choice about their work owing to that status.

In addition, supervision of lower-status occupations has come to be driven by Theory X ideas, while management of upper-status occupations has come to be driven by Theory Y ideas. These properties were the result of the structure of the occupations, not who was in them. However, as time went on, it was assumed that Theory X ideas were necessarily descriptive of the lower occupational categories. This view was probably helped along by Protestant ethic views about work status and its links to moral character and by the way the jobs themselves were resisted by people (not because they did not like work but because the jobs were divided up into small pieces and lacked integrity). Similarly, it came to be assumed that people in the higher status occupations could be managed according to Theory Y ideas because of their character. These associations came to be seen as inexorable, even though such was not the case, and recent management thinking now finds Theory Y ideas appropriate for all levels of workers. Indeed, those closest to the job, it is felt, have the best opportunity for improving the way it is done.

## Work, Good Works, and the Needy

Differences in orientations toward work ripple outward. They have implications. One set of implications that is especially important for this discussion has to do with the relationship of attitudes toward work purpose, work process, workers, and work products to attitudes toward those in need and toward sharing.

The idea of sharing is embedded in the community-based view of work purposes and motivation of the Catholic ethic. Work is for self *and others*. It occurs in a social context. Need is part of the human condition. Therefore, in the Catholic tapestry of work norms and social views, sharing is natural and it is also natural to provide help through *good works*. The Protestant ethic often sees need as the result of nonwork and believes that help is best given through encouraging *work*. In this worldview, need is remedied through requiring people to work in exchange for their aid. The workhouses of the past are an example of this approach, as are today's work incentive programs, and some of the newer ideas of requiring volunteer labor in exchange for welfare assistance. The federal- and state-supported Work Incentive Program (WIN) forces welfare recipients to accept training for work. (Some think it no accident that a more straightforward reading of the program initials produces WIP ["whip"].) In Michigan, welfare families are being invited to volunteer for community projects.

In the Protestant ethic, as we have seen, work is good and not working is bad. One is entitled to individual possession of work products, and people who do not get enough sustenance from work products or who are not working are thought to have flawed character. In the Catholic ethic, work is important but the person is more important. Because the products of work are at least semisocial to begin with, sharing is easier and the provision of help less threatening to the perceived moral order.

-- there summary comparisons are truly silly and unhelpful --

## The Discourse of Need and Work

The ideas in the Protestant ethic that join the alleviation of need to work explain why the concept of work has become central to the discourse in the U.S. about why people become poor and how programs of aid should be contracted. For example, the debate in 1994 about President Clinton's welfare reform package had two strands of thought: nonwork and its perils, and work and its encouragement (DeParle, 1994), that is, it centered on work for pay and the fear/love continuum of motivation.

Everyone wants welfare recipients to work more because lack of work is seen to be the principal reason for poverty. Our daily newspapers routinely feature articles on various forms of "workfare." For example, one such article quoted Lawrence Townsend, director of the Riverside, California, Department of Social Services, saying, "A lot of individuals in our society have lost sight of the old-fashioned American work ethic." The article then described a Riverside program that "provides education for those who can't pass a literacy test; others are put in a job search. Anyone who won't do either faces a reduction in welfare payments. . . . Nancy Downs, 30, credits the program as helping her land a job . . . after a two-year skid through alcohol, drugs, and unemployment. *The key, she says, was being ordered to look for work or lose benefits*" (Welch, 1993, p. 6A; emphasis added). Work is shown to be the most desirable solution for neediness, but how feasible is it?

This history of welfare is of interest as we examine this debate because the Social Security Act passed in 1935 provided specifically for those who *could not* work (the old, the blind, and, later, the permanently and totally disabled) and those who *should not* work (mothers with children and the elderly). A transformation has occurred. Now welfare is seen as aid for those who "cop out" and refuse to work, rather than a means for everyone to "chip in" and give those in need a little help. So the debate now centers on how to get "those people" to work. Experiments are underway (in New

York State for example) to allow people to keep more of what they earn while on welfare (in part through retaining Medicaid coverage) so that they are encouraged to go to work. Various plans for reducing support to families where adults will not or have not worked are being canvassed (although a California experiment in this area did not survive a legal challenge, Lewin, 1994, p. A7).

Much of the welfare debate deals only indirectly with the questions of whether there actually are jobs for current welfare recipients that can accomplish what reformers want and how many welfare recipients are able to work or are equipped with even the minimal working skills necessary for a works program. (Another of the numerous difficulties in designing a program that is viable has been union opposition to programs that might take away jobs that union members could otherwise have.)

When an economic crisis has been severe and people's need considerable, then one solution has been to have government create jobs. During the Depression, the Works Progress Administration (WPA) provided person power for a lot of useful projects while providing income to the needy and thus satisfying the American desire that income for the needy be somehow work related. Notice the assumption in this thinking that the needy are not *entitled* to these resources. The resources must be part of some kind of exchange. Nevertheless, there were people from the very beginning who thought the WPA was a boondoggle and that the workers did not work very hard, and WPA also came to stand for things like "We Poke Along." In other words, not just any work will do in this exchange of income for work. It should be "real" work.

Provision of money to the needy even within the work-related compass has been difficult and complex. Another example of the difficulties is the view that if work is valuable and available, then paying people for not working with such programs as unemployment benefits is simply wrong. Of course, proponents of unemployment compensation and other programs that have made resources available for people when they are out of work do not think of these programs as paying people for not working. They see them as supplying funds that bridge the period between jobs.

Thus, while work continues to be a central concern and non-work an anathema in the Protestant ethic, the solutions to not working are complicated, fraught with concern about helping the wrong people or helping people in the wrong ways.

### The Discourse of Need and Good Works

Within the Catholic ethic, good works provided through either personal or institutional mechanisms are considered appropriate and natural. Neither giving nor receiving aid is anything to get too excited about. (Readers of Andrew Greeley's novels will see a small confirmation of this—the practice of mutual help and support through church, family, and community is one of Greeley's leitmotifs). A national approach to the poor and the needy based on the Catholic ethic would not *begin* by viewing work and nonwork as the division of importance and attempting to turn the nonworking into workers. Rather, it would be likely to begin with such elements as child allowances (which would cover everyone, including those now on AFDC—Aid to Families with Dependent Children) and family allowances and a "social wage" for people on the job. Then a jobs creation program to make work opportunities more available might be started. With a substantial social floor in place, aid to individuals who had extra or special needs (that is, a preferential option for the poor) could be provided under the aegis of good works.

### Current Trends

Discussions of archetypes—the emphasis here—often leaves one wondering whether scholars and researchers use similar concepts and whether average citizens respond to them in any way.

With respect to the scholars and researchers, it is clear that those who are studying work-related issues today are thinking in terms that link closely to those described here. Two studies can serve as illustration.

Wollack and others (1971) identified six factors that individuals might value in their work: *status of the job* (getting a good job), *activity in the job* (keeping busy), *striving in the job* (seeking to get ahead in the job), *earnings* (getting the best-paying job possible), *pride* (taking pride in doing the best job one can do), and *involvement* (getting internal satisfaction from work performance). While they did not look at specific differences by religion, these factors coincide with the ones discussed here as most valued by the Protestant ethic. That is, they found what one might expect to find in a society dominated by the Protestant ethic. Whereas the Protestant ethic would give extremely high values to these factors, the Catholic work ethic would give them moderate values. An antiwork ethic would score at the bottom.

Martinson and Wilkening (1983) divided work into two areas of "satisfaction"—extrinsic and intrinsic. Extrinsic elements included salary and the ability to earn more money without changing employers. Intrinsic satisfaction focused on elements such as feelings of accomplishment in the job; extent of independent decision making on the job; relationships (presumably positive ones) with others on the job; and work that allowed one to do what one did well. This is also in line with the ideas discussed here.

In terms of the second question, what average people think, some scholars have used religion as a variable when surveying people about work-related issues. Readers will recall from Chapter One that some early researchers in this field found some, but not overwhelming, differences between Protestant and Catholic individuals. It seems that such differences as there are tend to be modest and might have been more pronounced historically than they are contemporarily.

Ter Voert (1991) investigated attitudes toward "work as a duty," "job achievement," and the "Christian work ethic." The latter is of special interest. Work as duty was measured by preference for "hard" work; job achievement was measured by the preference for always taking a better job if you can get it, and the Christian work ethic was measured by the ranking of four "Christian" virtues: work hard (reflecting work as duty), strive for achievement; work orderly and precisely, and spend time usefully. (This definition of a Christian work ethic looks very much like the Protestant ethic.) Ter Voert's findings did not suggest strong relationships, but did identify Catholics as coming out lower on the scale of work as a duty than orthodox Calvinists (although Catholics were slightly higher than two groups—Dutch reformed and neo-Calvinists) and lower on the Christian work ethic scale. Catholics scored higher on the achievement scale, however, a finding made from U.S. data by Andrew Greeley on several occasions. So the picture is mixed.

Glenn and Weaver (1982) looked at changes in the work ethic over time. The question, asked in 1955, was whether respondents enjoyed their work so much they had trouble putting it aside. A healthy 50.2 percent of Protestants and 44.1 percent of Catholics answered in the affirmative. In response to a question whether the respondent enjoyed hours on the job more than hours not on the job, 40.6 percent of Protestants and 28.3 percent of Catholics answered in the affirmative. One reading of these results is that there was a split between Protestant and Catholic respondents in attitudes toward work. By 1980, when the researchers asked the questions again, positive responses to both questions had dropped considerably, and the Catholic versus Protestant difference had disappeared. However, although both Catholic and Protestants were less enthusiastic about work in 1980, the biggest, most significant change, occurred among Protestants. Protestants were looking more like Catholics than the reverse. This may signal a shift in ethics rather than a parallel diminution of their influence.

When reasons for work were examined by Yankelovich and Immerwahr in 1984, they found that 17 percent of the respondents viewed work as an "unpleasant necessity"; 9 percent viewed work as a "transaction (the more I get paid the more I do)"; 21 percent saw work as "interesting but [with] limited claims (I find work interesting but I would not let it interfere with the rest of my life)"; and 51 percent took the "intrinsic moral value view of work (I have an inner need to do the best job possible, regardless of pay)" (1984, p. 21). The differences reflect the kind of division we would expect to find insofar as "the inner need view" appears to correspond to the Protestant ethic and the morally neutral "interesting but [with] limited claims" view appears to describe the Catholic ethic.

If U.S. Protestants and Catholics are moving closer together in terms of work orientation and both seem to be committed less to work than each was historically, how can this be understood? Yankelovich and Immerwahr (1984) suggest that it is less the commitment to the work ethic that is changing than the conditions of the workplace. Workers are ready to work but lack trust in their employers and feel that their rewards are rarely commensurate with their investment and effort in the workplace (Yankelovich, 1981).

The workplace is a cauldron of competing values. On the one hand, there are those who believe that performance should be, and is, rewarded with appropriate cash rewards. On the other hand, there are those who believe that pay is allocated on almost every other basis than merit (with "merit" defined as individual productivity). And there are arguments about how much pay one should get for performance, assuming performance could be defined to everyone's satisfaction.

Then there are questions about the very basis of this thinking, the tight connection between status of work and status of income. Christopher Jencks declares, "We must reduce the 'punishments for failure and the rewards for success'" (Jencks, 1982, p. 8; cited in Bellah and others, 1986, p. 106). It is not clear how many would agree with this idea now, but certainly there is movement at the margins to do just what Jencks suggests. And some modification of the extremes of wage distribution is occurring through setting minimum wage scales at one end and tempering executive compensation at the other.

It is timely for us to be considering the values of the Protestant and Catholic ethics. The empirical situation in the workplace and the perceived connections between work and money appear to be changing. Shifts are occurring that may eventually bring people who once had different views closer together. Looking at the history of some of our deepest values about work and money and examining the deep structures that underlie these values and will continue to shape them even as they respond to other cultural influences can give us some necessary wisdom about ourselves and our possibilities for conscious choices.

So basically no diff's tween Prot's + Cath's or any 7 true — I'm pretty sure Wuthnow's about study But this author just moves right along!

## Money

Money says, same thing —

Money has become a universal medium of exchange. Without it, we find it hard to accomplish the myriad tasks that constitute daily living. While money will not buy everything, it buys a lot of things. However, beyond these basic elements, having money means different things to different people. To some, money means having a regular income. To others, it means having enough to indulge in things the person and his or her family desire that are beyond ordinary needs—a fine house, fine cars, fine clothes. These different views have been variously influenced by the Protestant and Catholic ethics.

### The Protestant Ethic: You Can Never Be Too Rich

In the Protestant ethic, money is clearly a hallowed product which derives from participating in work, the sacred ritual. After the Reformation, energy that had gone to securing grace according to the Catholic ethic went to securing money according to the Protestant ethic.

Money in the Protestant ethic and grace in the Catholic ethic have a lot in common. You can never have enough of them. They can be "devalued" in an instant, so you had better keep a lot in reserve. In the Protestant ethic tradition, as discussed earlier, money is the worldly sign of success at work. Thus, the wealthy person is the morally superior person. The person who has pursued his or her calling by working is close to God, is probably predestined to be saved, and for that reason is of higher elevated character. Its sacred significance made money itself sanctified, like grace.

As the sacred product of a sacred process, money became detached from need. In the Protestant ethic, the fact that somebody lacked the cash for necessities was not what determined whether or not that person should get assistance. Similarly, the fact that someone did not *need* a raise in order to buy necessities was irrelevant to whether or not he or she should get one. Raises, like grades in school, were to relate to work performance.

## The Catholic Ethic: Money Is Probably Good but Not Great

The Catholic ethic had an instrumental perspective on money. Money was probably good; more money might be better. Money allowed you to get the things you needed to live and also things that you might want beyond those needs.

However, one also had to be careful about money. It could have dangerous properties. Too little was obviously problematic. But too much was also likely to be problematic—derived from exploitation or from illegal or immoral sources or from working to the point of ignoring family and community. A person with a lot of money might forget that money cannot buy everything and seek to offer money instead of self in important relationships. Money could compromise a person's sacred status. The gospel warned: "It is easier for a camel to get through the eye of a needle than for a rich man to enter the kingdom of heaven" (Matthew 19:24). Jesus asked people to give up everything to come with him.

In the Catholic ethic, then, money is approached ambivalently. Having more money does not make you a better person, and it could easily make you a worse person. It is partly for this reason that some religious officials (priests, nuns) take vows of poverty.

Part of this ambivalence stems from historical tradition—Christianity first developed among people who were poor. Part comes from a sense that those who had much money probably made it through exploitation. How could one enjoy resources forced from others? Part also emanates from Christianity's early communal perspective, the idea that goods are, at least in part, community property because it is the community's responsibility to provide at least the basics of what its members need. This principle is most clearly operative in formal religious communities of priests and nuns. But it is true in a somewhat looser sense in all Catholic communities. If a community member has few resources, the community will step in and help out. Up to a point, then, community members can rely on the community to supply resources rather than rely solely on themselves. However, excessive individual resource acquisition can threaten community membership and personal self-esteem. One should have what one needs. If what one can get on one's own falls below that, the community will help out. But if one has a lot more than that, questions about the provenance of one's resources might well arise.

Fanfani (1936) summarizes the Catholic doctrine on the acquisition of wealth in this way: "Man has necessities, needs that must be satisfied, and, if temporal goods can satisfy them it is duty and legitimate to seek to acquire such goods bearing in mind two rules, first that they must be acquired by lawful means, and secondly, *that the amount acquired must not exceed the need*" (p. 128; emphasis added).

The "pizza king" Tom Monaghan is a case in point. He has had fabulous financial success. However, this devout traditional Catholic is filled with guilt because of the prosperity he enjoys. In the press, he frequently mentions his feelings of guilt and his wish to perform charitable acts as a way to "atone" for his wealth. For example, he once announced, "I'm the biggest hypocrite there is. So anything that gives me pleasure for purely selfish reasons, I'm selling." The pleasurable goods included "an $8 million Bugatti; a $12,000 wristwatch, $14,000 paintings, and $7,000 vases. Also Monaghan's helicopters, planes, and yachts" (DeSmet, 1991, p. 12A).

Monaghan's various statements and activities illustrate several points in the Catholic attitude about money. One point is that there is a "proper" use of financial resources. They are not yours to simply do with as you wish. Thus, Monaghan seeks to use his money for good works, and he also gives to churches and to missions.

Fanfani points out that in the Catholic tradition, economic activity is second to people, a relationship similar to that which obtained with work in the traditional Catholic view: "Catholic theology and philosophy posit a religious criterion as the supreme rationalizing principle of life, even in its economic aspects and, again, Catholic philosophy subordinates economic rationalization to political rationalization, in that it relates the material well-being of the individual to the material well-being of his neighbor, and subordinates purely economic well-being to individual and social well-being in the widest sense of the word" (1936, p. 93).

Fanfani also sees that the Protestant ethic/Capitalist ethic changed this relationship: "Once it has been asserted that there is no conflict between the intensity of economic action and man's final end, the restrictions imposed by religious morality cease to exist. . . . And the new attitude is possible when the principle of subsistence, or, better, of sufficiency, is repudiated" (pp. 22–23). Moreover, "once a man has become imbued with the capitalist spirit, his chief concern with regard to work is indeed to achieve the maximum results with the minimum means. . . . Such a man . . . secretly substitutes material of inferior quality for material of good quality. . . . In the same category we may place attempts [at] reducing the quality of workmanship" (pp. 56–57). And finally, "The law of competition, which is the law of self-defence, makes it incumbent on all to put away any excessive concern for others" (p. 62).

## Money and Welfare

Money is hard to dispense under the Protestant ethic precisely because it is a sacred product. If money did not mean so much, it would not be as hard to give it away or to let other people use it for a while. But because it is so meaningful, all kinds of strings and checks must be placed on the giving of it to ensure that recipients "deserve it," that they are not "double dipping" (working while getting welfare benefits), and so on. So revealing of self are people's feelings about money that a number of researchers who rely on surveys have learned to put questions about attitudes toward money last on their questionnaires. These questions have a high potential for upsetting people and interrupting the flow of an interview. (The only more sensitive questions relate to body weight!)

At some level, as suggested earlier, providing money to people as a form of assistance can seem like providing them with extra points on an exam or even taking the exam for them. It can seem to be a means of distorting a fundamental indicator of a person's intrinsic value. When money indicates personal achievement, people constantly worry that they might be providing illegitimate aid to upward mobility or supporting lazy people.

Within the Catholic tradition, however, sharing is the expectation and it extends to money. Fanfani observes: "that which [a person] acquired [that person] was bound to dispense . . . to those in need; *to give it back to be used by the society to which it belonged.*" Capitalism, conversely, "has one principle: individual economic utility" (1936, p. 137).

If money were not a sacred symbol and proxy, then the "problem" of welfare would look much different to us.

One approach to need could be a social wage, meaning that people could make enough from work to support their needs. Fanfani explains, "It is this conviction" that there is a social use of wealth "that leads Catholic writers to speak of a just price in transactions . . . in this case a just price will be a just wage" (p. 134).

Paul Schervish (1991), a scholar who thinks a lot about what economic justice might look like, looks at similar ideas with contemporary methodology. First, he defines "justice" in wages this way (drawing on the 1891 social encyclical of Pope Leo XIII, *Rerum Novarum*, nos. 32, 63, 65): based on Church teaching, justice, as it applies to remuneration for human work, "required a wage to be 'not less than enough to support a worker who is thrifty and upright,' . . . a wage 'sufficiently large to enable him (a worker) to provide comfortably for himself, his wife and his children'" (p. 5).

Using a concept of "ordinary economic rights," Schervish calculated that it would cost $37,124 (in 1991) for a thrifty family of four to achieve those rights. Only one-fifth of that amount would go for food, the rest would have to go to other needs for the family to achieve ordinary economic rights. With this information, he recalculates the definition of poverty. Currently the poverty line in the United States is based upon the assumption that a worker spends one-third of her or his income for food. With this multiplier in mind, the Department of Agriculture shops for the foods that would constitute a nutritionally basic diet and multiplies that cost by three. Four levels of food expenditure are defined: low, thrifty, moderate, and high. The thrifty level is used to calculate the poverty line. The department then figures the proportion of families with an income below that line.

Because Schervish calculates that only one-fifth of the family's income goes to food, he multiplies the cost of a thrifty diet by five instead of three. This change "raises the percentage of the population in poverty from the current 13 percent to over 30 percent of the U.S. population" (p. 13). For example, if it costs $100 to buy food for a thrifty diet for a month and if the assumption is that people living at a thrifty level will use one-third of their income on food in relation to their expenditures on their other needs, then $300 a month would be needed to avoid falling below the poverty line. If the assumption is that they use one-fifth of their income for food, then $500 a month is the poverty line.

Schervish's conclusion, made in the frame of the Catholic ethic, is that wages should go up.

The Catholic ethic, then, takes a more relaxed attitude toward money than the Protestant ethic. In certain respects, money is not too different from a bowling score. There is definitely a plus to having a higher bowling score, but no one would think you are a better person because of it. Shaquille O'Neal (the basketball player who will make $40 million over seven years with the Orlando Magic) suggests this attitude when he says, "I make more money in one year than my father made in his entire life, but that does not make me a better person than him. . . . To be able to [buy] stuff for the ones you love is the best thing about having money" (O'Neal, 1993, p. 7). The Protestant ethic is tougher and harsher in its view of money. It assumes that money is a vital indicator of a person's inner self and inner character. If the rich are different, as F. Scott Fitzgerald said, the Protestant ethic says the rich are better. The converse is even more troubling—the poor are not only different from other people, they are worse.

## Conclusion

The Catholic ethic and the Protestant ethic have different perspectives on work and money. While the Protestant ethic perspective has long been dominant, each perspective has merit and meets one set of social concerns. Each perspective opens up important questions about how we might define need and how we can get resources to that need when those resources are affect-laden.

## Chapter Four

# An Emphasis on Family, Community, and Mercy

In human society, one of the great tensions is that between family interests and individual interests. Cultures provide guidance and perspective for their members on questions of "right" relations and "right" thoughts about the respective roles of the family and the person. Greater emphasis can be placed upon the person (an individualistic emphasis) or on family and community (a communalistic emphasis). Religions, as cultures, directly and indirectly take positions on this issue.

One useful overview of possible orientations affecting this extremely large area of our lives was developed by Reisman, Glazer, and Denny in *The Lonely Crowd* (1961). They proposed three major foci, each of which characterizes a life orientation. One is *tradition-direction*, in which guidance from the past is the central feature. The second is *inner-direction*, in which guidance comes from looking inside oneself and coming to one's own decision. The third is *other-direction*, in which guidance comes from checking and clearing decisions with those in your family and community (both residential and workplace).

Both the Catholic ethic and the Protestant ethic are tradition-directed in part. In terms of emphasis however, the Catholic ethic is more other-directed, stressing commitments and natural ties to family and community, while the Protestant ethic is more inner-directed, accenting self-reliance and individualism, the responsibility to the solo self.

Linked to the issues of inner and outer directedness is each person's view of the nature of cause, fault, and responsibility, and of course, judgment, mercy, and forgiveness. The story of the prodigal son, for example, illustrates forgiveness in a family context. Religious cultures take varying positions here. How merciful should we be? How much accepting is acceptable? In this chapter, we will discuss all these issues.

## Family Orientation

The Catholic ethic is profamily. Its support of such economic measures as allowances to families with children comes from that profamily value base. The current Catholic positions on contraception and abortion come from that value base as well, even though the same base is used by others to support quite different positions, which tells us that the term profamily itself requires definition. Specifically, in the Catholic ethic, a familial orientation means that the family is a point of reference for an individual's decision making, and other members' views are always taken into account. For example, an offer of a job that would require you to leave town would also require you to consider the offer very seriously in the light of family interaction and the loss of family connections. Because "self" is at least partly defined in terms of the family/community nexus, leaving family, extended family, and community for purely personal advancement, while certainly not prohibited, will be extremely stressful, requiring much thought and doubtless many family debates. Greeley calls this familial orientation and consultation the "the gallantry of the Catholic family" and also remarks that it was taken "for granted" by Catholics (1991, p. 111), which is another way of asserting that the Catholic ethic puts family and family obligations above self.

Indeed, at times, the strength of this family commitment transcends any "rationalistic" approach (to use Weber's term), allowing the idea of family to justify foolish sharing of resources or tolerance of abuse. Greeley tells of a priest receiving "a call from a parishioner, whose oldest son, home from first year at an Ivy League law school, had brought a girlfriend home without warning. The woman was five years older than their son, did not wash or use deodorant, was foul-mouthed, insulted the other children, and smoked marijuana. 'You should not put up with this behavior,' the priest said. 'But he's our son!' the father replied" (1991, pp. 280–281).

Anyone living in this tradition knows that family is not a place you have to go; it is almost always, in spite of problems, a place you want to go. Contrast this to the flinty approach to home described by Robert Frost in "The Death of the Hired Man": "Home is the place where, when you have to go there,/They have to take you in" (1971, p. 156). This very different view implies grudging acceptance rather than joyful welcoming at a place you "have to go" to.

A story about the twentieth-century artist Jean Dubuffet illustrates how extreme distances can arise between family members when individual needs come first.

[Dubuffet] once told an American journalist that he hated his "merchant family" and he appeared to have eventually severed his relations with them. When he was well into his late years, Dubuffet traveled to Le Havre to inspect a museum retrospective of his work, and, as he rounded a corner, encountered an extremely old woman examining a painting. The woman turned out to be his mother, not far from her hundredth birthday; they had not met for years. As he related to Glimcher, they had "a very nice conversation." Then he went back to Paris and never saw her again [Dudar, 1993, p. 81].

Today in the United States, we even have "throwaways," children who have been tossed out of their homes by parents for a variety of reasons. They make up a part of the homeless population that roams contemporary America.

### From Family to Community

The Catholic ethic enlarges the family. Family includes an extended family and community, that is, the local community centered around the parish (Greeley, 1990, also notes these "communal" elements).

The Catholic ethic sees the individual, the family, and the community as parts of an integral whole, a mosaic. Individuals feel a strong sense of linkage to the family and then to the community. Gregory Baum of McGill University has pointed out (personal communication, August 1994) that the Catholic conception of community as organic means that it includes a place for everyone—high and low, rich and poor—and that all the members of the community are "God's children." Family extends through generations and gradually includes members of the church congregation, ethnic group, local neighborhood, and larger community. In these extended families and linked communities, people know each other and know each other's business. Obviously such interconnections were once enhanced by concentricity of work, home, and community in the rural village and family farm. But through modern communications media, family and community linkages can now be maintained in the absence of physical proximity.

In addition to emphasizing families and communities, the Catholic ethic is also a communalistic ethic. Recall that Lester Thurow (1992) uses the concept of communal capitalism to characterize European capitalism. In communal capitalism, both individuals and corporations consider themselves citizens with a sense of membership in the community. Corporate citizens are sensitive to family and community connections and obligations. More broadly, the concept of communalism reflects the relationship (mainly positive or at least potentially positive) between the community in which you live and your own well-being. The Catholic ethic emphasizes this orientation.

Thurow contrasts communalistic capitalism to individualistic capitalism, which he sees as characteristic of the United States. Individualistic capitalism emphasizes personal gain and profit (whether the actor is an individual or an organization). And that characterization fits this country's dominant religious ethic. In the

Protestant ethic, personal and individual orientations dominate. Family and community orientation are present, of course, but less prominent. In the Protestant ethic, personal advancement may well supersede family loyalty, oftentimes with the family's approval. Although, in contemporary American society, in line with our new interests in examining value systems, we are achieving something of a balance between personal and family interests. The days when IBM was said by its employees to stand for "I've Been Moved" and when businesses uprooted people with no concern for their families seem to be passing.

## From Community to Society

Familial identification within Catholicism has never seemed to result in bonds extended across national boundaries, however, as has been the case for Jews, for whom religious identification has usually come before any national identification. For Catholics, the national identification seems stronger, with religion being the modifier. The so-called hyphenated Catholic is well known—for example, Irish-Catholic, Polish-Catholic, French-Catholic, Italian-Catholic, Black-Catholic, and Hispanic-Catholic.

In Quebec, for example, there are hundreds of towns named after Catholic saints, and the entire province celebrates the day of its patron, St. Jean Baptiste, with a legal holiday, illustrating an interconnection of religion, community, and family. In addition, until the early 1960s, the Catholic Church in Quebec operated schools and welfare programs serving the primarily Catholic French Canadians at the request of the government. (Protestants ran their own programs, as well.) Now that approach is changing from a religious to a provincial base. However, because of this accommodation, cross-national identification among all Canadian Catholics was not as great as it might have been. On smaller scales, communities (in Europe, and later in the United States and Canada) of Catholics have usually grown up within ethnically segregated enclaves.

The importance of ethnic communities, however, is consistent with the Catholic ethic tradition's emphasis on family and community. (Readers of fiction will find an evocation of the Irish-Catholic parish and its sense of familial solidarity in Andrew Greeley's novels, a feeling that Chaim Potok captures for Hasidic and other Jewish communities in novels such as *The Chosen* and that even the series of mystery novels by Harry Kemelman evokes.)

## Gemeinschaft and Gesellschaft

As the context of social relationships changes, the relationships change. Movements from family to extended family and from extended family to community emphasize communal values. Movements from community to society, however, change the nature of those relationships. A number of years ago, the German sociologist Ferdinand Tönnies ([1887] 1957) described this division between communal, personalistic relationships (*gemeinschaft*) and societal, impersonal ones (*gesellschaft*), and there have been many applications of this concept over the years.

One is temporal, suggesting that as modernization occurs, societies move from communal to societal bases of relationships, from barter and exchange to money, from "belonging" to "entitlement." Another approach suggests that the division involves the movement from rural life to urban life and from the personalization and smallness of the rural village to the impersonalization and bigness of urban existence. A third approach focuses on the shift from clan organizational forms to hierarchy and bureaucracy, from belonging to rules, as a basis of interaction.

In addition, I suggest that the Catholic ethic links to gemeinschaft orientations. That is, membership, personal connection, and affectional bonds are the important relationships between people. The Protestant ethic links to gesellschaft orientations. That is, citizenship, position, rights, and duties are the bases of relationships. Thus, a family orientation is also a community orientation and a self-orientation is also a societal orientation. It may be that more impersonal relationships of society require individualism or, alternatively, that individualism is fostered by the impersonality of societal interactions. Whichever way the causality goes, Tönnies's concept captures one dimension of difference between the Catholic ethic and the Protestant ethic.

Yet this also seems an appropriate point to recall that conflicting viewpoints can exist within the same ethos in a dominant-subdominant relationship. The following illustration suggests the way in which dominant and subdominant emphases might look.

| Dominant | Orientation | Subdominant |
|---|---|---|
| Catholic ethic | ← Family  Community → | Protestant ethic |
| Protestant ethic | ← Self  Society → | Catholic ethic |

Furthermore, these two approaches, family and community on the one hand and self and society on the other, suggest where we will find class consciousness and where communal consciousness. In the Protestant ethic, class consciousness is dominant, indicated by the focus on the individual and consciousness of individual *position*. One affiliates horizontally, with others in a similar position. In contrast, the Catholic ethic promotes the family and community and consciousness of *connection*, one links oneself to others in one's family and community in all directions, regardless of position.

## Solo Self and Ensemble Self

The communal focus in the Catholic ethic is not distinct from a concept of the self but completely intertwined with it. When we think of the self, conditioned by the Protestant ethic, we are most likely to think of an individual person, a sort of self-contained self. However, recent social psychological thinking has explored different ways in which a self can be defined or constructed. One approach, indeed, is to think of the self as a solo self, a person who is her or his own main point of reference, who is inner-directed, and whose very self-concept is autonomous.

Alternatively, though, we can construct a self through interweaving strands and fibers of family and community, so that the self is not *distinct from* those connections but *meshed with* them. Sampson (1985) calls this communally interwoven self an "ensemble self." The concept of the ensemble self reacts against the picture of "human nature as being autonomous, independent, individualistic, and rational . . . [and instead, defines] the self in terms of relationships" (Smetana, 1991, p. 494). The concept of the ensemble self fits well with the existing Catholic ethic, for it is fundamentally in the family and community that the self in the Catholic tradition draws its strength, meaning, orientation.

The concept of the community-based, ensemble self as an effective self has the potential to mitigate the intensely individualistic, work- and wealth-oriented self that is the effective self within the Protestant ethic. That does not mean that people living out the Protestant ethic are not attached to one another, but individual identity is not ineluctably bound up in those attachments. Rather, identity comes from achievement and accomplishment via work, which is something one does alone. Action is taken with the self as a point of reference.

Individualism—the free-standing social self—is a relatively new concept historically, and it represents the high point of the Protestant ethic, especially in the United States. It has had many positive outcomes. For one thing, it emphasized independence and self-reliance in a country where that perspective was an extremely functional one. For another, it legitimized the drive for individual gain necessary in a competitive environment. If one is seeking to wrest goods and resources from others, then a guilt-free approach to this activity is surely a plus. Concerns about competing for resources could be, if one was so inclined, discarded with the kind of thinking summed up in the simple aphorisms: "All's fair in love and war"; "A penny saved is a penny earned"; "Business is business"; or "May the best man win." This kind of individualism allows (but does not require) exploitation of others and throws up barriers against sharing.

Individualism within the Protestant ethic tradition did not totally prevent the development of a charitable orientation. Individuals could have a sense of obligation to designate some of their resources for others, and some did this on a large scale, building libraries (as Andrew Carnegie did) or universities (as John D. Rockefeller did). But such thinking was an individual definition of obligation, rather than a sense that resources are partly claimed by the community. And it is this kind of belief system that Ryan (1981, p. 50) calls "counterfeit equality," meaning that the community, even the family, may lay no legitimate claims on an individual's resources.

An apt illustration of the individual orientation to resources is the maxim often heard today on college campuses with respect to the financial condition of the various units and departments: "Each tub sits on its own bottom." It means that where money is concerned, there is no campus community and that no legitimate claims may be made, say, by a school of social work on the revenues of, say, an athletic department or law or business school, even though the former may be falling on hard times and the latter flush with money. The individualism of Protestantism and the Protestant ethic finds itself at home in a community that agrees that each tub sits on its own bottom.

In cultures guided by the Protestant ethic, community emphasis, as mentioned earlier, is based on a notion of exchanges not sharing, while the charitable impulse seems most excited by a disaster such as a fire or flood. Then neighbors rally round and chip in. It is when more permanent arrangements are contemplated that people become ambivalent.

By transforming the context of daily life and the meaning of work, individualism shifted society's emphasis on the importance of the *connections* between nodes (family member nodes, community nodes, or, as sociologist Georg Simmel puts it, "the web of group affil-iation" [Wolff, 1950]) to an emphasis on the *nodes themselves*. Even work, as I mentioned, is done alone and one symptom of that emphasis has been the downgrading of collective work efforts.

Nevertheless, again, there is evidence that we are opening ourselves to new values. Countervailing cultural models are being advanced, and one that is now achieving some credibility in the managerial world is the concept that teamwork is often more pro-ductive than solo work. The feminist movement is also support-ing a shift in contemporary perspectives. Carol Gilligan (1982) and other feminist thinkers argue for a more connected, more relationship-based sense of self and feel that such a perspective is more characteristic of women's socialization and posture than is the solo self.

However, though the language may be new, the concepts are old. After all, it was Aristotle who said, "Man is a political [that is, social] animal." To the extent that Aristotle's ideas were picked up by ancient culture and became part of the Catholic ethic, it is the Protestant individualism that is new, and our discovery of the ensemble self is a rediscovery.

## The Family and Community Team: A History

Family and community are each important in their own right within the Catholic ethic, but in addition, they function as teams and they are manifestations of a team orientation in the Catholic ethic. A person's basic identification in this ethic comes from the bonds of the family team and of the community team. There is a sense that everyone is in life's situations together. Family and com-munity members have a sense of permanent membership, ongoing belonging. They are family and community members on temporary assignment until something better comes along.

The importance of this aspect of the Catholic ethic becomes clearer if we look at the status of the family in pre-Christian times.

In those days, support for the family unit was highly variable. Not only was the legal status of women and children questionable, their very lives were often endangered as well. The death of many children before reaching adulthood and of many women in childbirth may have made even the idea of strong, enduring family relationships hard to sustain. On the lack of attention given to children, Hamel (1990) comments: "Little children, especially daughters, hardly appear in the sources. Jewish marriage contracts did occasionally stipulate that the husband was to provide care for his daughters, whose right to maintenance was not clearly established . . . children are rarely mentioned in Greek marriage contracts and inheritance clauses that come from other areas of the Mediterranean" (p. 41).

Early Christianity was communal Christianity. Christians had to depend on each other because almost everyone else was an enemy. Thus, communalism and interdependence were part of the very foundation of early Christianity and have survived and prospered to this day. The ancient church's emphasis on family as part of this communalism and on the role of women in the family should be regarded as extremely progressive, for at that time women and children had almost no rights whatsoever. In Christianity, the family now had a place, a function, a role. It was linked into the social structure in ways that had not been the case in most cultures of the ancient world (although the Jewish culture had emphasized the family as well). When Christianity began, the change to a family emphasis was probably revolutionary.

Women and children are each one-third of family. If their status is not protected or is placed in serious jeopardy, then there really is no family—there are just independent groups of fathers, mothers, and offspring. Connections are matters of convenience. The development of the concept of the family and the emphasis placed upon it is a case of the creation of social categories to provide support for those who previously had no protection. Although the emphasis of the Catholic Church on the family has come to be thought of as oppressive to women and perhaps limiting to children, it is actually an example of a social success turning to social failure as times change. Its success was to find a socially creative way to redefine and ennoble groups whose status had often been marginal and abysmal.

The redefinition of family in the Catholic ethic tradition appears to have been as radical as the Protestant redefinition of work or of the poor 1,500 years later. It may well have been one of the first charitable acts of the Catholic Church, elevating two key groups of humanity from oppression to worthy of social concern.

At the same time, familial feelings were being established within the body of Christianity. Meeks (1986), for example, speaks of the "unusual emphasis on solidarity and intimacy of [early] Christian fellowship. . . . [T]he rhetoric of [a letter from St. Paul] is so composed as to arouse the affection of the readers for one another, for the writers, and for Christian groups in other places, with which they have had some direct or indirect connection. . . . More than a metaphor is involved here, for the Christians are evidently expected . . . to cherish fellow members of the sect with the same care as they would natural siblings" (p. 129).

Family life has never been easy. Even with the emphasis on the family in early Christianity, women and children continued to suffer disproportionately from life's hardships. One of the more moving descriptions of the perils of family life is given by Mollat (1986) when he reflects upon the harshness of the early Middle Ages and the way "we can guess from the high proportion of child remains in the cemeteries that the infant mortality was quite high. Abandonment of newborn infants was common. . . . Marble basins were placed in the churches of Tours and Angers to receive babies left by their parents. . . . [I]n Paris there was the 'bed of Our Lady' at Notre Dame, and in Poitiers the 'bed of Our Lady of the Straw' at Saint-Cyprian" (pp. 288–289).

Marriage too, especially for women, carried no guarantees. In the middle ages, "marriage in the West, like marriage in the East, had not acquired the force of a durable bond: one wonders how many so-called widows were in fact abandoned wives" (Mollat, 1986, p. 28). Thus, even though the hazards of life for women and children had doubtless declined since the birth of Christ, reinforcement of the importance of women and children through the concept of the family was needed, and it was provided largely through the notion of the Trinity and the Holy Family first and then through corroborative church nomenclature. This continuing transformation of family was woven into the Catholic ethic.

### The Holy Family

Catholic devotional practices introduced and reinforced the development of familial structure. A root expression of these orientations and practices is the Blessed Trinity of God the Father, Christ the Son, and the Holy Spirit. This relational structure is reflected in the Holy Family of Jesus, Mary, and Joseph—a child, a mother, and a father. As time went on, Mary's status became extremely exalted and she, unlike Joseph, rose to close-to-deity status (see, for a popular contemporary example, Ostling, 1991). Along with the disciples and all the saints and martyrs, the celestial hierarchy thus formed a sort of extended family that was a bedrock for the church.

The family roles in this hierarchy provided an opportunity for familial intercession with God the Father. While a person's sins might be all in the (Holy) family, the Father might still be too scary to approach directly, and thus a person seeking forgiveness might want to speak first to a softer, more understanding family member, such as Mary, to see if she would intercede. The Holy Family may well be a projection of the traditionally accepted family roles with the father the harsher member and the mother more accepting. Whatever the Holy Family's origin, it daily reinforces the family system advocated by the Catholic ethic.

God viewed through the Protestant ethic, by comparison, is also somewhat stern, but He is unfamilial. Protestantism, unlike most religions, has no female figures whatsoever to serve as mediators with God for the petitions of the religious and those in need on earth. Ostling observes that "Protestants see no biblical basis for praying to [Mary] for favors, and they believe that veneration of her can slide into worship that is due to God alone. They also reject the idea that human beings, Mary included, can contribute to humanity's salvation" (p. 66).

## Church Nomenclature and Doctrine

In addition, the nomenclature of the Catholic Church has long embodied and reinforced family orientation. Priests are addressed as "father," nuns as "sister," heads of convents as "mother superior," some monks and members of other religious orders as "brother." Imagine the impact of these phrases, repeated millions of times each day over hundreds of years. If repetition reveals emphasis, then church nomenclature reflects the Catholic ethic's support for the importance of the family.

This metamessage, or underlying message, in the Catholic nomenclature particularly stands out when we compare the nomenclature of other religious traditions (Tannen, 1990). In Judaism, for example, the religious leader is a "rabbi" (that is, teacher), a form of address that stresses learning and knowledge rather than family. Among Protestants, the honorific "reverend" indicates a bond of respect and esteem, even deference, but does not indicate a family relationship and family feeling. In neither the Jewish nor the Protestant case is family specifically reinforced through the names of holy persons (see also Ostling, 1991; Woodward, 1991).

The Catholic Church has taken many doctrinal positions that support its kind of family emphasis. In addition to encouraging members to marry within the religion, as most religions do, the Catholic hierarchy has remained steadfastly in favor of families staying together and has opposed divorce, despite widespread flouting of this view among Catholics. Although interest in the ensemble self seems to be increasing among all individuals, other traditional doctrinal aspects of the family emphasis in the Catholic ethic are also being questioned by Catholics. The family emphasis is patriarchal, suggesting superiority of men and subdominance of women. The church opposes women priests and is unsympathetic to women's issues generally. The church's official views on abortion and birth control also reflect its strong emphasis on family members' interests over individuals' interests, even though these views are also ignored by many otherwise devout Catholics.

One important contemporary argument is that the latter views are actually antifamily, in the sense that they allow family size to expand beyond the level that parents can typically support. However, this is one of the reasons why the Catholic tradition supports family allowances. If the community and the extended family really joined together to care for children, seeing them as a community not just an individual responsibility, and if a social wage was in place along with family allowances and/or child allowances, then the antifamily aspects of larger families would be diminished. Thus, the Catholic ethic's support for charity and the welfare state, for family allowances and child support, is consistent with the devotional practices and beliefs of the Catholic Church. (However, support for the family has not been extended to include acceptance of new types of families, other than mother, father, and children, and unmarried couples, merged families, and gay and lesbian couples are still not considered families.)

Today's Catholic Church continues to emphasize the overall importance of family. As Gremillion (1976) comments, "Vatican II strongly reaffirms a—perhaps the—basic tenet of Catholic social teaching: 'The family is the foundation of society. In it the various generations come together and help one another to grow wise and harmonize personal rights with the other requirements of social life. All those, therefore, who exercise influence over communities and social groups should work efficiently for the welfare of marriage and the family'" (p. 111).

## Family, Community, and the Sharing Impetus

The emphasis in the Catholic ethic on family and family relationships, symbolized in the Holy Family and reflected in the simple structure of a parish headed by a "father," carries the concept of family into the concept of community, supporting the idea of helping and sharing. It looks positively on efforts to extend help within the communal group and surely is one source of the sharing orientation in that ethic.

Resting on ideas of family and community and communalism, the ethic does not support an adversarial relationship between the nonpoor and the poor. To use Ryan's terminology (1981), people are seen as collective and similar, not individual and different. Sympathy and help for others are more likely when the others are thought of as included in one's family and community.

Since family is where most individuals gain experience of giving and receiving care and learn the importance of mutual assistance, an orientation that emphasizes the importance of family is also one that supports the giving and receiving of aid. The emphasis on helping family members leads to support for, especially, unrelated women and children—the two groups long protected by the Catholic Church through its family orientation. Indeed, as Harry Murray (1990) points out in his discussion of the Catholic Worker movement, socialization in the family was considered practical preparation for taking up social responsibilities: "What the Catholic Worker position implicitly argues is that any member of society is capable of performing many of the tasks now claimed by various professions simply by virtue of being socialized" (p. 5).

An emphasis on family also supports the concept that giving or receiving aid between relatives is not extraordinary. It is not just something provided for those who cannot provide for themselves. The concept of aid inherent in the concept of family is that aid is a gift, provided out of affection and desire to help and emerging out of concern for connection and closeness rather than from a calculus of exchange. Fanfani (1936) states: "Capitalism requires such a dread of human brotherhood, such a certainty that man's neighbor is merely a customer to be gained or a rival to be overthrown, and all these are inconceivable in the Catholic conception of the world" (p. 142).

In sum, those raised in the Catholic ethic tradition will be more likely to support social welfare because the environment of assistance is positive and natural for them. Those raised in the Protestant ethic tradition will be more ambivalent about providing help to others and less likely to support social assistance.

## Mercy

Linked to ideas of family and community is a perspective on doing wrong, being forgiven, and forgiving. The Catholic Church is merciful. Its religious procedures allow for confession, mercy, and forgiveness of sins. The sacrament of penance allows one to access God's good graces. The very existence of such religious procedures indicates acceptance of a view in which the human condition is malleable and elastic. It is anticipated that individuals will flow into and out of states of sin and grace. Though a person may often get into trouble, he or she can always get out. The flexibility of the human condition is possible because celestial status is flexible. Therefore, "people deserve second chances," "nobody's perfect," and "there but for the grace of God go I" are phrases that express attitudes inherent in the Catholic ethic.

### Sin Happens

The Catholic view is that sin happens—daily. It is a part of the human condition. When Lee Iacocca, "confessing" his "sins," comments about his leadership at Chrysler Corporation, "If we went astray—you know people do go astray now and then in many areas—man, we got focused in a hurry" (Ingrassia and Stertz, 1990, p. 1), he is not accepting of sin per se but of the presence of sin in our lives and the need to accept the bad along with the good. Because sin is omnipresent, some way to deal with it is required that works and is easily accessible. While sin itself may not be eradicable, sinners can be rehabilitated; souls can be repaired. Through arguing that *sin is bad* but *sinners can be forgiven*, the Catholic Church and hence the Catholic ethic separate the sin from the sinner (just as they separate the work from the worker).

## The Cycle of Sin and Forgiveness

The Catholic view stresses, then, that sin, or evil, is always at work in the world, fighting with good. Overall, the outcome is certain. Good will win. However, in individual circumstances, evil and sin may be stronger than good influences. Good people stray and need a way to get back on track. In the Catholic Church, this is accomplished through forgiveness in this world and through Purgatory and eventual forgiveness in the next world.

We can see similar thinking in nonreligious situations as well. For example, while not a Catholic, President Clinton has expressed a highly similar view of sin and forgiveness, showing how perspectives from one ethos or another are now moving relatively freely around in people's value systems. Observing that "the President told members of his inner circle, 'character is a journey, not a destination,'" Klein comments: "This is not an insignificant statement. It is, first of all, an insight into [Clinton's] religious faith. Life is a pilgrimage; sin is inevitable; redemption is always possible (Clinton got into trouble, early on, by proposing that even Saddam Hussein might redeem himself). It is also a matter of personal experience. In the President's life displays of character have usually involved perseverance rather than principle" (1994a, p. 20).

Another example occurred in Poland in the summer of 1994, as the country completed a week of celebration of the Polish Uprising, a resistance movement of citizens against the German occupation in which the Polish people suffered 200,000 casualties. The president of Germany, Roman Herzog, had been invited to the ceremonies, amid great opposition. In a speech called by many to be profoundly moving, Herzog *apologized, and asked the Poles to forgive those World War II atrocities.* Polish leader Zbigniew Brym replied: "We as a Catholic nation are always ready to forgive, but, as in the Bible, we need the prodigal son to come and say, 'Father, I have sinned.' Until now we did not have that" (Murphy, 1994, p. A11).

The ubiquity of sin means that it is likely to touch all our lives. We all slip. However, the fact of sin does not create an indelible mark on the cloth of one's soul. It is like the dirt one picks up through the day; it can be washed away. Therefore, sin does not have implications for a person's character. People are not *either* bad or good but both bad *and* good. There are no sharp distinctions between sinners and other believers. Indeed, in Ireland today, you can still hear "sinner" used as a synonym for "human." Compare that view with Weber's description of the Protestant ethic: "The God of Calvinism demanded of his believers not single good works, but a life of good works combined into a unified system. *There was no place for the very human Catholic cycle of sin, repentance, atonement, release, followed by renewed sin*" ([1904–1905] 1956, p. 117; emphasis added).

In both ethics, sin is present in the world, and for both, it is to be avoided. The Catholic ethic, however, has a greater recognition of temptation's power. For the Protestant ethic, that power is not the issue. The Protestant ethic does not conceive of procedures that allow a person to flow back and forth between states of sin and states of grace. Status, as I discussed earlier, is immutable. If one is saved, one knows it or experiences it as a profound psychoreligious transformation. One does not earn salvation or work up to being saved; it happens. One either is or is not in this condition.

The differences in the Protestant and Catholic views of sin extend to definitions of what sin is in its essence. The Protestant ethic's individualistic orientation includes personalization of the religious experience. Sin, therefore, is personal. "The concentration was on the individual self and experience. . . . 'It is I who am the lost soul, sinful and defiled, in need of cleansing and renewal'" (Welch, 1972, p. 28). Social sin was not a concept of any currency. (The social gospel among some Protestant denominations did not develop until around the turn of the twentieth century).

The Catholic tradition considers sin in light of its effects on the family or community, and some thinkers go further, arguing that sin is separation from community rather than violation of any specific rule (see Cone, 1986). In this line of Catholic thinking, putting self over the needs of the community is sinful.

## Implications for the Poor and the Needy

Because the Catholic tradition is not prone to making clear distinctions between good people and sinners, it also does not make sharp distinctions between those who need help and those who do not. Negative judgments and hostile actions are to be tempered, an idea that continues to be emphasized in Catholic teachings. For example, the Catholic bishops' 1986 pastoral letter strongly and specifically cautioned against negative, judgmental thinking about the poor. In contrast, the Protestant ethic, as I have discussed, finds it appropriate to assign responsibility and to blame people as well as credit them.

In urging temperance, the Catholic ethic draws on a tradition of mercy stretching back to the gospels. Questioned by the Pharisees about how to punish an adulteress, Jesus urged them to "let him who is without sin be first to cast a stone at her" (John 8:1–7). When the Pharisees left the woman unpunished, Jesus told her: "Neither will I condemn thee. Go thy way. But from now on, sin no more" (John 8:11). Mercy is given to the sinner, who is separate from the sin.

Tolerance for sinners supports the provision of material help for those in need; it is a source of the sharing spirit of the Catholic ethic. While *absolution* (complete remission of sins) can be given only through the rituals and under the authority of the Catholic Church, the foundation of the process of absolution and forgiveness, the idea that people need and can be given help, can be applied to anyone. The tradition of cleansing sinners translates into the idea that charitable help can and should be provided to all (a point Murray, 1990, makes in a discussion of hospitality).

Moreover, the merciful culture of Catholic tradition assumes that moving between sin and absolution is a process, not a destination. Therefore, just as a sinful path *can* be reversed, a suffering individual *can* be helped. And the process can be repeated over and over if necessary.

When people see sinning as commonplace, it is difficult for them to believe that there are sharp divisions between those with secular and economic problems and those without such problems. Needy individuals and those with plenty are not really very different, any more than are those who are tall and those who are short. Whatever differences there are between individuals pale compared to the commonalities.

### The Apparatus of Redemption and Sharing

The sense of the natural relations between human beings not only creates a bond between the poor and the well-to-do, it also means that mechanisms to help those in need are natural as well. The fact that the Catholic ethic thinks about religious problems and their solution in a certain way—sin is present, but so is forgiveness—suggests that it thinks about personal and social problems similarly—problems are present, but solutions are possible. The instruments for religious resolution of the issues of sin, the processes of forgiveness and their requirements, set the stage for the meeting of personal and social needs as well.

Forgiveness of sins occurs through the sacrament of penance. Although it has taken various forms over the years, penance essentially involves confessing one's sins to a priest and receiving absolution through the priest. The absolution generally requires specific penance both through prayer and through a genuine effort to right the wrong. There are several important accompanying ideas that translate into prosocial helping orientations.

First, there is the idea that penance is needed by all and open to all. This perspective can support the idea that social needs affect everyone and everyone needs help, at one point or another.

Second, there is the acceptance of the sinner. The statement of the sins, the repentance, and the completion of the penance assigned are left up to the individual. There is no checking or "micromanaging" of the penance transaction. This acceptance of people's motivation and condition at face value can extend to questions about whether individuals with social and personal problems are worthy of help. Just as the help of the confessional is available to any believer—and, really, to anyone—who comes, who seeks it out, distinctions between those needy who are worthy of help and those who are not become irrelevant. Need is need. Baum has pointed out (personal communication, June 1991) that there is no text of which he is aware in Catholic theology that distinguishes between the worthy and the unworthy.

Third, institutional help is available to anyone with spiritual difficulties. Groups affiliated with the Catholic Church have typically adapted this principle to provide help to those with earthly problems as well. In this century, the Catholic Worker movement opened its kitchens to anyone who was hungry. Indeed, in Murray's discussion (1990) of his own experience in that group, the development of restrictions at one house caused great conflict. Mollat (1986) has pointed out how Catholic hospices and leprosariums dotted the map of Europe in the Middle Ages. This openness has continued to be a characteristic of Catholic social institutions to this day. In a similar way, the Catholic ethic supports the provision of help for social and personal problems in hospitals, schools, and the many offices of Catholic social services.

Fourth, Catholic religious practices include the practice of sharing concerns with others in the context of providing spiritual relief for sinners. In penance, the rituals of the confessional and the intercession of the priest are the vehicles through which forgiveness is provided. However, within this interaction the very real dilemmas faced day to day are examined and discussed. From the penitent's point of view, this process reinforces the notion that sharing problems with others may be helpful.

A fifth significant feature of penance is atonement. Something must be done to undo the consequences of sin in order to secure forgiveness. Prayer is one element of atonement generally mandated by the confessor. In addition, penitents are usually required to take steps to relieve the suffering their sins may have caused. The tradition of atonement supports the idea that although helpers cannot undo bad things that have happened to others, they can indeed make bad better.

## Penance and the Criminal Justice Systems

Most of the examples I use to illustrate the Catholic ethic of sharing concern welfare or health. However, it is also informative to compare the mechanisms of penance, of sin and redemption (bearing in mind that they influence social mechanisms for helping with social problems), to the U.S. criminal justice system, another social mechanism for dealing with social problems. While the penance system and the criminal justice system share elaborate rituals, they have different assumptions about the human condition.

*Reconciliation versus punishment.* The most obvious difference between the two systems is that the penance system of the Catholic Church has reconciliation as a central element, while the U.S. criminal justice system emphasizes punishment. The sacrament of penance attempts to bring the sinner back to the church, to restore the communal bond, as opposed to separating the individual from family and community. The emphasis on remorse in penance is an important element in restoring that communal bond, and it is not found in the criminal justice system. There, the accused's remorse is more or less irrelevant, although the judge may take it into account in sentencing. (In Japan, where there is more emphasis on rehabilitating the criminal, repentance is among the more important concerns of the criminal justice system.)

*Good faith versus adversarial proof.* The penance system trusts the good faith of the penitent's remorse. The criminal justice system seeks to prove guilt or innocence in an adversarial process between the accused and the state. In the United States, fault is paramount to all other considerations. (A different approach is taken in juvenile court, although this different process is now and has been under challenge.)

*Recompensing versus ignoring the victim.* Penance requires recompense; the sinner is to make right the wrong. The U.S. criminal justice system has traditionally sought to make the guilty suffer and lets victims cope on their own. Indeed, the victim has been almost extraneous to the proceedings. However, the idea of compensating victims is now attracting more interest, and statements from victims about their experiences and the impact of those experiences are now being shared with the court at sentencing time. Two versions of compensation are being employed in several different jurisdictions: one involves sentences of community service; another requires direct compensation to the victim. Some states are also working on victim assistance programs.

*Embracing complexity versus electing either/or judgments.* The penance system recognizes the complexities of human motivation and weakness while the criminal justice system seems to want to reduce complex issues to either/or terms of guilt or innocence. These two systems evolve from different views of the human condition and how to deal with our experience of it. They recall Theory X and Theory Y (see Chapter Two): Theory X assumes force and constraint are needed to control human behavior; Theory Y assumes people want to be good but may need help in doing so. Our criminal justice system is a Theory X system. It takes a dim view of the human condition. The penance system of the Catholic tradition is a Theory Y system.

Given the dominance of the Protestant ethic in the United States, it is not surprising that the criminal justice system appears to be influenced by that ethic rather than the Catholic ethic and the sacrament of penance. The emphasis on guilt or innocence as an either/or designation parallels the Protestant emphasis on being either saved or damned. The ignoring of other complexities and of ways a person might be restored to membership in the community he or she has harmed parallels the Protestant emphasis on fault, on personal responsibility for one's act.

We can find comparable tendencies in organizations. "Find the problem and fire him" remains a prime managerial tactic. However, as the late management consultant and statistician W. Edwards Deming pointed out, punishing the worker is useless when most problems are systemic. Punishing someone who makes a mistake is like killing the messenger; that person is just delivering the message of the system.

## Conclusion

The Catholic ethic views the world through the lenses of family and forgiveness. The Protestant ethic views it through lenses of individualism and immutability. In the Catholic ethic, life in this world is a process, a journey, in which forgiveness is always possible. In the Protestant ethic, one's efforts to "succeed" may help in this world but have less influence on the next. Each person is a tub on its own bottom.

The merciful culture of the Catholic ethic has many elements that make the sharing of resources natural and ordinary and that temper hostility toward the needy, and these elements guide the daily decisions of those who are influenced by this ethic. In addition, in the church itself, the rituals of confession and requirements of penance work as an influence on behavior. Ideally, then, the set of assumptions that make the Catholic penance system sympathetic and understanding of those in need of forgiveness of sins, ramifies to sympathy for the poor and enhances willingness to offer practical help to improve the welfare of the poor.

*Chapter Five*

# This World and the Next
# in the Catholic Ethic

All religious cultures have perspectives on life after death (the after-life) and what influence, if any, an individual has on that afterlife. In this chapter, I bring together previously discussed strands of the Protestant and Catholic perspectives and introduce some additional concepts and ways of thinking about salvation, ways that have im-plications for a sharing orientation or a work/worth orientation toward helping others.

Its orientation toward Heaven (*otherworldly*) or Earth (*this-worldly*) is a defining characteristic for any religion. An otherworldly orientation directs individual believers to focus on life in the next world and diminishes the importance of temporal concerns. The prospect of Heaven and eternal life with God is of paramount importance. A this-worldly orientation emphasizes the importance of conditions during life, and individual believers' attention is directed more to the here and now, partly because it may not be thought possible to influence the status one has after death.

## Protestant and Catholic Ethic Orientations

Protestants have a this-worldly orientation and Catholics have an otherworldly orientation, a point stressed by Max Weber ([1904–1905] 1956). These attitudes are in some sense "derivative." That is, Protestants and Catholics did not *set out* to have these orienta-tions. Rather, these orientations emerged as by-products of other ideas in the religious culture. As Mack, Murphy, and Yellin (1956) put it, "The Catholic ethic propounded a culturally established emphasis on otherworldliness; the rationale for the performance of tasks was otherworldly" (p. 295).

The Protestant ethic, however, looked to this world for justification of actions. Because of that this-worldly orientation, measures of worldly success, especially those connected with work (the "calling," as we saw earlier) and money, took on more meaning. In the Catholic ethic, the symbols of success in this world were less sacred, possession of them or lack of possession, less central. The Catholic ethic saw the social order as just that—a social order, not *a moral order*. The social ladder was not Jacob's ladder, reaching to Heaven. Thus, Catholics were expected to remain slightly detached from this world. Conditions would be better in the next.

## Why Is There a Difference?

The simplest answer to the question of why there is a difference is that there are perceived differences in the amount of control one can exercise over one's heavenly destiny and the amount of control one can exert over the here and now. People put their energies into areas where they think those energies will tell in some way. Therefore, controllability becomes paramount in the way a religious culture thinks about this world, the next world, and the relationship of these two worlds. The Catholic ethic is oriented toward the other world because Catholics can influence their status to come in that world. The Protestant ethic is oriented toward this world because Protestants find their status in this world influenceable and revelatory. For Catholics, the emphasis is on *creating* one's salvation status; for Protestants, the emphasis is on *discovering* one's salvation status.

An important key to the Protestant ethic, as discussed earlier, is predestination. While it is almost certainly true that only a minority of Protestants today believe in "pure" predestination, this issue is still important in a number of denominations. In the fall of 1993, for example, a group of Baptists calculated that about 46.1

percent of the people in Alabama were going to Hell (Associated Press, 1993, p. 1). (The act of making this calculation is not that different from the Puritan practice of having the saved sit in special locations in church.) The later offshoot of the doctrine of predestination—that grace is a *gift*, which can be discovered but not earned—has many adherents. And the gift of grace is, like predestination, an either/or concept; one has it or one does not. A person does not gradually acquire the gift of grace. The importance of this either/or-ness is, first, that it creates an ethic of focusing on this world. Although salvation and damnation are predestined, they can be "divined" through this-worldly status. Second, it is influential because its very way of seeing only two opposing sides to an issue has crept into many social evaluations. The either/or-ness of American racial concepts described earlier is one example.

It is also important that Protestantism lacks a bureaucratic buffer between beliefs and believer. The power of belief is visited directly on the individual believer, unmediated through such interpreters as higher authorities and Papal encyclicals. The individualism of belief and practice is one manifestation of the individual orientation of Protestantism, which has an "entrepreneurial" rather than a hierarchical perspective. Clergy, too, have shared this individualism, splitting off and taking their congregations with them. Because God is manifest in history but does not act in history, the whole of life in this world becomes a puzzle in which the Protestant labors to discern God's design. The meaning of events in this world reveals the plan for the next. Then, too, events in this world make an actual difference in individual status in this world.

In the Catholic tradition, salvation is to be pursued, and there are many things one can do to gradually influence that salvation, that state of grace. One can generate grace through religious actions such as prayers, the lighting of candles in church, attending special masses, invoking the saints, and so on. The sacrament of penance places one in a state of grace, however briefly, until one errs again. When one is dying, the sacrament of extreme unction can assure all sins are forgiven and assure salvation. With such an array of heavenly opportunities, a focus on the next world is understandable.

Thus, actions in this world are aimed toward controlling (as opposed to revealing) the next. Good works such as helping others out and sharing resources are not only good for those who are helped. Such good works carry salvation credit. Although performed in this world they look toward the next.

### Acquiring Versus Sharing

The this-worldly and otherworldly orientations differ in tone, approach, implications, and impact. They generate variations in approaches to human conduct, helping to determine whether a person has an acquisitive orientation or a sharing one, helps himself or herself or helps others.

If the goods of this world are so valuable and so revelatory about a person's character, then possessing them is important, and the person would want to have as many as possible. And if the person sees in those acquisitions that God *is* helping him or her, then the burden of discovering his or her either/or status will be somewhat reduced. The this-worldly orientation that results from this view of the significance of worldly success is likely to be associated with a negative view of those in need. If it is true that God's will is manifest in the structure of this world, then the various levels of status in this world might, however subtly, reflect our eternal destinies. The poor, in this orientation, are not a group beloved by God but a group with problems that reflect inner flaws.

In contrast, if worldly goods are not that valuable or significant, then sharing what one has is no big deal. Indeed, such sharing might help pave one's way to Heaven, as good works often do. Nevertheless, one must be cautious not to get overinvolved in this world, even when performing good works. Liberation theology, for example, focuses on alleviating the extreme poverty of people who live with oppressive structures and corrupt politics that are central to the creation of that poverty. Yet it has been criticized by some traditionalist, conservative Catholic thinkers who argue that it focuses too much concern on conditions in this world and that people should not let even severe worldly privations blind them to their eternal destination.

Since everyone is moving toward the same heavenly goal of salvation, too much concern with the things of this world (including poverty and oppression) is, more than likely, an impediment to the journey. Thus, the lack of material possessions is not only a status without stigma but some individuals in some situations may even desire poverty, knowing it is best to pack lightly for the salvation journey. Poverty helps you keep your eyes on the prize. The tradition of voluntary poverty and vows of poverty among members of some religious orders come out of this perspective.

### Internal Versus External Control

The idea that people put their energies where they think they can exercise control in cultural and religious matters is related to the perspectives social psychologists have taken on this same topic. Psychologists frequently use categories of "internality" to describe an orientation in which people feel they can influence some aspect of their world and "externality" to refer to an orientation in which people feel that "what happens, happens" (see, for example, Rotter, 1966). The result is that people are sorted into either/or categories according to control orientation. However, it is possible that each of us has *both* internal and external orientations, applying them in different regions. People's this-worldly and otherworldly emphases are a case in point.

In the Catholic ethic, internality describes the orientation toward the other world. That is where the action is; that is what is important; that is what can be influenced. The orientation to this world, however, is an external one, because of this world's lesser importance and because of the perceived practical difficulties of influencing it. In the Protestant ethic, the reverse is true. Lack of control over otherworldly destinations supports externality; God will do what God will do. However, the redoubled effort at control over the here and now where effort can pay off supports internality. Table 5.1. outlines the different perspectives.

## The Heavenly Calculus

Whether a person exercises control or exerts his or her energy toward this world or the next stems in large part, I suggest, from his or her perception of the resources available, and more importantly, the perception of the availability of those resources to him or her specifically and the regularity of that availability. If we see resources as scarce, then acquiring them and keeping them is important. If we see resources as plentiful, then putting lots of energy toward winning them is foolish and sharing them is reasonable, as more will be coming. That is, the dissimilarity between the "acquisitive society" (Tawney, 1948) and the sharing society, between people who "need" to optimize (have it all) and people who "wish" to satisfice (have enough) relates to perceptions of the supply of desirable goods and services. This area of thinking is one Weber did not stress, but clearly, it is an important dimension of both ethics and connects to the ways they characterize worldly resources.

A logical place in which to start asking questions is supply. How much salvation do the different ethics believe is available? If salvation is thought to be abundant, enough for all, then no one need worry. In this Garden of Eden perspective, everyone has a chance to be saved. Alternatively, if salvation is in short supply, available only to members of an elite club, then everyone should be worried about her or his own position relative to the scarce sacred goods.

If one asks enough questions of this sort, heavenly calculi emerge that help to explain the origins and persistence of the Catholic and Protestant ethics through such varied circumstances

### Table 5.1.  Internal and External Control Orientations.

|                  | *Otherworldly* | *This-Worldly* |
| ---------------- | -------------- | -------------- |
| *Catholic ethic*   | Internality    | Externality    |
| *Protestant ethic* | Externality    | Internality    |

over so many centuries. These calculi are part of the deep structure of the Catholic and Protestant ethics. They are assumed rather than consciously believed.

Furthermore, these heavenly calculi can be seen as models for economic calculi, or sets of equations about market relations. This hypothesis reverses conventional assumptions regarding the flow of influence between the secular and spiritual worlds. The customary view is that the sacred world is modeled on the secular one, that the Holy Family, for example, is modeled on the "typical" Christian household. Many Catholic devotional practices treat saints and sinners, angels and devils, as sisters and brothers, uncles and aunts, plain people with their own virtues and flaws—connections that psychologists call projections.

However, the connections between the sacred and profane worlds can also be seen the other way around. Heavenly relations and perceptions can be a model for the real world. In this formulation, the person who sees salvation to be plentiful will also see material goods as bounty and earthly resources as plentiful. While temporary and local shortages of needed resources will be recognized, overall the Earth will be seen as an abundant place. Conversely, the person who sees salvation as scarce will extend this view to earthly resources. They too may be thought of as scarce. In short, the norms and values governing salvation relations become a model for the norms and values governing economic relations.

### What Is a Calculus?

A calculus is a set of relational or interactional postulates. Ideas in the form of "if . . . then" expressions produce rules and regulations through which one learns to understand, explain, and control the object of the calculus. In this way, a calculus explains the nature of a reality and defines cause and effect within the scope of that reality.

A heavenly calculus views the uninterpreted world (including both this world and the next) as an ambiguous decision field, one that could support the widest range of interpretations or "truths." To resolve this situation, the terms of the calculus crystallize a particular concrete perspective that reduces ambiguity and allows decision making. Specifically, the heavenly calculus deals with propositions and explanations about what happens after death, and how one can control, if at all, death's terms, one's destination after death, and one's accountability at the time of death.

A simple secular example illustrates how a calculus functions as a set of metarules that guides behavior and is so deeply embedded as to be applied more or less automatically. Think about what happens when two drivers meet at an unmarked street crossing or two walkers must pass on a narrow sidewalk. A complex set of metarules applies: who arrived first, who displays greater urgency, who is bigger, what social codes are relevant? Then, in nanoseconds, these many and sometimes conflicting rules are weighed, ordered, and configured to instruct the behavioral system. While society-specific codes are involved, many of the rules seem more general, in that they do not depend upon or relate to specific cultural contexts, such as smaller gives way to bigger.

In short, over time, many sets of rules have emerged as ways to organize human interaction. These rules are based upon perspectives on and assumptions about the nature of life in this world and sometimes in the next one. The heavenly calculi implied by the Catholic and Protestant ethics are examples of these sets of deeply understood rules.

## The Protestant and Catholic Calculi

The calculi based on the Protestant and Catholic ethics reflect the different attitudes toward money, work, family, and so forth contained in these ethics. In general, the argument has been that the Protestant ethic is more rigid, less forgiving, more individualistic, and more supportive of acquisition than the Catholic ethic, which is more forgiving, more communal, and more supportive of sharing. These general features suggest that the heavenly calculi will take positions on questions of salvation relating to supply, interdependency, anxiety, economy, and power, among others. That is, asking whether salvation is abundant or scarce, whether one person's access to salvation can bump someone else out of line or whether one person's salvation has no effect on another person's opportunity to be saved is only the start. Determining how much salvation is available, and how numerous the slots are, says nothing about how to achieve salvation nor about whether salvation can be bargained for or is given freely. In addition, questions of the power relationships between individuals seeking salvation and the savior providing it must be answered in any heavenly calculus. God, after all, is not bound by human rules or conventions. Individuals have to ask how, or if, they can earn salvation, whether it can be guaranteed, and whether each person is on his or her own in the search for salvation or can seek help from others. A number of these key questions (there may be others yet to found) are discussed below.

***Supply: Is Salvation Abundant or Scarce?*** How much salvation is there? According to the Catholic ethic, salvation is plentiful, and all an individual must do is ask for it and accept it. According to the Protestant ethic, salvation is available only in limited amounts; paradise is an opportunity, but not for everyone. Pagans and those of other faiths might not get in, and even all Protestants will not get in. One common Protestant criterion for salvation is to be "born again" and "accept Jesus Christ as one's savior." The Protestant view that salvation is scarce makes supply questions crucial in a heavenly calculus and requires assessments, both by oneself and by others of one's acceptability or unacceptability. As

Morgan (1958) tells us, 20,000 people came into the Plymouth Colony in the middle 1600s, "and every soul was checked off as saved or damned" (p. 79).

### Interdependency: Is Salvation a Zero-Sum or Non-Zero-Sum Game?
A second question is whether an individual's salvation takes away the salvation of someone else. At first glance, this question might seem to be a subset of the first question, but it inquires into the abundance or restriction of slots rather than the abundance of salvation itself. Think of salvation as a supermarket: there may be much food or little food on the shelves, but if a limited number of shoppers are allowed in, then regardless of how much or little is in the store, each person in the store limits the entry of someone else. This model sees salvation as a zero-sum game: for each winner there is a loser. The alternative view, that salvation is open to all, is the non-zero-sum model: one individual's salvation does not affect any other individual's access to salvation. The notion of open access to salvation is characteristic of the Catholic calculus, while the idea of Heaven as limited in size is characteristic of the Protestant calculus.

### Anxiety: Is the Way to Salvation Clear?
All Christians are interested in questions of access to salvation: how is it to be achieved? The Catholic ethic sees clear and unambiguous routes to salvation, although it is also clear that understanding how to achieve salvation does not ensure success in achieving it. Many of the devotional practices of Catholicism are based on a fixed notion of how to attain salvation. This clarity and the existence of a bureaucratic process of salvation through confessions, forgiveness, atonement, and last rites (recall that ritual *transforms*) are a part of the Catholic calculus. (Even periods in which excessive bureaucratization, such as the selling of indulgences, trivialized aspects of the process, they did not substantially detract from the belief that there was an effective process available.)

The Protestant ethic lacks uncertain procedures for access to salvation: it is not clear what, if anything, one needs to do to assure salvation or even a place in line. While in some denominations one needs to be "born again," the exact process by which that actually happens and the control one has over the process is not established or institutionalized. That salvation has occurred is indicated through a saving experience. But what if one does not have a saving experience? The Puritans faced this problem when it became apparent that "too many founders' children did not have the 'saving experience' which would qualify them for church membership. The clergy found the answer in the 'first principles of New England.' In *their* case, they decided, the churches could grant provisional membership by *inference* of conversion" (Berkovitch, 1975, p. 94). The uncertainty of salvation procedures and, in some Protestant interpretations, the assertion that such procedures are irrelevant because of the very nature of God's judgment is a factor in the Protestant calculus.

### Economics: Is Salvation a Gift or an Exchange?  Is salvation free or is it available at a price? "Free" does not mean that salvation is abundant, or non-zero-sum, but rather that it is a gift, and the giver—God—chooses the recipient in His own wisdom. If salvation is free, there is no way for an individual to earn it without God's intervention. A state of grace is a condition of the soul, not the balance in a salvation bank account. This point of view figures into the Protestant calculus.

The Catholic ethic implies that access to salvation can be earned through a variety of procedures. It has a price of sorts. This approach is the exchange view, which sees God as a friendly shopkeeper. It is very different from the Protestant view of God as inscrutable, as the distant upper management that distributes salvation in a mysterious way. However, there is opposition to the exchange view. As Rauschenbusch (1907) puts it, "When the capitalistic impulse tries to accumulate a cash balance in heaven and do business with the Lord on a debit and credit basis, commercialism poisons religion" (p. 169). The extreme form of this impulse, as already mentioned, literally sells indulgences to sinners.

***Power: Is Access to Salvation Capable of Certainty?*** How much power does each side have in making agreements about salvation? One view is that there are binding agreements based on the exchange model: "I do my part; you, God, do yours." Under this control-of-God model, God is obligated to fulfill His side of bargains made with individuals. This perspective, reflecting a part of the Catholic calculus, is doubtless very reassuring and is a central part of what many call faith.

However, many people adopt a view of the world as chaotic and disordered. And they see religions of the world, like the world itself, as full of betrayals. They observe powerful figures who do not keep their word and who act for inexplicable reasons of their own. They see bad gods and bad people go unpunished and see some people burdened with more than their share of grief. Harold S. Kushner's book *When Bad Things Happen to Good People* (1983) recognizes this issue. People do hope that if they are good, good things will happen in return, and then they have to deal with the fact that what they see around them does not support their hope. Social psychologists have looked closely at the idea that there is a parity between actions and results in life in that good acts get good results and bad acts get bad results. It is called the "just world hypothesis" (Wortman, 1976). But Protestants in particular see deals and arrangements in this world are undependable. Therefore, the Protestant calculus contains the view that God holds trumps: no matter how good your hand *looks*, it may not be *good enough*. Alternatively, however, one can think that the seemingly good and worthy person who came to ruin was really just good on the surface and was genuinely bad and undeserving underneath. The person appeared for a time to be helped here by God (and therefore destined to be saved), but this was a misperception. When Ryan (1971) talks about "blaming the victim," it might be just this kind of psychology/theology that he is surfacing.

***Existential: Are Problems of Salvation to Be Faced Alone or with Help?***  How does an individual face the problems surrounding salvation, and what does she or he anticipate the moment of salvation will be like? Is this a time when each tub sits on its own bottom or not? Is each person alone before God? Are all losses personal, and all gains personal as well? That is, if there is no obligation to share, there is no obligation to help, either; the fate of others is not connected to the fate of any single individual. This perspective is a part of the Protestant calculus.

The Catholic ethic, however, says that the major questions of life, including salvation, are faced within a collective context (a rising tide lifts all tubs): individuals can count on institutional help from church and religious hierarchy to win salvation and can also count on a network of family, friends, parish, neighborhood, and community to help with both spiritual and temporal matters.

***The Salvation Economy.***  Table 5.2 contrasts the elements of the Protestant heavenly calculus and the Catholic heavenly calculus, illustrating the different assumptions and concerns about salvation.

## The Heavenly Calculus and Market Relations

The two alternative heavenly calculi, or models of the salvation economy, provide a paradigm for understanding Catholic and Protestant views of other economies, including in particular the economy of daily life in this world.

I suggest that the view of salvation expressed in the Protestant calculus inspires a view of a worldly economy that is competitive, that requires acquisitiveness and hoarding, and that is bound by few

Table 5.2.  Heavenly Calculi: How Much Salvation Exists and
How Can I Be Saved? Two Patterns of Response.

| Question | Catholic Calculus | Protestant Calculus |
|---|---|---|
| Supply | Abundant | Scarce |
| Interdependency | Non-zero-sum | Zero-sum |
| Anxiety | Clear procedures | Unclear procedures |
| Economics | Exchange | Gift |
| Power | Certain access | Uncertain access |
| Existential | "I have help" | "I am alone" |

rules. In contrast, the heavenly calculus inherent in the Catholic ethic tradition inspires a view of a worldly economy that is cooperative, and that supports sharing. This economy stresses the importance of regulated transactions—everyone needs to come out with his or her fair share.

Is this extrapolation from salvation to worldly economies realistic? Do people really think according to these models? In some ways, yes. A philosophical and an everyday example follow.

Parker J. Palmer, the author of *Scarcity, Abundance, and the Gift of Community* (1990), finds that "the world operates on the assumption of scarcity. It denies and defies the gospel truth of abundance. Our standard economics textbooks begin with the explicitly stated principle that the primary problem of every economy is scarce resources. We act as if the basic necessities of life are scarce—when the truth is that a handful of people take more than they need and *create* scarcity for others" (p. 1). Palmer clearly recognizes that different calculi operate in the world and also recognizes in particular that the central dualism of abundance and scarcity is not only an actual phenomenon but also a social construction. Palmer emphasizes that "we must recognize the very quality of our lives depends upon whether we assume a world of scarcity or a world of abundance" (p. 2).

Palmer adduces the parable of the loaves and the fishes to explain the results of the different attitudes. After describing how the disciples suggested to Jesus that He send the people into the market to buy something to eat, Parker comments: "Look at how they try to solve the problem of scarcity. This [proposal] is one of the earliest examples of Reaganomics. They want to disperse the crowd, break it up into isolated individuals, and send them out into the marketplace. Let competition and the cash economy take care of this human need. . . . The disciples said '*They buy.*' Jesus said, '*You give*'" (p. 3).

Palmer sees the calculations behind the disciples' suggestion: competition and the cash economy. When worldly things are scarce they must be bought. Only when they are seen as abundant can they be given. Palmer then ties this view to a view of community: "Community and its abundance are always there, free gifts of grace that sustain our lives" (p. 5.). (To avoid any confusion, I should point out that Parker is using "gift" here in a different context than I have used it. He means that *the fact* of abundance is a gift, grace in the form of God's bounty. In the same way, salvation in the Catholic view is a gift *in that it exists*, that God chose to make it available. However, the right to avail oneself of that gift must still be earned with a celestial exchange system. That is, one must find an acceptable way to get to the gift.)

An illustration of the reality that we all frequently think in terms of secular abundance and scarcity comes from a newspaper article by Susan Watson (1991) about the generational differences in viewpoints between her and her somewhat older husband: "The difference in our outlooks is not based on money management. Rather, *it is based on the possibility of running out of things. It has more to do with supply than demand.* . . . In the early years of our marriage, news reports raised fears that the Midwest might suffer a meat shortage. . . . When I heard the reports I figured we'd eat frozen fish dinners. My spouse rushed out and bought meat" (p. C1; emphasis added). In other examples, she explains that after a storm caused her family to loose electric power, she decided they would not need power to run the refrigerator as long the restaurants were open, while her husband responded by buying a generator. When she had a cold and blew her nose in the middle of the tissue, he instructed her in a method of using each corner, then the middle, thus getting the most out of each tissue.

Such behaviors and orientations reflect different mentalities, different calculi. On a much larger, religious scale, the Protestant calculus sees the world as a draining pond with only so much water, requiring caution and thrift in that water's use: resources are scarce, and thrift and hoarding are appropriate and prudent. The Catholic calculus sees the world as a replenishing spring blessed with constant restoration: the world is plentiful, and any person's basic needs can be met with minor adjustments of resources.

## The Heavenly Calculus and the Social Construction of Reality

When an individual's outlook incorporates elements of the calculi described here, the real world can be made to conform to and illustrate that perspective, regardless of the objective state of the world.

In objectively and resource-deprived poor areas, some people will perceive and define (and construct) riches. In areas of relative abundance, others will perceive and define (and construct) scarcity. Social construction of reality results from selective perception. This perception may not even see material wealth and scarcity as important. For example, if a person believes that "the best things in life are free"—the waves, the forest, the sunrise and sunset—then material abundance or scarcity is not an issue. Similarly, God's love is not something we can see and count, like acres of land or dollars in the bank. If one believes that such love is *the* key resource, then material wealth and poverty are beside the point.

In addition, individuals and cultures often define abundance of material resources in ways that "create" scarcity. There may be plenty of food, but if the culture defines much of it as sacred and unable to be eaten, then scarcity exists. If a culture defines ownership patterns in terms of each tub on its own bottom, then one member of that culture, say "Jim," has no access to resources possessed by another member, "Chuck," even though Jim may need some and Chuck has more than enough. People see what they want to see. Often, what is there is what they put there.

The Protestant ethic and the Catholic ethic have powerful perspectives on celestial abundance and scarcity that, I suggest, translate into this-world views of what reality is. (There may, of course, be additional influences on different individuals—exposure to yet other ethics, experience of severe economic depressions, the relative affluence in which one grew up, and so on.)

The Protestant calculus perceives the celestial world with scarce salvation resources, so disposition, acquisition, and hoarding make sense: no one could ever have more than he or she needs. In addition, each person is on his or her own, making the struggle for survival and success all the more tenuous. The Catholic calculus sees the celestial world as relatively full of salvation resources. Those who adopt this point of view believe that things will work out and feel able to rely on a continuous supply of grace as the need arises.

Our present world construction tends to be shaped by the views created by our ideas about the celestial world. We think what we want to think, then we see what we want to see, and find what we want to find. We create what we think is there. But the fact that we *feel* or *believe* that resources are scarce does not mean that they *actually* are.

Yet what we perceive can make us act consistently so that we can describe modal types or orientations toward abundance and scarcity. If resources actually are scarce and one acts as though they are scarce, one is probably thought to be *thrifty*. If resources are scarce and one acts as if they were abundant, then one is *profligate*. If resources actually are abundant and one acts as if they are abundant, then one is *generous*. If resources are abundant and one acts as if they are scarce, then one is *miserly*.

## Implications of Abundance/Scarcity Perspectives

Individuals' different ideas of whether salvation is abundant and/or scarce may affect their worldly views in a number of areas where they find that concepts of abundance and scarcity can also be applied. Different philosophies will lead them to very different sets of actions in this world and different attitudes toward sharing.

First, thrifty and miserly types are going to be less likely to share than profligate and generous types.

Second, if a person sees resources as scarce, then he or she is likely to be willing to compete for them. Those who survive are the "fittest" to survive. In a competitive environment, it is tough to share with the "less fit." In contrast, if resources are seen as plentiful, then it is not necessary to compete for them.

When resources are thought to be scarce, people are encouraged to adopt a zero-sum philosophy in worldly actions. If I get some of the resources, you do not. If you win, I lose. Many commercial relationships are seen in this way (I get the contract; you do not). Even romantic love can develop as a zero-sum relationship (see Larry Kersten and Karen Kayser Kersten's *The Love Exchange*, 1981). Sharing is very hard to do from a zero-sum perspective.

Another obvious example of an area in which many people have a zero-sum orientation is sports. Victory is considered scarce. Winners take all, and second place and below are losing. As football coach Vince Lombardi once said, "Winning isn't everything; it's the only thing." A tie is not the same success as winning. In the words of another coach, "A tie is like kissing your sister." Even when you are ahead, you keep plugging away to extend your position by ever more favorable margins. Losing is so bad that a hit Broadway musical, *Damn Yankees*, was built on the Faustian premise that someone would sell his soul to the devil to ensure the victory of a baseball team. Many parents have watched other parents succumb (or have succumbed themselves) to the powerful attraction of winning as opposed to sharing when their children start playing competitive sports. As a coach for my daughter's soccer team, I had parents shouting at me to play their children, to run up the score, to crush the opponents, as if they personally would not be validated unless their children's teams won and their children were stars.

And there are other aspects of sports that may stand out because they reflect the terms individuals must deal with in a heavenly calculus. One aspect is the destiny versus effort theme. A team can be seen as "predestined" to be the national champion, or team members can be seen as working hard and earning their spot. One can focus on the competition between opponents or the cooperation between teammates. A team may optimize (in victory) or satisfice ("Just do the best you can"; "We played as well as we could—tomorrow is another game"; "Wait till next year!"). The solo self (represented by the quarterback or the pitcher) is lionized and publicized, but the ensemble self (players seen as part of a team) is valued also. The energy that sustains attention to these aspects of sports has, of course, its own obvious motivations, but practices that, although secular, evoke a heavenly calculus are likely to gather intensity and energy from that evocation.

An individual's salvation economy gives him or her a way of interpreting this-worldly and otherworldly concerns, of putting them into some larger, yet practical perspective. Among those concerns are attitudes toward the poor and toward sharing. A scarcity perspective, a desert island approach, makes one ambivalent about sharing. After all, one wants to help others, but one wants to have enough for oneself as well. And one can never tell what might happen, so hoarding is a good idea too. If a view of celestial scarcity leads to a focus on the importance of this world, it increases ambivalence toward sharing the goods of this world.

Conversely, an abundance perspective makes sharing easier. In the Garden of Eden, sharing is not only accepted, it is expected.

After all, there will always be more. And since goods in this world will not help you in the next world (you can't take it with you), there is no barrier to sharing them here.

## Conclusion

Fear of death and its aftermath and a focus on the meaning of life in view of death are central concerns of all religions. The depth of this concern is revealed by the attention given to the possibility of salvation. The salvation economy is the set of assumptions and relationships that a religion teaches about access to salvation. Differences in these teachings form major distinctions between religious traditions. In each tradition, the specific equations describing the access to salvation form a heavenly calculus.

The Protestant calculus is based on the assumption that the amount of salvation is limited and that access to what salvation there is, to places in line, is also limited. Salvation or grace is given, not gradually earned through action, and there is no clear procedure for acquiring this gift. Moreover, each believer is alone in any spiritual endeavors. The Catholic calculus, on the other hand, assumes that salvation is in ample supply and accessible to all and that there are numerous but clear ways to earn it, to enter an exchange relationship with God. Believers are not alone but can rely on friends, family, and church in all spiritual matters.

These salvation economies have become transmuted into common perspectives on the workings of the market economy in this world, affecting people's actions and the ease or difficulty with which they share what they have with others.

*very odd that the examples of PE & CE are not identified as Prot or Cath, and sometimes they are clearly the opposite of the ethic they manifest!*

# Part Three

---

# *The Catholic Ethic and the Culture of Sharing*

*has not done this*

In the Introduction, I suggested we can have confidence in the concept of a Catholic ethic when we can identify beliefs and attitudes that are more typical of Catholic tradition than they are of other traditions. The preceding analysis of Catholic and Protestant views on the five dimensions of money, work, family and community, mercy, and this-worldly and otherworldly orientations has shown a number of the required distinctive beliefs and attitudes in the *NO* Catholic tradition. There is a Catholic ethic. It is cohesive—that *BS* is, it is internally consistent. It is a cultural perspective that is intertwined with, but separable from, the Catholic religion and institutional Catholicism.

This is, of course, an initial investigation. Later efforts may reveal more dimensions to be investigated. Also, while the differences between the Catholic and Protestant ethics are visible and important, it is not clear how much difference these differences make as cultural guides for thinking about the world and for guiding action. Again, later efforts may get closer to some specific measurements.

Then there is the question of "reality." What do actual Protestants and Catholics believe and do? We are looking at two cultural "recipes," discussing their ingredients, speculating about how they might turn out. To complicate things, there are no completely authoritative sources for the recipes. Thus, one constructs framework recipes (before deconstructing them) and hopes to be fair in both processes.

Nevertheless, despite the state of the investigation, everyone wants to know how the final product really tastes. Once again, do actual Catholics and Protestants think and behave this way? Do Catholics value work differently from Protestants? This kind of assessment is necessary, but at this stage, examinations of the reality will be tentative. No single real instance will prove the ethics discussed here are wrong or right, any more than any single poor meal means that the recipe was wrong. Because multiple events and forces impinge upon behavior (what ingredients you can get, how your stove cooks), each real instance will vary in some way from theory.

Religious cultures influence people's thoughts and actions in concert not only with each individual's unique religious experience but with cultures of race, gender, workplace, and generation. Thus, a search for empirical tendencies and patterns will be more rewarding than a search for individuals who conform in every particular to the behavioral patterns predicted by the Protestant and Catholic ethics.

In the next two chapters, to explore the Catholic ethic further, I focus on a second ring of properties that a cultural package might generate, implicate, or drive. Max Weber did a similar analysis with the Protestant ethic. He first described the ethic as he saw it; then he looked at some of the sequelae that were linked to the ethic as described. His primary contention was that the Protestant ethic was essential to, and indeed caused, capitalism. Others since then (Heaven, 1980; Ganster, 1981) have sought to show relationships between the Protestant ethic and a range of other variables.

Does the Catholic ethic have similar connections to other con-structs? I contend that it has. It is supportive of a sharing orien-tation, and it is supportive of the poor and of those in need. It is willing to provide help to them, willing, even, to use the welfare state as a vehicle for the expression of sharing and pro-poor goals and commitments. In the Introduction, I discussed why I chose the word *sharing* over such words as welfarism and charity. Sharing sug-gests that need is a legitimate state, that is, it is not a cause for shame or blame. Moreover, sharing implies a certain communal-ism, that everyone has some claim on resources that are basically collective. Individual holders are trustees not owners. Chapter Six describes the long Catholic tradition of sharing (what actual people thought and did). Chapter Seven looks at the structure of the Catholic Church (which has a number of organs through which sharing is exemplified to Catholics) and explores some lessons from theology.

*Chapter Six*

# The Tradition of Sharing

oh, correct

If the Catholic ethic does indeed support sharing, then we should see evidence of sharing practices over the history of the Church itself. And indeed, from the very earliest times, Catholic theology, organization, and practice emphasized helping others. The biblical examples of the good Samaritan and the prodigal son, among others, speak to the problematic as an enduring, fundamental element in the human condition and support the parallel provision of help and support whenever the inevitable problems are encountered. Having trouble is not a special part of life; it is life itself. Providing help is nothing special either; it is just what one does. We can find the truth of this across the history of the Catholic Church.

## The Early Church

Much of the original impetus for sharing in early Christian times probably came from Judaism, which has continuing precepts of, among others, mitzvahs (good deeds) and righteousness. The early Judeo-Christian precepts of sharing or communal aid were doubtless geared to the important goal of communal support and survival. All community members were entitled, through membership, to some share of the community's "GCP" ("gross communal product"). The question of being deserving or meeting some bureaucratic standard of need did not arise. Rather, need appeared to be self-defined and giving appeared to be an act of membership in the community rather than something driven by sympathy for and concern about individual plights.

Apart from those early traditions, there was doubtless a very practical aspect to early Christian sharing. The early Christians were an outcast group, much like the Jews. If they were not for themselves, who would be for them? Most out-groups contain many people with different needs. But the idea of helping "the down-trodden" loses much of its meaning and utility when your entire group is the downtrodden. Early traditions and early conditions, therefore, would have cemented the tradition of charity in the form of sharing within the nascent Catholic ethic.

Moreover, founding activities are of special sociological importance. Arthur Stinchcomb (1965) argues that habits and behaviors associated with and in a way imprinted in the founding ethos of an organization have great power over time and apparently continue to reinvent and reinvigorate themselves as the generations roll on. Sharing was such a founding activity in the early church.

## The Medieval Church

From the founding period up until the Reformation, the institutional church and its affiliated organizations were among society's major supporters of sharing and providers of social aid. Alms areas in monasteries provided food and lodging for both locals and travelers, mainly pilgrims on their way to holy spots. The poor were seen as particularly close to Christ, as one phrase for them, *pauparum Christi* ("the poor of Christ"), suggests. Most churches had poor tables where contributions were taken and then given out to those in need. Hospitals developed, leprosariums sprang up, and other forms of aid were delivered to the needy and to the sick. In the Middle Ages, Catholic sharing was almost the only sharing that existed. It is perhaps also important to emphasize that sharing in general and helping the poor in particular was not a distinction made as sharply then as now. Most people were poor; helping almost always helped someone who was poor. However, the structure of the medieval social system, involving, as it did, reciprocal obligation, did tend to bind members of the society together in a social giving-getting compact. In this sense, the obligation to help was a part of the larger cycle of giving and receiving.

## The Reformation: Changing Views

Whether as a result of the Reformation or as part of its genesis, attitudes toward the poor changed at the time of the Reformation. The poor were singled out and stigmatized.

Before the Reformation, "the poor of Christ" had been a hallmark and calling card. Poverty was seen as an accepted status, and one which required help. And as mentioned, being poor put one in a rather large group of almost everyone. The question whether people deserved help or not did not come up, because the concept of the deserving poor had not been invented.

But with urbanization and mercantilism, the status of poverty was transformed and inverted. For the new Protestant groups, to be poor was to be increasingly distant from God. A link between poverty and criminality began to develop. This new perspective that poverty could lead to crime and other occasions of sin was suspicious of the poor and saw them as copping out rather than chipping in.

In Protestant nations and areas with significant Protestant populations, the new negative and hostile view of the poor seriously conflicted with the old view, although in largely Catholic areas, the old view obtained. The contrasts clearly reveal that the Reformation was a fork in the history of ideas about the poor. It was during this time, then, that the poor became divided into the worthy poor and the unworthy or lazy poor.

The driver of this approach was a characterological rather than a life-course view of poverty. A citizens' committee report issued in London during the middle of the sixteenth century, for example, argued for various categories of poor—the casualty poor (those who were poor due to fires, flood, and other casualties), the impotent poor (people we would call handicapped or disabled), and the shift-less poor in their own homes (the famous "lazy bums" in the modern poverty litany). In England at that time, policy conflicts about poverty abounded that are illustrative of poverty policy conflicts generally. On the one hand, forced contributions and then taxes funded poor rates, so there was some sense of public welfare. On the other hand, there was whipping, beating, branding, and enslavement of those who seemed to be poor over and over again (de Schweinitz, 1943).

## The Nineteenth Century in Europe

The twin streams of poverty orientation developed and matured during the nineteenth century. On the Catholic side, there was increasing development of Catholic social action, Catholic political parties, and Catholic lay associations, and the numerous helping orders attracted people who worked for the poor in hospitals and elsewhere.

On the Protestant side, the English Poor Law reform of 1834 continued the development of a negative orientation toward the disadvantaged, tempering the development of the public sector. "Outdoor" relief was suspended (meaning aid to people in their own homes), and workhouses were introduced as well as houses of correction. The link between poverty and crime was more or less complete.

The attenuation of public effort led to the development of private social welfare agencies and was an important beginning place for the profession of "social work." By the end of the century, the Charity Organization Society had been established. Nevertheless, despite such private developments, support for the poor was clearly seen as problematic and difficult. Indeed, there were even some suggestions—offshoots of social Darwinism and the thinking of Thomas Malthus—that helping the poor interrupted a natural cleansing action of illness and disease that systematically removed the poor through death. Help, it was said, merely enabled those who were less fit to survive (the expression "survival of the fittest" was a catchphrase then as now), and added a burden to society in the form of possible and actual demands for additional support, care, alms, and the like. Concern about the possible inverse results of social helping has been a constant feature of critiques of social aid from at least the time of the English Poor Law reform until today. (Albert O. Hirschman calls this posture the "perversity thesis, [because] the attempt to push society in a certain direction will result in its moving all right, but in the opposite direction," 1991, p. 11.)

As the nineteenth century drew to a close, concern within the Catholic community about industrialization, wages, and who owed what to whom, was brought together in one of the most famous documents in social welfare history, the first of the papal "social encyclicals," *Rerum Novarum*. In that document, Pope Leo XIII argued for just wages and appropriate and respectful relations between employers and employees. The document had all of the earmarks of the Catholic ethic. It respected but did not lionize work. It respected but did not lionize money. It talked about mutual and communal obligation and saw structural and systemic concerns (as well as more individualistic ones) as an appropriate level of analysis.

## The Twentieth Century in Europe

The twentieth century saw the heyday of the welfare state. In Europe, Otto von Bismarck, the so-called Iron Chancellor of Germany, supported pensions and health care on the argument that a strong Germany needed a strong workforce and these protections were essential to that workforce. Government social programs began to spring up in other Western European countries.

In England, by the beginning of the twentieth century, the system of (limited) public and private charity was clearly not working. In England, A royal commission was appointed, with a chair from the private welfare sector, Charles Stewart Loch. The 1909 report of the Royal Commission on the Poor Laws and the Relief of Distress pitted the Charity Organization Society perspective, championed by Loch, against more communally oriented thinking voiced and supported by Beatrice Webb and the Fabian socialists. The commission split, issuing majority (Loch) and minority (Webb) reports. Although the majority report did repeal the negative tone of Poor Law reform of 1834 (de Schweinitz, 1943), it did not go as far in terms of providing the undergirding structural and governmental protections as Webb's minority report advocated.

However, by the 1940s, many features called for in the minority report had begun to be implemented. Sir William Beveridge was asked to prepare a new report that took into account the new implementations as well as the fact that Britain was at war. The Beveridge Report, issued in 1941, is often thought of as the document that introduced the British welfare state. But in a sense, the welfare state it announced had already begun, telegraphed by the minority report of 1909. Other European countries, as well—France, Germany, Sweden—had also begun to introduce wide-ranging social benefits.

## The Catholic Ethic, the Protestant Ethic, and Social Expenditures in Europe

Many countries were moving in the direction of the welfare state, even though they expressed different ethics. Great Britain, for example, was a Protestant ethic country (with a Catholic ethic subtext), while France was a Catholic ethic country (with a Protestant ethic subtext). But they both established important social benefits. Protestant Sweden was an active welfare state leader. How should we understand these developments? *Good question.*

I suggest that these different experiences are a testimony to the power of sharing traditions within the Catholic ethic. That requires some explanation. *— I'll say.*

If the Catholic ethic is associated with a helping orientation, with pro-poor, pro-charity, and welfare state activities, then Catholicism should be associated with increased welfare state activities. And it is. Harold Wilensky (1981) studied the social expenditures of a number of European countries over many years in the twentieth century and found that when Catholic parties were in power, government welfare expenditures went up (see Misner, 1991, for specific social program detail with a focus on France).

When we look at other countries, however, what we find is that some, like England and Sweden, had been historically Catholic and had been forcibly changed to a state religion of Protestantism for political reasons. These countries perhaps retained latent elements of the Catholic ethic in their tradition and culture informally and in minority religious expression formally. That is, the historical perspectives and interests did not just go away but rather were expressed in *functionally substitutable ways*. Wilensky makes this specific argument for Sweden, that some of the pressure for socialist or welfare state activities came out of the history of the Catholic ethic in that country. Blocked for most people from direct religious expression, it came out through governmental programs. That happened in England as well. Also influential in England were the Protestant groups of the Quakers and the Salvation Army, who differed from other Protestant groups in retaining the helping/sharing perspective of Catholicism.

The communal aspects of the Catholic ethic emerged in secular garb. Socialistic community pressures developed and pushed state governments to act as the Catholic Church once had—large secular bureaucratic organizations replaced the large religious organization that was no longer an official nationwide force.

Similar twin streams of development occurred in the United States. While it began as a Protestant country, and while in the New England Colonies, experience in determining the elect and the nonelect could easily have affected committees dealing with social welfare, encouraging them to determine worthy and unworthy poor, later Catholic immigration brought the Catholic view into local and national government.

One way to visualize the historical flow of events is shown in Figure 6.1. The strand that is Catholic charity and sharing begins in pre-Christian times with Jewish charity and is augmented by early Christian traditions. The traditions are institutionalized and expanded during the medieval period. At the Reformation, a split occurs. The Protestant view of the poor and of sharing diverges sharply from the Catholic view, taking a negative, judgmental stance. However, in the twentieth century, the Protestant and Catholic views begin to intertwine, like rope strands, remaining separate yet acting together.

The interweaving of older and newer views probably gave authorities in each of the religions some pause. It was at this time, the late nineteenth century and throughout the twentieth century—that the Papal social encyclicals were issued, documents written by various Popes stating Catholic doctrine and beliefs on social issues. It was perhaps important from the Catholic perspective to restate the Catholic view, fearing that, in mixing, uniqueness might be lost.

## Further Developments in the United States

In the twentieth century in the United States, Catholic charities became a relatively big business, helping the immigrant Catholics who were flocking to cities in large numbers, and the Catholic community continued to be an important source of support for Catholic social aid, which is especially significant because, until 1935, there was no public welfare. The social programs that we today think of as "public" simply did not exist. Catholic concern, therefore, was heavily oriented toward its own community and to the waves of immigrants from Germany, Ireland, Italy, and Poland who needed immediate assistance.

Protestant activity proceeded somewhat differently, although it,

### Figure 6.1. Historical Evolution of Catholic and Protestant Attitudes Toward Sharing.

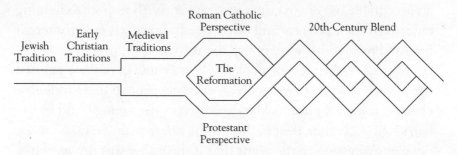

too, was largely private, at least partly because of the deep suspicion of governmental actions that still characterizes the United States. For example, a mid-nineteenth century attempt by Dorothea Dix to interest the federal government in taking a social welfare role by setting aside 10 million acres of federal land for the care of the indigent insane was vetoed by President Pierce in 1854, in words that have become an important document in U.S. social welfare history: "If Congress has the power to make provision for the indigent insane without the limits of this District, it has the same power to provide for the indigent who are not insane and thus to transfer to the federal government the charge of all the poor in all the states. . . . The whole field of public beneficence has been now thrown open to the care and culture of the federal government. Generous impulses no longer encounter the limitations and control of our . . . fundamental law" (Pumphrey and Pumphrey, 1961, p. 132).

Of course, Dix's bill had passed Congress, and she had also succeeded in getting a number of states to pass similar bills, so even in those times, the U.S. attitude could be influenced toward a pro-poor stance in some circumstances. Nevertheless, the overall attitude toward the poor was negative, and that negativity was certainly augmented by the Prohibition campaigning throughout the nineteenth century, since alcohol was widely thought to be a major cause of poverty. Government action in the form of local antidrinking and "dry" ordinances and a constitutional amendment to prevent citizens from being exposed to this cause of social problems did seem an acceptable use of governmental power. With respect to helping citizens in their poverty and other needs, however, governmental laws and regulations were not thought to be appropriate.

Moreover, the view of alcohol use as a cause of poverty painted the poverty discourse over with an even deeper and more indelible characterological patina. The depiction of the young child in the bar, singing, "Father, dear Father, come home with me now," was a popular expression of the point that if the father was not working, income was not coming in, and the family was probably poor. Even if the father was working, excessive drinking could soon use up his pay packet. Such moralistic as well as self-reliant and individualistic attitudes of the Prohibition movement infected popular ideas about poverty relief.

It is no surprise, then, that the thrust in the United States was private rather than public. In the middle of the nineteenth century, the institution of the social agency as we know it today jumped from England to the United States. Associations for the Improvement of the Conditions of the Poor were formed, and in 1877, the very first U.S. Charity Organization Society was founded in Buffalo, New York (Charity Organization Society, 1927; Edwards, 1995, p. 2634). The private programs were heavily individualistic; much of the poverty relief they offered was geared to individual transformation and, indeed, salvation. When funding for private agencies became a problem, federated fundraising, also private, began. The United Way started in Denver in the late 1800s as a means of community federated fundraising. The profession of social work began to develop its middle-class mission to the poor with the hallmark of friendly visiting. ("Friendly visiting" was what the early social workers did. It involved going into the homes of the poor and providing advice and counsel on how the poor could improve.)

A different—and more social—approach was taken by the social gospel movement. An explicitly religion-based movement that sprang up around the turn of the century (see White and Hopkins, 1976), its members not only saw some of the causes of social problems in the structure of society rather than in personal character but they also believed in taking action to correct these structural causes.

White and Hopkins quote historian Carl Degler's observation that "the acceptance of the social gospel spelled a transformation of American Protestantism," and they comment: "Always more than a traditional religious movement, the social gospel stepped outside the churches to intersect the political, social and economic sources changing America. . . . Toward the end of the progressive era the social gospel was defined by one of its adherents as 'the application of the teaching of Jesus in the total message of the Christian salvation to society, the economic life and social institutions . . . as well as individuals'" (p. xi).

The social gospel movement was important in several ways. It took account of collective forces—both in terms of responsibility for social conditions and for their amelioration—as well as individual ones. It provided fuel for municipal reformers and others who were seeking to improve the social order. While not the dominant element of American Protestantism, the philosophy of the movement represented and expressed subdominant elements within it, as did the Quakers and the Salvation Army.

Other examples of social concern that operated within Protestant settings and influenced the Protestant ethic as we see it today include the institution of the social settlement (like Hull-House) and the social reform view of the political movement embodied in the Progressive Party (or more popularly, the Bull Moose Party). The party was successful in sponsoring conservation and national parks but not in helping persons in need. Hull-House was the famous Chicago settlement house organized by Jane Addams, which sought to provide education and help to the poor. It was both conservation and social-action minded.

Walter Rauschenbusch, a pastor among the working people of

New York City at the turn of the twentieth century, looked deeply into the social causes of poverty in his book *Christianity and the Social Crisis* (1907). Rauschenbusch argued that the Christian church needed to be more active on "the social question," meaning not only the social problems emerging as a result of industrialization but also the social problems resulting from the oppression of peoples at any point in history. He picked out some of the forces discussed here as forces unleashed by Protestantism, and he recognized that they were not simply individual choices but were social forces impelling individuals: "the farther a man goes in comprehension of the questions before us, the more will he realize that the great leaders of industry are not committing mischief for the fun of it, but that they themselves are the victims of social forces. In underpaying and overworking his men, and employing women and children, the man with kind intentions is pushed by the entire group to which he belongs. In competition, the most ruthless man sets the pace. Corporate management eliminates personal sympathy" (p. 360). Not only did Rauschenbusch identify social culture and structure as influences upon what had been thought of as individual action, he also talked about helping the poor, observing that if the person preaching on social questions "follows the mind of Christ, he will be likely to take the side of the poor in most issues" (p. 361). Rauschenbusch exemplifies the Protestant thinkers who worked from the subdominant side of the Protestant ethic, the reformers, the settlement house workers, and the social agency and friendly visiting workers who picked up that strain and made it their own.

The generosity of the Quakers was also evident in the United States, as was the vigor and devotion of the American Friends Service Committee to social justice activities and to providing help to those in need. The Salvation Army in the United States has been a mainstay in providing assistance to the poor historically and is one of the largest poverty assistance agencies today. Each of these organizations drew their sustenance from subdominant portions of the Protestant ethic, configuring a charitable and helping stance from them.

## Nineteenth-Century Buffalo, New York

Buffalo, New York, was the place where private social work in the United States got its sendoff. There are also good data available from Buffalo, in part because of the early existence of the Charity Organization Society there. Therefore, a look at charity and hospital care in that city tells us a good deal about attitudes toward the poor and the shape of attempts to help them.

The Buffalo Association for the Improvement of the Condition of the Poor (AICP) was founded in the 1840s. However, as the historian of the Charity Organization Society in Buffalo comments, "Little is known about it and it did not last. This is perhaps fortunate for as Mr. Johnson says (Alexander Johnson, author of *Adventures in Social Welfare*), 'In every city where one of the old relief societies existed, when charity organization was attempted it met with bitter opposition; not only from the officials of the old societies, but from many of the best people'" (Charity Organization Society, 1927, p. 15).

Among the early agencies that succeeded or supplanted AICP was the Buffalo Association for the Relief of the Poor (founded in 1853). It was one of the most active and well-organized of all antebellum Protestant relief organizations. However, it had many problems.

[It] was bedeviled by difficulties in raising funds, and perhaps even more, by the impossible effort, through home visitations of relief applicants, to separate the "worthy" from the "unworthy" poor. During the home visit, "friendly visitors" would seek to get some sense of the persons in need, and the nature of the need. If it seemed that the poverty was through no fault of the victim's own, then they were "worthy" of getting some assistance. But if there seemed to be some lack of effort on the part of the family in question, then aid could be denied. The passions for rooting out the latter impaired the ability of the Buffalo Association for the Relief of the Poor to reach people too proud to have middle class American investigators snooping about their homes and into their lives [Gerber, 1984, p. 131].

This Protestant ethic perspective can be contrasted directly to the Catholic ethic approach in Buffalo because many Catholics had arrived in Buffalo in the middle of the nineteenth century and the Catholic order of the Sisters of Charity was already running a hospital without regard to "worthiness," serving people of all faiths and classes. Furthermore, "when angry groups of unemployed led by Irish workers and ward politicians gathered in the depths of the 1857 to 1859 depression to demand 'work or bread' from municipal officials, Protestants had special reason to be grateful that the Sisters of Charity were giving out food to everyone, 'worthy' or not, at their soup kitchens" (Gerber, 1984, p. 131). This was at a time when "poor relief by individual [Protestant] congregations tended to be limited to neighborhood Protestants" (p. 131, n. 25). Even when Protestant Buffalo did develop a hospital for the poor, Gerber relates, its death rate was much higher than the rate at the Sisters of Charity hospital. The Protestant hospital seemed to be not only restrictive in its operation but problematic in its operation.

These actions contrast a *culture of distance* to a *culture of acceptance* in religious efforts to help the poor in Buffalo. The members of the dominant culture were hesitant about helping the poor, not only because of their aversion to the poor but also because the very processes of help were suspect. "Indeed, what was done for [the poor], in the form of charity, was widely believed to create dependence and sap initiative" (Gerber, 1984, p. 132). In addition, the papers were full of condemnation of those in poverty and expressed "contempt for the poor, particularly those begging, accepting charity, residing at the poorhouse or engaging in 'work or bread' demonstrations" (p. 133). Experiences in nineteenth-century Buffalo exemplified ways in which Catholic thinking about the poor tended to be more open and sharing while Protestant thinking tended to be more judgmental and restricted.

## The Twentieth Century

Compared to the countries of Western Europe, America was a welfare laggard. In 1854 when President Pierce vetoed the bill to provide for the indigent insane, America was a largely Protestant country. But some historians believe that the religious picture was changing by the end of that century and that Protestant views were receding somewhat.

> It was still Protestant America. Small islands of Roman Catholic population had been incorporated within the nation by successive annexations of territory, and a broadening tide of immigration had brought large Roman Catholic communities into being in the cities. The whole mood and spirit of the country, however, seemed . . . indelibly Protestant.
>
> The outward indications of Protestant strength and well being, however, were deceptive. They represented little more than the high tide of Protestant advance which had been carried forward. . . . In spite of the busyness of the churches the halcyon years of the two decades bridging the turn of the century actually marked the end of an era [Hudson, 1961a, pp. 126–127].

American society overall retained its reliance on private social agencies and on ethnic/religious charity and sharing (particularly among Protestants, Catholics, and Jews). However, there were two large, potentially important exceptions to private prosocial activity: the Civil War pension program and the Freedman's Bureau. The first provided aid to the widows and other family members of Northern veterans of the Civil War; the second aided freed slaves. These programs were administered out of the War Department. Both, however, died, for complex reasons. On the surface, legislative mandates and budget problems were a factor, but at a deeper level, social antagonism to programs of social helping was certainly involved.

Sometimes such negativism was disguised as actual helping. Illustrative of a Janus-faced social policy is the plan, developed in Chickasha, Oklahoma, in the 1930s by John B. Nichlos of the Oklahoma Gas Utilities Company (Schlesinger, 1957, p. 179): "By the Nichlos plan, restaurants were asked to dump food left on plates into five gallon containers; the unemployed could qualify for these scraps by chopping wood donated by farmers." Nichlos wrote to his friend Patrick J. Hurley, the Secretary of War, "We expect a little trouble now and then from those who are not worthy of the support of the citizens . . . but we must contend with such cases in order to take care of those who are worthy." Schlesinger relates that "Hurley was so impressed by the plan of feeding garbage to the homeless that he personally urged it on Colonel Woods. . . . Anything was better than the dole, a word invested with every ominous significance. . . . It was better, Calvin Coolidge said philosophically, 'to let those who have made the losses bear them than to try to shift them to someone else.' 'Unemployment insurance,' said Henry Ford, 'would only insure that we always have unemployment.' 'If this country ever voted a dole,' said Silas Strawn, now head of the United States Chamber of Commerce, 'we've hit the toboggan as a nation.'"

This attitude has by no means dissipated. Its continuing presence is depicted for example in Liebow's *Tell Them Who I Am: The Lives of Homeless Women*, a depiction summed up by a reviewer as "a provocative portrait of the coercive and demeaning aspects of social work, even when provided by thoroughly well meaning and admirable professionals. In the name of therapy, the last vestiges of personal privacy are invaded; in order to avoid creation of 'dependent personalities' those professionals mete out punishment to the poor, laden with powerful moral overtones" (Newman, 1994, p. 44).

The Great Depression of the 1930s was a watershed event in the United States, the confluence of several streams of change and development that set a new course in assistance to the needy.

First, of course, was some decline of Protestant ethic influence, as already noted. Parallel to that, and no doubt related, was the rise of Catholic ethic and Jewish ethic influence, through the substantial Catholic and Jewish immigration to this country that began in the middle of the nineteenth century. Catholic social thinking, sharing thinking, began to be expressed in the political arena. The social action department of the National Catholic Welfare Conference, established in 1919, published the *Bishops' Program of Social Reconstruction*, a document written by Msgr. John Ryan, first director of that department (from 1920–1945). "This was a comprehensive call for social reform, including public insurance against sickness, accident, unemployment and old age" (O'Brien, 1987, p. 32), and it contained the key elements that later emerged in the Social Security Act.

Second, there was the greater activity of government in the lives of the population in ways apart from specific social programs. Governments are always more active during war and the threat of war, and the Civil War, the Spanish American War, and World War I all saw increases in governmental influence and the creation of a more visible, powerful public sector.

Third, the idea that there were civic problems (not just individual ones) and there could be civic helping was developed and extended. The so-called muckrakers of the time (journalists and authors who exposed social problems) showed the civic issues in, for example, the meatpacking industry (Upton Sinclair's *The Jungle*) and municipal government (Lincoln Steffens's *The Shame of the Cities*). The use of government muscle to break up large business trusts and to create national parks began to be accepted. While Prohibition was not a social program, it was an example of the use of government authority to shape social behavior. Legislation was more difficult to pass in the area of child labor. However, concerns about children led to the concept of the juvenile court in 1899 (in Chicago first), and to the creation of the Children's Bureau in the Department of Labor in 1912. While the bureau did not provide programs itself, its research and public expressions of social concern put the cause of children in the limelight.

While all these changes were going on, the role of the private voluntary agency was growing through the Charity Organization Society. Aid to the needy through structured means was given impetus by this developing role. As David C. Adie, Executive Secretary of the Buffalo Charity Organization Society wrote in 1930, in describing a wide range of Buffalo agencies and charities, "the past 50 years [from 1880 to 1930] have witnessed the dismissal of Madame Bountiful, with her condescending smile of pity. In her place we find a great company of men and women who through training and experience are better able to understand the social needs of the individual and the group. . . . Charity 50 years ago was a thing of the dole indiscriminately awarded to those who were definitely below the subsistence level, utterly devoid of spirit and given a badge of calumny" (p. 14). However, Adie was waiting for government action, too. He comments on New York State's revision of state poor laws, and is looking forward to the report of a new commission to study aid to the old.

It is widely thought that it was the severity of the Great Depression that broke the back of American resistance to governmental poverty relief and diminished negative attitudes toward poverty relief in general. American society ushered in a form of the welfare state with the passage of the Social Security Act and its signing on August 14, 1935. And the way had been prepared by the rivers of change and development just described. Although it was and remains controversial to some, the Social Security Act, as amended, is the centerpiece of U.S. social welfare policy and is the enabling legislation for what is commonly referred to simply as "social security" (Old Age, Survivors, and Disability Insurance) and for unemployment insurance, welfare (Aid to Families with Dependent Children), Medicare, Medicaid, and child welfare programs.

In spite of these developments, negative and suspicious attitudes toward those in need linger to this day. Welfare especially continues to occupy a place of apprehension and concern, receiving much media attention from all points of view. As mentioned, President Clinton's proposal "to end welfare as we know it" recognizes the river of distrust that continues to flow.

While the public response to need was developing during the 1930s and later, private responses continued to grow. Sectarian social work as a kind of private social agency work expanded and flourished. By 1977, there were 103,026 nonprofit agencies with one or more paid employees (Tropman and Tropman, 1987, p. 829). Of these, about 52 percent were involved in social, legal, and health services. In 1980, these agencies consumed $113.8 billion, of which about $38.4 billion came from governmental sources (Tropman and Tropman, 1987, Tables 2, 5, pp. 830, 832).

Within the Catholic community, a great emphasis on sharing activity and concern for the poor was expressed, suggesting a positive answer to the question about Catholics' actual sharing behavior. At the most basic level, there is the embracing of poverty among some who work with the poor. While the idea of choosing to make do with less seems antique in these consumer days, many Catholics and also other Christians and members of other religions choose to forego comfort and luxury to pursue spiritual values. Dorothy Day and the Catholic worker movement are one example (Miller, 1982). Catholic Worker houses, still scattered across the United States, "usually adopt three major activities: hospitality (the provision of food, clothing, and shelter, usually in skid-row areas); direct nonviolent protest against social injustice; and publication of newspapers and newsletters. The hospitality involves actually sharing one's own home with the poor; full-time volunteers live in houses and, in the 'richer' houses, may receive $10 or $20 a week stipend. The houses . . . have no paid staff" (Murray, 1990, p. 6).

While helping the poor is as fraught with conflict and ego as any other human enterprise (Murray documents the fights, staff break-ups, and bitterness that accompanied his sojourn with the Catholic Workers, for example), the philosophy of voluntary poverty has sustained the Catholic Worker group and has enabled that organization to continue its selfless service to the poor since the early 1930s. In addition, priests and other religious individuals take vows of poverty, reflecting in an intensified form the way the Catholic ethic deemphasizes the value of earthly success and, in that way, encourages its adherents to share more with others.

Moreover, organized Catholic charity is an enormous undertaking. In a 1992 personal letter to me, Tom Harvey, former chief executive of Catholic Charities USA, wrote (at times echoing the earlier description of the efforts of the Sisters of Charity in Buffalo, New York):

> The Non-Profit Times (November, 1991) listed Catholic Charities USA as the largest network of human service organizations in the country today. With 91 percent of its agencies reporting, Catholic Charities USA expended 1.6 Billion to deliver social services to over 8,000,000 individuals in 1990. Unlike [the period] of massive immigration of the 19th century, the vast majority of these clients would not be identifiably Catholic. Philosophically, Catholic Charities believes people have a right to service on the basis of need, not religious affiliation. In addition to size, Money magazine (December, 1991) listed Catholic Charities USA as one of the 10 most efficient nonprofits, with 92 percent of its resources going to program rather than overhead.

Thus, there is considerable practice of sharing, as well as talk about it, within Catholic culture.

Catholic sharing activities and fundraising to help those in need continue worldwide. But it is not only in the area of specific social service that developments are occurring. Social action and community organization efforts are going on as well. In South America, the development of liberation theology harkens back in many ways to the orientation of the early church toward the poor, with its concern for the structures of social oppression and sympathy for the downtrodden.

## Conclusion

As the twentieth century draws to a close, we see in the United States a country now spending hundreds of billions of dollars for social programs and still disliking the poor. The dollar amount is not as significant as the antiwelfare attitude that still seems dominant among politicians and the general population. However, we also see the Catholic ethic vigorous. Catholic Charities USA is raising and spending over $3 billion a year just in the United States. We see U.S. and Canadian Catholic bishops talking about problems of the poor and urging a preferential option for the poor. These bishops have also taken world leadership in articulating the traditional and historical view of Catholics toward the disadvantaged.

The United States has become a welfare state, in spite of great early resistance to that concept; however, for the most part, it has retained a "poor-fare" culture. We help the poor, but we do not like the poor. We are willing to provide low-income housing but not in our neighborhood. We take an arm's-length view of the disadvantaged, which contrasts to the Catholic view of greater inclusion.

The Catholic ethic is a sharing ethic because it supports the idea that the human condition, ever beset with problems as it is, will always require help. The provision of that help is part of the basic framework of the Catholic ethic. Yet one does not particularly lose or gain status by being, respectively, one who receives help or one who gives help. If there is any judgmental tilt within the Catholic ethic, it is toward the poor and toward a suspicion of great accumulation.

Working within the framework of acceptance of other human

beings and "doing unto them as you want them to do unto you" is a tradition that began early and continually reinvented and reexpressed itself in a variety of ways and in a variety of countries and cultures, remaining fundamental to the Catholic ethic to this day. The papal social encyclicals (discussed further in the next chapter) represent one means of this expression, but they did not arise simply from recent developments; they grew out of a long tradition of concern and caring and a lot of experience with practical concern and caring as well, as the extent of the work of Catholic Charities USA and Catholic charities worldwide illustrates. There is little question that the Catholic ethic is a sharing ethic.

## Chapter Seven

# The Institutional Church and Theology

Catholic religious practices and traditions are one thing—they have developed over hundreds of years and been refined and customized in thousands of ways. The Catholic Church as institution is something else. The institutional church is a network of organizations, staffed with officials (priests, nuns, brothers, and so on) who run the corporation of the church. Throughout that network, those who hold power in the church develop church policy through councils and other policy machinery and disseminate it to the faithful, the semifaithful, and others worldwide through papers and newsletters and local parishes. Church structure plays an important role in supporting the idea of sharing.

Additionally, of course, there is the large amount of church policy that can be loosely called theology ("theo-policy," perhaps, is a more accurate term). An examination of these writings can show whether there is an intellectual rationale for the sharing perspective.

## Church Structure

Catholic organizational structure expresses, reflects, and reinforces the charitable, sharing orientation of the Catholic ethic. Many structural features of the Catholic Church have influenced the development of the Catholic ethic tradition, including some not specifically related to a pro-poor, pro-welfare, or pro-helping stance. The present discussion emphasizes those that are related to that stance, looking at formal church structure, lines of communication, Catholic schools and other church-related organizations, the confessional

147

exchange, and global activities and reach. The opposition to the Catholic Church during the Reformation and the more recent nativist opposition in America are also considered. Consideration of theo-policy includes an examination of specific theology, the papal social encyclicals, and the 1986 pastoral letter from the Catholic bishops on economic justice.

## Formal Structure: Isomorphism to the Welfare State

The institutional Catholic Church is a large organization with many levels of authority, ranging from the parish to the Vatican. Members of the Fortune 500 would envy the Catholic Church's formal organizational structure. Indeed, Pascale and Athos (1981) argue that the Catholic Church structure was the *model* or *prototype* of the formal bureaucratic structure we take for granted today. Basically, the church structure has three levels: priests, bishops, and the Bishop (the Pope). Each lower level is guided by the one above it. The Catholic Church also has people with special designations (monsignors, cardinals) and groups with special responsibilities (the Jesuits, for example). And this structure has sustained itself. Of the largest American organizations at the turn of the century, only one, General Electric, remains. The church dwarfs its organizational competition.

Directions about behavior and belief come from all church levels. The church's bureaucracy resembles any other modern corporation or government, with departments and levels, direct and dotted-line reporting relationships, flows of authority and information, and trained functionaries (priests) to speak for the church, subject to its imperative authority in Rome. The structure the Catholic Church has developed is a large-scale need-meeting system. It provides support to those in trouble, and offers them forgiveness and grace as well as practical help.

Catholics are accustomed to this bureaucratic structure and were familiar with it long before the invention of the bureaucratically structured welfare state. The support for progressive social welfare policies that has developed in the Catholic ethic may owe much to the way the structure of the Catholic Church itself has accustomed church followers to the uses of a need-meeting bureaucracy.

The departments of social services found in most governments are essentially secular versions of the Catholic Church structure. Local welfare offices are not unlike parish churches: in both individuals make contact with vast organizations that help the needy. Both offer "services"—one, religious; the other, social. Both offer practical assistance with food, shelter, and clothing, although the growth of the public welfare apparatus has reduced the need for parishes to provide as much practical help as in the past. Parish "services" can include anything from sanctuary for political refugees to business contacts for the well-to-do. Of course, parishes provide spiritual help as well.

In some ways, then, the Catholic Church apparatus and its operation and purpose are parallel to the welfare state, making the functions of the welfare state familiar and acceptable to Catholics.

### Effective Chains of Communication

Any organization needs an effective means to communicate its values, and the Catholic Church has such a means. Values flow from the top to the bottom, from the Pope to the parishioner through the organizational levels. Missives from Rome, or from national hierarchies, have a weekly locus of dissemination in the parish pulpit and in countless church bulletins. In this way, the core values of the organization can be moved quickly, regularly, and massively to the members of the organization. Later in this chapter, I will explore the social encyclicals as an exemplar of sharing culture.

### Catholic Schools and Other Church-Related Bodies

A third major structural feature of the Catholic culture that has supported the development of a charitable orientation is the system of church-related organizations, especially the Catholic educational system. Catholic schools, ranging from primary schools to colleges and professional schools in the United States and in many other countries, have extended the influence of the church's teachings into spheres that could not be reached otherwise. Students in Catholic schools are exposed to the values of the Catholic ethic in classes and through the modeling of those values by the members of religious orders who teach at and lead most of these schools. These mechanisms of socialization support the values of sharing and compassion for human failings. Schools augment the church's system of communication, extending it into the Catholic culture that supplements the central church hierarchy. In addition, schools deal with children, a special population that might miss the message at mass or might not come to mass.

When Catholic schools are linked with a parish, as has been typical in America, they underscore communal elements of the church's teaching, developing the communal view in the Catholic ethic. The communities of church, school, and neighborhood overlap perfectly for most young children attending Catholic schools and their parents, reinforcing social ties and encouraging mutual assistance. The togetherness of the typical American Catholic parish, reflected so well by Greeley (1991), is strengthened through the interwoven connections between church, school, and neighborhood. Will the current closings of numerous Catholic schools bode ill for the Catholic ethic? That is hard to say. On the one hand, it is certainly true that fewer children will be exposed so intensely to that culture. On the other hand, if the Catholic ethic is indeed spreading among parts of the general population, there may be other sources that will be endorsing and enacting values of sharing.

The school is not the only church-related organization of importance in spreading core values. There are mission organizations (organizations driven by a single purpose, often deeply felt, such as feeding the hungry), Catholic printing presses and publishing houses, and semiofficial formal bodies like the Knights of Columbus, a Catholic men's organization devoted to fellowship and benevolent activities. A host of organizations, like the St. Vincent De Paul Society and the Catholic Charities USA, are specifically oriented toward sharing. Each of their meetings becomes an occasion to express and embody, to ritualize and reinforce, the sharing perspective.

## The Confessional Exchange

Some of the sharing that underlies and is communicated by the Catholic system of penance—confession, forgiveness, and atonement—has already been outlined (Chapter Four). The exchange that occurs between parishioner and priest during confession (that is the formal confession of one's sins), is a ritual that in addition to its primary function of absolving sins, generates some structural consequences that influence the Catholic ethic.

One consequence is the legitimation of the helping process, whether the help needed is sacred, secular, or some combination of these two. Because help accompanies the "metamessage" of the sacrament of penance, experiencing the sacrament makes it acceptable in general for good people to get help, which makes it acceptable for good people to have problems in the first place. John Tracy Ellis (1969), an authoritative historian of American Catholicism, comments: "As any Catholic Priest will bear witness, the confessional is a place to which many penitents carry more than their sins; they frequently bring their personal and domestic problems. Thus the reception of the sacrament of penance afforded a natural channel for guidance and direction" (pp. 59–60). Another way to regard this is that the Catholic confession is interpersonal rather than intrapersonal; help is provided to the penitent by another. This dynamic further amplifies for members of the church the changing roles all individuals can legitimately play in the world, from beneficiary to benefactor, from sinner to saint.

A second influential feature of the sacrament of penance is its universal application. It encompasses all believers: everyone needs it; no one is exempt. Even after discarding the narrow, immature construction of sin often maintained in popular media portrayals of Catholicism ("I failed to pray yesterday"), a perspective few Catholics consider reasonable or truly devout today, most Catholics still believe that all individuals are prone to sin and that grace is something everyone needs. When distinctions between grace-full and grace-less persons are thus muted, so, by extension, are those between the needy and the non-needy.

A third consequence of experience of the sacrament of penance derives from the way the sacrament of penance directs Catholics toward considering sin in light of its social aspect. That is, in the Catholic view, the treatment of others is the instance and perhaps the measure of sin (for an early and interesting discussion of this issue, see Niebuhr, 1932). Pride, anger, covetousness, and other sins are defined by how they affect an individual's relations with others. The stress falls on the hurt sinners cause others, as opposed to the hurt they cause themselves. Such an emphasis, by building sympathy for the victims of the consequences of sin, serves to build sympathy for all others who have been hurt or who suffer in some way.

In addition, penance requires penitents to provide actual help to others to undo the consequences of sin. This focus on reconciliation not only stresses the act of helping, reinforcing its importance, but also stresses atonement as an acted process, not just a mental exercise. (The kind of process meant is illustrated by the earlier example of the Polish leader who publicly forgave Germany, once forgiveness was asked.)

Finally, the confessional exchange provides a model for the secular counseling relationship. Though the rituals of the secular helping professions are mostly devoid of sacred elements, they share with the sacrament of penance a structured process of sharing fears and concerns and receiving support and advice.

All these various structures in the confessional exchange have long functioned to generate a Catholic ethic that is tolerant of human weakness and offers help to individuals with problems.

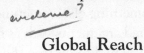

## Global Reach

The practice of sharing that the Catholic ethic encourages is a universal practice, in large part because of the global reach of the Catholic Church. There are some features that are distinctly North American, to be touched on below, but first, it is necessary to look at the values of the Catholic Church from a historical and international position.

All over the world, Catholics have similar and recognizable devotional practices. Until recently, even when local languages were different, the use of a Latin liturgy in all church services gave Catholic travelers in foreign churches a sense of being at home (perhaps similar in a very broad way to the familiarity an American might feel at a McDonald's restaurant in Tokyo). The universal character of the Catholic Church means that the same or similar values are embraced in many places around the world, despite local differences in languages and cultures.

But the worldwide culture of Catholicism does not exclude differences. Hofstede (1980), in one of the few international and cross-cultural investigations of Catholic identifications and values, studied the worldwide network of employees of one large multinational corporation. Controlling for intranational, or ethnic, factors, he found that religious differences are of some importance. (However, while there are interregional and country differences, there are intraregional distributions as well. So a Catholic is very likely to find Catholics like himself or herself in terms of perspective and orientation—liberal, conservative, and the like—wherever he or she goes.) These differences are significant in relation to the values of the Catholic ethic and the existence of opposition to traditional values.

## Opposition to Traditional Catholic Values

Value systems change over time. They decay and vanish; or they decay and develop into something else, sometimes even into inversions of themselves. Tortured arguments such as the ones heard during the Vietnam War—"We had to destroy the village in order to save it"—are public expressions of such value warping.

Values may also continue, improve, and continue to be vital. The tradition of sharing and a positive orientation toward the disadvantaged is one such continuing value. It has gone on existing and spreading in spite of other church activities that went in opposite and sometimes awful directions (the Inquisition, for example), and some explication is demanded for sharing's vitality. After all, it is one thing for a group of outcasts in an age of opulence to emphasize simplicity and sharing. But for these values to continue for two thousand years is something else again, a feat so remarkable it deserves close attention.

One force in the endurance of the value of sharing, as noted in Chapter Six, is the special power of founding values (Stinchcomb, 1965). Founding values are stronger and more vital than other values. They are often at the core of revitalization efforts, providing the legitimation needed to reinvent the organization. Sharing, as shown earlier, was a founding value of the Catholic Church.

Another reason the value of sharing has endured is more surprising. That reason is opposition. Paradoxically, values are more likely to be sustained, with increasing strength, in a climate of opposition and challenge than in a climate of universality and acceptance. If others around me support and validate what I believe (climate of universality and acceptance), then I experience *extrinsic reinforcement*. If others question what I believe and differ with me (climate of diversity and opposition), then I have to articulate it: I have to express it, and I experience *intrinsic reinforcement* (see Martinson and Wilkening, 1983; and the discussion of work and money, p. 58).

Both kinds of reinforcement need to operate if a values system is to be sustained over time. If there is only extrinsic reinforcement, the value system may decay, distort, and drift from lack of attention. If there is only intrinsic reinforcement, the value system may warp and drift from the continuous pressure on it. And drift differs from change. It is unminded and reactive rather than planned and directed.

In a sense, Catholic culture was thoroughly lucky that the Reformation came along. That new social and religious force provided the opposition needed to strengthen and revivify Catholic beliefs and the Catholic ethic. The Reformation stimulated the Counter-Reformation and new energy for new approaches, much as playing tennis with a capable and wily partner improves and hones one's own game. Some competition is essential. Because Reformation theology took a different, more negative attitude toward the poor and the needy than the Catholic Church, it encouraged, indeed demanded, a revitalization of sharing norms within the European Catholic culture. At the opposite extreme, one result of the absence of opposition can be seen in South American Catholic culture. It is essentially a pre-Reformation Catholic Culture, encapsulated and developed apart from the reinvigorating influences of the Reformation challenge. Such a culture has historically been more autocratic in orientation, more fused with the culture at large, looser about rules, and less intellectualized.

In the United States, opposition accelerated Catholic concern for the disadvantaged. This opposition was the hostility and rejection that Catholics and Catholicism encountered in a country that had been dominated by Protestants for over two hundred years before large numbers of Catholics (and Jews) immigrated to it. The presence of this hostility reversed the historical position of Catholicism in Europe, providing the Catholic Church with one of its most serious occasions of opposition since the Reformation. As recent immigrants, Catholics had religious practices sharply different from the practices of the dominant Protestants. From the Protestant point of view, the features that set Catholicism apart included ornamented churches, celibate priests (who wore peculiar clothes), ownership of local church property by distant authorities, and extranational allegiance (to Rome), the latter suggesting to many Americans a potential for disloyalty to America (an issue that came up during the presidential campaign of John F. Kennedy in the form of, inter alia, worry about a "special phone" to the Pope).

The immigrant Catholics not only had to face organized nativist anti-Catholicism that flourished as a political orientation for a considerable time (Billington, [1938] 1964), but they also were poorer than the so-called natives. They also, as we have seen, tended to gather in close ethnic communities. The resulting combination of oppression, isolation, and poverty among these immigrants meant that the Catholic Church in the United States had to move quickly into the helping business (Ellis, 1969). Much of the energy of the early U.S. Catholic Church was focused upon helping the early immigrants adjust to their new lives. Thus, the sharing propensity of the church was prominent in many immigrant Catholics' lives, reinforcing that value for them.

## Theology of Sharing

In addition to the organizational structures of the church that support a culture of assisting the poor rather than judging them, are theological structures that move in the same direction.

Gregory Baum is a professor at McGill University in Canada and a theologian and sociologist who has written, among other books, *Theology and Society*. I asked him to assist me in analyzing the issue of theology and sharing for this book. His comments (personal communication, 1993) follow, but first, the boundaries of his analysis must be set. The specific question he addressed was, in his words, "simply whether present in classical Catholic teaching was a peculiar ethos, a characteristic ethical stance, a special, possibly largely implicit understanding of the human vocation." He looked only at "what Catholic theologians taught." He "paid no attention whatever to what Catholics, including their priests, bishops, and popes, actually did," and in no sense did he try "to answer the question whether or to what extent Catholics allowed themselves to be affected by their theological tradition."

My brief analysis has shown that there is such a Catholic ethic ["a characteristic ethical stance"] and that it is different from the Protestant ethic. In Catholic teaching, the process of justification, including the forgiveness of sins, is not the trusting response of the alone to the Alone but it includes a turn to the other, to the community. According to Catholic teaching, faith is not salvific unless it is spirited by hope and love. In their faith believers experience themselves as interdependent beings and not so much as self-responsible ones. Catholics hold that all the good things, including divine grace, come to them mediated by others.

According to Catholic teaching, the love of God, which is both divine gift and abiding disposition, includes the love of neighbor. Loving God co-implies love of the community. The effects of this love include especially the identification with and the compassion for the poor and downtrodden, a religioethical stance today often called the preferential option for the poor. Caritas, or the love of God, even includes loving oneself and affirming unashamedly eros, i.e. the deep desire of the human spirit for beatitude and fulfillment. According to Catholic teaching, only disordered self-love is sinful. The theological virtue of love, in which God is graciously present to the Christian, is here seen as capable of integrating the service to the community with the just concern for each person's own fulfillment. This is deemed possible because, according to Catholic teaching, the human being is essentially other-oriented, oriented toward God and neighbor, and hence by moving toward his or her fulfillment, he or she is liberated from self-centeredness and increasingly longs to serve and be present to the other. Divine caritas is here the principle of integration destined to heal the human family from its sins, its wars, and all of its oppressive operations.

While in Protestant teaching justice referred mainly to the God's justice (equals mercy) by which the sinner was justified and to the justice (equals righteousness) of the forgiven sinner exercised in his or her religious practice and ethical engagement, in Catholic teaching justice referred principally to the virtue of justice, thanks to which people are committed to render to all and each what is due to them. Distributive justice, in particular, demands that the citizens help their neighbors in need—here alms-giving is understood as acts of justice—and that the public authorities serve the material and spiritual welfare of all. According to Catholic teaching, divine revelation promises that the natural virtue of justice, fragile because of the sinful human condition, is lifted up and perfected by the gift of God's love. Built into Catholic caritas is the impetus to social justice and public welfare.

If the above analysis is correct, the comparison between Catholic and classical Protestant teaching on justification, love and justice reveals that present in Catholic teaching is a conception of the human being as other-oriented, interdependent, embedded in community, bonded especially to the poor, and co-responsible for the welfare of all. This orientation 'ad alterum' [to the other], this Catholic ethic, is presented as the fulfillment of each person's telos, not as radical self-forgetfulness.

Baum's analysis suggests that sharing as used in this book is an important element within the very theology of the Catholic Church.

Theology, of course, is not something churches produce off the cuff. Typically, it is not only reasoned but it also builds upon the ideas of former thinkers. Sharing is a theological tradition in the Catholic Church.

### Social Encyclicals

Out of this theological tradition come the social encyclicals. Leo XIII (whose papacy lasted from 1878 to 1903) is sometimes called the "first encyclical pope." Encyclicals are letters intended for the "faithful" and are communicated directly (as well as through the bishops) to priests and lay members. Leo XIII's encyclical concerned the living conditions of poor working classes. Its original Latin title, *Rerum Novarum*, literally means "new things," but owing to its contents, it is most often called *On the Conditions of Workers*. It became the classic model of the social encyclicals. His advocacy for poor workers and his confronting of rich industrialists were so radical that the next two popes (Pius X and Benedict XV) and broad sections of the church tried to silence his social message. However, forty years later, in 1931, Pius XI commemorated the first social encyclical by issuing a renewed protest against the living conditions of poor people. All together, six social encyclicals have been issued (English titles are not literal translations of the Latin originals, but refer to the main theme of each encyclical):

| Year | Pope | Latin Title | English Title |
|------|------|-------------|---------------|
| 1891 | Leo XIII | Rerum Novarum | On the Conditions of Workers |
| 1931 | Pius XI | Quadragesimo Anno | The Reconstruction of the Social Order |
| 1961 | John XXIII | Mater et Magistra | Christianity and Social Progress |
| 1971 | Paul VI | Octogesima Adveniens | A Call to Action |
| 1981 | John Paul II | Laborem Exercens | On Human Work |
| 1991 | John Paul II | Centesimus Annus | The 100th Year |

The analysis of the social encyclicals made by Schwab (1991) on behalf of the Catholic Ethic Project reveals consistent support for both a Catholic ethic and a sharing orientation. Schwab concludes that the encyclicals demonstrate "the existence of a uniquely Catholic way of structuring the fabric of society. A Catholic ethic undoubtedly does provide value orientations for a vision of society which evinces numerous and critical characteristics of the concept of 'welfare state'" (p. 21).

Schwab gives several examples, but the material on property and money is illustrative. Schwab observes that the following quotation from Saint Ambrose becomes of pivotal importance in the social encyclical of Paul VI: "You are not making a gift of your possessions to the poor person. You are handing over to him what is his. For what has been given in common for the use of all, you have arrogated to yourself. The world is given to all, and not only to the rich." Schwab goes on to explain that "private property, in fact, is under a 'social mortgage,' which means that it has an intrinsically social function, based upon and justified precisely by the principle of the universal destination of goods" (p. 42).

The encyclicals represent a recent, consistent, sustained effort to communicate a set of values to the organization of Catholicism—values that constitute at least part of the Catholic ethic. But the more important point is that they were *social* encyclicals; they talked about the need to share, the importance of family, the sense of social obligation, and the need for limitations on the synergy of private property. This is clearly a culture that is willing to alleviate poverty.

Calvez (1987) also draws several germane conclusions about the social encyclicals. First, he observes that "Catholic teaching, has persistently linked justice with a demand that society provide at least minimum living standards for those left out [of] or crushed by the economic system. . . . [T]he church insists that all members of a society must be ensured a decent standard of living" (p. 23). Second, he also observes from the documents that while competition is supported, there is grave concern over its unbridled expression. State intervention to control its operation and modulate its effects is legitimate. He argues that this shows that "the church is never content with economic solutions that simply increase the level of production, or even of distribution. Its basic interest is for any form of organization to permit, at the same time, advantages of a more personal kind to be achieved by as many people as possible" (p. 23). In other words, more goods is not the goal; a better life for the many is what is important. Finally, he comments on the international scope of Catholic social teaching, concluding that it has "exerted real influence on economic and social history."

### Pastoral Letter on Economic Justice

Few documents are more illustrative of the development of the culture of sharing in the Catholic ethic than the 1986 document drafted by U.S. Catholic bishops: *Economic Justice for All: Catholic Social Teaching and the U.S. Economy* (Gannon, 1987). It stands as a culmination of the interaction of the Catholic ethic and the Catholic experience and perspective within an American context.

As many readers will already know, this pastoral letter talks about the economy in terms of its human impact, "how it touches human life and whether it protects or undermines the dignity of the human person." It emphasizes that "the life and words of Jesus and the teaching of his Church call us to serve those in need and work actively for social and economic justice" (section 1). Even more, "All members of society have a special obligation to the poor and vulnerable. . . . As followers of Christ we are challenged to make a fundamental option for the poor—to speak for the voiceless, to defend the defenseless, to assess life styles, policies and social institutions in terms of their impact on the poor" (section 16).

*Economic Justice for All* not only emphasizes the importance of caring for those in need and emphasizes that all actions and policies may be judged in part at least on the basis of their impact on that need. It also expresses a communal focus: "Human dignity can be realized and protected only in community. . . . [T]he human person is not only sacred, but also social" (section 14).

The bishops' goal is practical, and aimed at implementation: "The Church's teachings cannot be left at the level of appealing generalities. . . . [T]he time has come for a 'New American Experiment'—to implement economic rights, to broaden the sharing of economic power, and to make economic decisions more accountable to the common good" (section 21).

The bishops' suggestions did not come out of thin air. As O'Brien (1987) points out, there is a tradition of church involvement in these areas. Early on, "preachers told their immigrant flocks that their worth and value did not depend on their riches. . . . In 1840, after warning against 'the prevailing temptations of our land . . . the pride of luxury, the speculations of avarice, the love of riches and the inordinate desire for gain,' the bishops urged their people to be 'content with the modest acquisitions of honest industry'" (p. 30).

As described earlier, formal Catholic charities had been developed, activists like John Ryan had been encouraging sharing, and church support of social welfare had been ongoing via the Catholic Worker movement, Catholic Charities USA, and the hundreds of other Catholic instrumentalities. It is from this background that the bishops' letter emerged. It represents a policy document that has had, and will have, great influence both in stating a position of social consciousness and in making concrete suggestions about what should be done.

*Are bishops more focused on sharing than, say, the NCC? I doubt it*

## Conclusion

The institutional/organizational church is a setting where many of the sharing concepts and ideas contained in the Catholic ethic achieve expression. Such structural pieces as the ability to communicate locally and globally and the presence of a variety of organizational venues are among the instrumentalities that create a living influence. Additionally, theological arguments and church policies and documents support the culture of sharing.

# Part Four

---

# *The Catholic Ethic and Society*

If the Catholic ethic is a viable concept, what are its uses? What ideas might it illuminate? I think of this approach as the *heuristics test* because it tests the "fertility ratio" of an idea. It asks, Does the idea spawn other ideas? When a concept opens up new lines of inquiry, the results from these new investigations often provide support for the integrity and validity of the original concept. They add plausibility if not certainty to the original idea.

Two such lines of inquiry are considered in this section. One approach, considered in Chapter Eight, has to do with generalizing the concepts of the Catholic ethic and the Protestant ethic, placing them in the more universal or generic context of values conflicts rather than seeing them as religious conflicts. While initial and experimental, this approach has some exciting promise, allowing as it does not only a more general formulation of the Catholic and Protestant ethics but also a way of seeing how we could combine Protestant and Catholic ethics within ourselves (and something of other ethics too).

The Protestant ethic was an idea that stimulated much new

thought. It is to be hoped that discussion of the Catholic ethic will do the same. In Chapter Nine, I seek to answer three questions that may suggest how the Catholic ethic can allow us to reexamine current issues and see them in a new light: What have we learned? What does it mean? and What can we do with it?

## Chapter Eight

# Conceptions of Self and Society

In this chapter, I explore the ethics we have been discussing not as two religious traditions but as two general cultural perspectives or attitudinal dispositions, which I call the Alpha and Omega attitudes.

Many religious people feel guilt and disloyalty if they entertain the idea that some other faith may have its good points or be "valid." Other practitioners find themselves able to identify with one or another element in the value streams of other religions without feeling guilty, exactly, but wishing that there was a way they could embrace that particular perspective *along with* their current belief. Often, they secretly feel that in some way they have embraced it; that the "outside" element is already a part of them.

The problem is that one cannot have two religions. That would, supposedly, set up competing if not actively dueling faiths within one. Such exclusivity is the view in the West at least; in the East, blending, dualism, and multiplicity seem more accepted. But because of the way we in the West think about religion, as an exclusive identification or commitment, it is hard to conceive that people might have some values of, for example, both the Protestant and Catholic ethics (and probably some values of other religious ethics as well). The purpose of this chapter is to suggest an approach that explains how such a thing is possible and in fact already present.

As I investigated the Catholic ethic, I posed the following question: What would happen if one both expanded and generalized the ideas in the Catholic and Protestant ethics and removed the *religious names* from the generalized core? My answer was that one would be left with two "value systems," not "religions," with an array of properties and perspectives. These two value systems can be called the Alpha and Omega attitudes.

With neutral names, with the religious identification removed, the exclusivity drops away. It is much easier to see the ideas as "just" two value systems. Think of them as food preferences. Most of us like many different kinds of food. We may have a dominant orientation (preferring Italian, for example) and a range of subdominant orientations (Mexican, Japanese, or Indian). Few among us feel guilty if, despite our preference for Italian food, we occasionally have Chinese food. Both nourish us.

Pretending, then, that religion as we conventionally think of it is not a factor in the present discussion, consider the two value sets that we will call Alpha and Omega. They have a number of common dimensions, but within each dimension, there is an Alpha perspective and an Omega perspective, one subdominant as the other is dominant (as discussed in Chapter One).

The Alpha and Omega attitudes represent different ways of looking at the world. Each results from values tempered in the cauldron of human interaction. They are hard-fought and represent cultural conclusions of substantial importance about crucial dimensions in human affairs. They represent different viable answers to questions that continually arise within the context of the human condition. And most of us have a preference for one or the other of them.

However, problems come immediately to the fore when we select one or the other. If one picks Omega values, downsides develop that can be addressed only by Alpha values. If one picks Alpha values, then troubles will pop up that need to be mitigated by Omega values. Thus an Alpha dominant would likely be an Omega subdominant, and the reverse would also be true.

Put in these terms, nobody would have much difficulty accepting the notion that most of us have a set of Alpha/Omega values (that is, we have all or some of each attitude) and that we spend a considerable amount of time applying those values differently to specific cases depending upon the situation. No one would have much trouble, either, in accepting the idea that for some individuals and in some cultures, the Alpha set might be dominant and the Omega set subdominant, while in other cultures and in other persons, the Omega set might be dominant and the Alpha set subdominant. In other words, the concept of dominance and subdominance allows us to deal with the obvious issue that each of us, probably, has most of both sets of these values.

## Seven Dimensions of Competing Values

Before looking at the specific values, we need to pay some attention to the dimensions themselves; that is, the areas of our lives to which the values relate. These dimensions are broad enough to contain competing or contradictory approaches to the same life issue. There are many areas of our lives that are potential dimensions. I have conceptualized seven, based on the earlier discussion, as important to stress here. They represent seven important questions to which all societies need to provide answers. The sum of those answers is what we call culture.

1. *Self-concept.* How do I construct my "self"?
2. *Treatment of others.* How are others to be regarded and treated?
3. *Relevant social rules.* What are the rules of the game in this society/place?
4. *Relevant social process.* How do things work around here?
5. *Goal achievement/accomplishment.* How should I approach achieving goals?
6. *Responsibility.* How is responsibility conceptualized and blame/fault regarded/assigned?
7. *Basis of help.* What is the approved basis for helping others?

Let us briefly consider these dimensions and then the competing values they contain.

## Self-Concept

The self-concept dimension asks the questions: How am I defined? How do I know who I am? How do I construct my "self?" That is, What are the important templates or reference points that help me establish my identity? There are different approaches to constructing the self. The solo self and ensemble self, discussed earlier, are one set of alternatives. In each case, the self exists, but the ways in which it is defined differ. The solo self has an individualistic and personal reference, while the ensemble self is anchored in family and community and uses family and community as elements of identity construction.

Lykes (1985) noted a similar dualism in ideas about the self when men and women were compared, stating: "My investigation of two alternative bases for ideas about the self in men's and women's experiences of individualism and collectivity provides evidence of a reconstructed and synthesized notion of the self, [which is that of] social individuality [for women]. This view contrasts . . . with the interactionist perspective rooted in the assumption of an autonomous entity interacting with other entities [for men]" (p. 357). Thus, there is support for the view that the construction of the self can be divided along lines of individuality and collectivity. Moreover, I suggest that gender is not the only possible influence on whether one sees oneself as largely separate from others or largely influenced by and connected to others; the social culture is a factor as well.

## Treatment of Others

Cultures need to provide directions for interacting with and relating to others on a daily basis. These directions need acceptable justifications as well because the basic principles for interacting with others differ from group to group. Some of the basic questions to be answered are: How are others to be regarded and treated? How should I approach individuals in the world around me? Have I been taught to see others in the world as part of a team, all working cooperatively toward a similar large goal, or do I work alone, contesting everyone? Are others obstacles or resources? Theory X and Theory Y are again relevant, Theory X regards workers as obstacles (they need to be forced to work) while Theory Y regards workers as resources (they want to work and will help other people or a company to work).

On the one hand, one can view others as helpers, possessors of needed resources with whom one should and needs to share. On the other hand, one can view others as contenders for resources, who need to be beaten out in some resource race. Much depends on whether we have been socialized to perceive resources as plentiful or whether we have been taught that there is only so much to go around, and we better get ours, because if we do not, somebody is going to take our share in addition to his or her own. One view emphasizes competition; the other stresses cooperation.

### Relevant Social Rules

The third dimension has to do with rules for behavior in community and society, as well as their prominence and enforcement. People need to know the rules in their society or situation, just as they need to know the rules when they play a game.

One can, for example, set up a game—that is, a system—in which the rules completely dominate. In that kind of system, whatever the rule says has to happen has to happen. If a move is to be made in one minute, taking anything over a minute disqualifies you. No adjustments are made for any reason. This approach, the *fair play* principle, is means oriented. The rules are the rules—if you step outside the line, you do not get the touchdown. It is as simple as that. In this case, the means are supreme, and the ends are secondary.

Another approach to rules takes as its point of departure the ends desired. Rules, under this argument, do not always serve the ends they were designed to serve. The idea might be for everyone to receive something, but other things get in the way. Therefore, in order to be sure that everybody gets his or her *fair share*, we might have to make some adjustments at the end to make sure that things come out all right. Every parent who has tried to divide up cake among competing children knows the fair share principle. (See Ryan, 1981, for a discussion of this duality.)

### Relevant Social Process

The process dimension addresses the question: How do things (the value system) work around here? One determinant of the kind of process system one espouses is attitude toward changeability. Some value systems take the position that you are either this or that— either you are Jewish or you are not, or you are black or white, straight or gay. There is no in between.

Other value systems take a more fluid view of the way the world works. They see change as constantly occurring. As a result, people move into and out of statuses and move up and down within various status dimensions.

### Goal Achievement/Accomplishment

Cultures contain different approaches to meeting goals and objectives. How does one construct or construe an acceptable goal to reach? Does one have to reach the pinnacle, and always do so? Does one have to optimize or can one approach at least some life goals from a "good enough" perspective? Can one "satisfice"? Obviously, there is likely to be a mix of answers. But the dominant and subdominant elements in that mix will be different depending on one's value systems. In the sports subculture, for example, as I previously suggested, optimization is the goal. Being number one is what everyone pushes for. Business subcultures of marketing and sales also have this orientation. However, in some areas of sports—Little League, for example—the ethos is, at least officially, based on intensity of effort and personal improvement rather than winning. Does one "optimize" or seek to "satisfice"? When Little League players' parents try to replace this satisficing goal with an optimizing goal, what occurs is *values leakage*, in which a set of values that is dominant in one culture erupts into areas where it is supposed to be subdominant (see March and Simon, 1958).

## Responsibility

Responsibility is often differently conceived in different cultures. Therefore, we ask: How is responsibility conceptualized and blame or fault regarded or assigned? Some particular areas in which responsibility is likely to be an issue are causes of problems and conditions of persons. Suppose someone presents you with a problem. Your first impulse might be to ask, "How did this happen?" Such an approach is fault or cause driven in orientation. In the kind of value system that promotes this kind of concern, the foremost impulse is to assign responsibility.

One could approach the problem differently, however, by asking: "What do you need? How can we help?" In this case, the condition of the person or the imperatives of the situation become the driver and the offer of assistance follows closely. Interest in cause or fault or blame does not disappear, but it becomes less prominent.

## Basis of Help

A final dimension that contains conflicting values is the basis upon which others can be given help. Are people assessed on the basis of certain criteria? For example, a norm we often use in the United

States is worthiness. Do people meet certain standards? *Needing* help is not enough; one has to *deserve* to be helped.

In contrast, once again the need for assistance rather than the character or condition of the one in need can be the touchstone. Here, one seeks to address the pressing concerns of the person or situation, and the question of whether a person or situation is worthy or deserving becomes secondary.

## Alpha and Omega Competing Values

In the Alpha and Omega attitudes, the seven dimensions discussed in these pages contain the competing values shown in the following list:

| Dimension | Alpha Attitude Value | Omega Attitude Value |
|---|---|---|
| Concept of self | Solo self | Ensemble self |
| Treatment of others | Competitive | Cooperative |
| Relevant social rules | Fair play | Fair share |
| Relevant social process | Either/or | Up and down |
| Goal achievement/ accomplishment | Optimizing | Satisficing |
| Responsibility | Cause | Condition |
| Basis of help | Worthy | Needy |

As noted, the Alpha and Omega attitudes are not polar opposites. They are different emphases available for approaching the sets of basic questions that value systems need to address. A value system retains its integrity, meaning, purpose, and vitality when it meets the needs of the people who hold it. In order to meet those needs, it has to provide a comprehensible, understandable, usable framework for daily life.

But it is important to understand that no value system meets all needs or is always applicable. We know this from everyday experience. For example, we know there are occasions when we have to draw on our identification with family and kin. We also know there are occasions when we have to draw on our internal sense of being and oneness. Each situation is thus more a question of dominance of one value system and subdominance of another value system within a particular vector than of either/or. It is only when exclusive labels, like religious labels, are put on particular value systems that the systems seem to be applicable only by themselves.

## Alpha Attitude

What does the Alpha attitude look like in these seven dimensions? First, the concept of self is the solo self. Because the solo self is inner-directed, that self becomes the measure of things. At the extreme end of inner directedness is narcissism. But a solo self need not be a narcissistic self. It can simply be a self that references itself as the basis for personhood. Personhood is thus unique, individual, and something apart from the "other." The person may link up and join with others, to be sure, but he or she remains alone in important ways that are reflected in the rest of the dimensions.

Competition is a hallmark of this inner-directed value system. Resources tend to be viewed as scarce, and thus they not only must be shepherded and acquired but this acquisition must also take place in the context of struggle with others.

There is an emphasis on rules within the competition, and fair play tends to be emphasized (although there may be other rules that prevent the operation of a view that "all's fair in love and war"). Equity obtains in the sense that the more one contributes, the more one should draw out. If one is a harder worker, one should get a

higher salary. Salary has to do with effort put in and, more importantly, results produced.

A sense of either/or-ness emphasizes sharp boundaries between
statuses. There are the elite and the masses, the favored few and the
unfavored many. There is an us-and-them orientation.

In getting and giving help, worthiness is a key factor. Those
who get assistance need to demonstrate that somehow they "deserve" what they are getting. Emphasis is placed on the causation
of situations rather than the conditions of situations. The goal orientation optimizes, seeking the very best results, being first, being
number one.

## Omega Attitude

Now consider an alternative set of beliefs and values, the Omega
attitude, that begins with the concept of an ensemble self. Here,
the self is developed, grows, and is extended within the context of
community, neighborhood, and family. The importance of larger
identifications as intrinsic to and intermeshed with the self are so
powerful that one can almost not conceive selfhood independently
of those other identifications. For example, for some people with a
particular ethnic background, ethnicity is present and mentioned
but not central. For others of the same background, their origin is
an absolutely vital part of how they define themselves, think about
themselves, and act. It is absolutely fundamental to their sense of
who they are. This can be said for any racial or ethnic identity or
even regional identity. For some Americans, Yankee status is irrelevant; for others, being from Vermont is simply and integrally part
of who they are. People's sense that they are part of an ensemble
may be part of what allows a greater degree of cooperation within
the Omega cultural milieu. A sense of interrelationship and interdependency permeates the culture. We must look out for each other
and restrain ourselves from looking out only for number one.

Fair share (as opposed to fair play) is a hallmark of the Omega attitude. One should get what one needs, which in turn is influenced by what one deserves. There is a sense that basic needs ought to be recognized and that they are entitled to be met. Meeting needs is not some kind of extra, out-of-the-pocket, off-the-top-of-the-head approach but rather fundamentally and inextricably interlinked to the culture as a whole. Access to such support comes through membership in the culture.

Status within this culture is mobile, up and down. One is never one thing or another for any length of time. The "journey" of life has its ups and downs. One can be in the good graces of mom and dad or others and then fall out of them and then get back in them again. A sense of permanence in status is simply not present.

When presented with a problem, the person in the Omega culture looks at the conditions to be addressed, the issues to be resolved, the pain to be assuaged. The first question is, How can we help? not, How did this happen? Needs and the needy, therefore, occupy a prominent place, and it is one's needs that drive the response, not one's worthiness.

## The Ringtoss Analogy

One way to visualize this approach and the dimensions of the value sets is to think of these values as a set of rings. Suppose that each ring is made up of two colors, yellow and blue, shading from dark to light around the ring. The lines sit one on top of the other (which is top and which is bottom does not matter), abutting each other. The color of each point on the ring, then, as one looks through both lines of graduated colors, is determined by the exact mix of blue and yellow that obtains at exactly that spot. (See Figure 8.1.)

Now think of a set of seven rings, with each ring representing a dimension within which values can vary. For the colors, substitute two perspectives held in varying degrees. This arrangement of perspectives conveys three important features about the dimension.

**Figure 8.1. A Values Ring, Containing a
Representation of Alpha and Omega Orientations.**

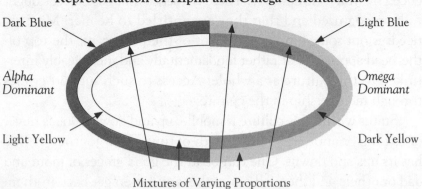

Dark Blue

Light Blue

*Alpha
Dominant*

*Omega
Dominant*

Light Yellow

Dark Yellow

Mixtures of Varying Proportions

First, each dimension has a pair of perspectives. Second, the perspectives are separate but abutting, not opposite. Third, there are degrees, or levels, of intensity, from low to high. So the perspectives are not different phenomena but different emphases.

Now, let's assume we stacked the rings on a stick. If the rings were all on the Alpha side, the configuration could describe an ideal-typical culture (or person) that was individualistic, competitive, fair-play-oriented, and so on. (See Figure 8.2.)

On the other hand, If the rings were all on the other side, the configuration could describe a culture (or person) that was ensemble-oriented, cooperative, committed to fair-share values, and so on.

Readers will note, however, that even in the case of the dominance of one perspective, there is a subdominant representation of the other point of view.

## The Blending of Values

It must be clear to readers that all of us have some of each of these value orientations within us. It is not a case of either/or but of how much of each one. The idea of exclusivity—that someone is all of

### Figure 8.2. Alpha and Omega Dimensions: An Ideal-Typical (or "Pure") Case.

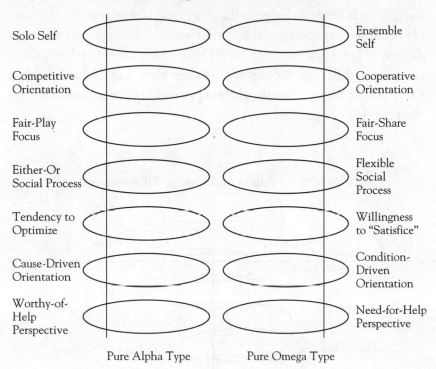

| | Pure Alpha Type | Pure Omega Type | |
|---|---|---|---|
| Solo Self | | | Ensemble Self |
| Competitive Orientation | | | Cooperative Orientation |
| Fair-Play Focus | | | Fair-Share Focus |
| Either-Or Social Process | | | Flexible Social Process |
| Tendency to Optimize | | | Willingness to "Satisfice" |
| Cause-Driven Orientation | | | Condition-Driven Orientation |
| Worthy-of-Help Perspective | | | Need-for-Help Perspective |

one and none of the other—would arise only if we were to identify Alpha values with the Protestant ethic and Omega values with the Catholic ethic. At that point, the religious nomenclature would make it difficult for us to understand how anyone could have two religions. And perhaps no one can. But certainly anyone can have value systems that draw from the traditions of those religions. Intermixed with U.S. society, the Protestant ethic is the dominant culture. In general, U.S. society is individualistic or solo-self oriented, competitively motivated, with an emphasis on fair play and optimization. But moderating or mitigating these emphases is a subdominant Catholic ethic that involves an ensemble self, cooperation, and a fair share. Thus we typically find ourselves focused on self-reliance and on the worthy poor and the causes of need at the same time as we have an underlying awareness that we ought to have an interest in helping those who do not appear worthy simply because they are needy, and that we ought to address the conditions of need and not just assign fault. At least two ethics, then, compete within U.S. society, within ourselves, and probably within the world at large. Visually, the rings would be distributed around the post. (See Figure 8.3.)

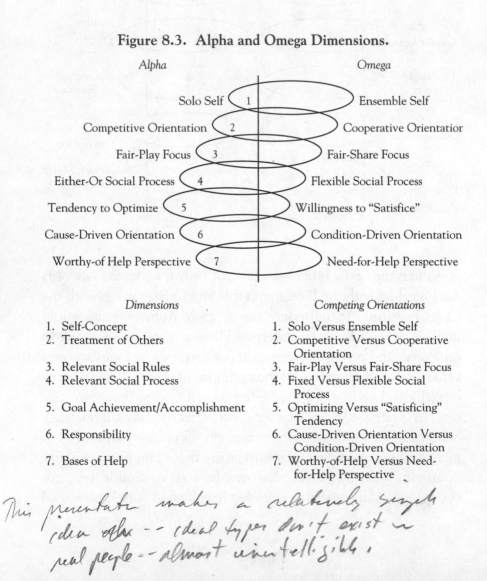

Figure 8.3.  Alpha and Omega Dimensions.

*Alpha*                                                    *Omega*

Solo Self — 1 — Ensemble Self

Competitive Orientation — 2 — Cooperative Orientation

Fair-Play Focus — 3 — Fair-Share Focus

Either-Or Social Process — 4 — Flexible Social Process

Tendency to Optimize — 5 — Willingness to "Satisfice"

Cause-Driven Orientation — 6 — Condition-Driven Orientation

Worthy-of Help Perspective — 7 — Need-for-Help Perspective

| *Dimensions* | *Competing Orientations* |
|---|---|
| 1. Self-Concept | 1. Solo Versus Ensemble Self |
| 2. Treatment of Others | 2. Competitive Versus Cooperative Orientation |
| 3. Relevant Social Rules | 3. Fair-Play Versus Fair-Share Focus |
| 4. Relevant Social Process | 4. Fixed Versus Flexible Social Process |
| 5. Goal Achievement/Accomplishment | 5. Optimizing Versus "Satisficing" Tendency |
| 6. Responsibility | 6. Cause-Driven Orientation Versus Condition-Driven Orientation |
| 7. Bases of Help | 7. Worthy-of-Help Versus Need-for-Help Perspective |

*This presentation makes a relatively simple idea ohh -- ideal types don't exist in real people -- almost unintelligible.*

## Religion as a Multilevel Concept

This analysis has suggested multiple levels of religious identification and commitment. One level, represented by the Alpha and the Omega attitudes, is a deep, or core, value level. The second level is that of the religious ethics—such as the Catholic ethic and the Protestant ethic. This level is a combination of religious values and religiously influenced values on such matters as work, money, and the possibility of penance. At still a third level are churches and sects, centers and abbeys, religious orders, and the like, each with its own orientation within the larger frame that is the next level. That next and fourth level consists of the policies of institutionalized churches. And the fifth level holds the specific practices each church recommends to its followers. The following list shows these five levels separated into Protestant and Catholic value set frameworks.

| | |
|---|---|
| Protestant practice | Catholic practice |
| Protestant policy | Catholic policy |
| Protestant churches and sects | Catholic churches and sects |
| Protestant ethic | Catholic ethic |
| Alpha Attitude | Omega Attitude |

Religion thus viewed is a multilevel concept, ranging from adherence to some very concrete, ritualistically specific procedures to an adherence to the cultural essence in the form of an ethic that discards the exoskeleton.

The presence of a core level (level 5) helps to explain situations in which different religions have similar results or downstream outcomes that can be associated with believers, beliefs, and their interconnections. When one thinks of the emphasis in the Protestant ethic on hard work, one has to think, "Well, of course that ethic produces wealth: people are working day and night, work is sacred," and so on. But other religions or the cultural ethics following from them may have a similar result. Robert Bellah (1957) has pointed out that the Tokugawa Shogunate belief system produces results similar to those associated with the Protestant ethic. Korea, Singapore, Hong Kong, and other "little tiger" centers are competing well today. They may have a set of results similar to that of the Protestant ethic because the essential cultural core produced by their beliefs is similar, even though much of the outward form of their belief system is different from Protestantism's outward form.

## Conclusion

It is reasonable not only to expect the Catholic ethic wherever there is the Protestant ethic (or an Omega attitude wherever there is an Alpha attitude), but also to see these two ethics as having larger, more encompassing representations and expressions than the formal religions behind the ethics.

This means that researchers must now be less certain of what religion is and what it is that they are measuring when they ask questions about religion. Religion is always a discussion of values. Sometimes this discussion is masked and made difficult because, by definition, values are ideas to which commitments are attached and that people have *feelings* about. Their ideas are "right." Others' ideas may be "wrong." Discussion is thus inhibited. Recognizing that constructs such as the Protestant and the Catholic ethics exist and have a certain complexity may make such discussions more possible.

## Chapter Nine

# Looking Ahead

In this concluding chapter, I address three questions: What? So What? and Now What? The answer to "what" is a summative reflection, a reprise mixed with some judgment and some conclusions. The query "so what" asks what it all means. Why does it matter that there is a Catholic ethic and a Protestant ethic? Why does it matter that the Protestant ethic has a dark side that makes helping harder? Who cares? I go beyond the basic conclusions and seek to show how these ethics illuminate old questions and pose new ones. "Now what" asks whether further explorations and investigations need to occur. In short, Where do we go from here? Finally, I conclude with some responses to common questions that have come up during the course of this investigation, ones that will probably occur to the reader also.

## What?

When they first hear the concept that there is a Catholic ethic, many seem to feel the idea is self-evident. Then the questions start. "Why have I not heard of this?" "What is it like?" "How does it relate to the Protestant ethic?" and "Do all Catholics believe it? It does not seem that all Protestants believe the Protestant ethic." As happens with many new ideas, initial enthusiasm quickly shades into puzzlement and then into skepticism.

The two major points of hesitancy are these. First, some people feel that "there is no such thing as the Protestant ethic because there are so many denominations." This argument suggests that differences within Protestantism make a common pattern of thought or behavior improbable. Second, some people feel that "there is no such thing as the Catholic ethic, because all Catholics think alike and practices are identical worldwide." This argument suggests that owing to what a social scientist would call "lack of variance," there is nothing to explain.

Both arguments are, of course, false. There are patterns within Protestantism, even though over time and space people have exemplified different elements of the Protestant mosaic. The obverse is true of Catholicism. There are lots of variations worldwide and historically, and the common pattern among these variations must be sought out.

*assertion, not argument*

## Development

One way to look at what the Protestant and Catholic ethics are is to look at their development. Each ethic developed, in part, in response to elements in the social environment that at times represented the thinking of the other ethic. The Catholic ethic began developing in ancient times in the context of Jewish thinking. The Protestant ethic arose, in part, in response to the Catholic ethic and to specific Catholic practices of the times. It thus emphasized different elements of a similar value matrix, giving a different orientation to concepts already present. Each ethic then addresses needs not emphasized or stressed by the other. Indeed, *complementary* might be more to the point than *opposing* as a description of the relationship of the two ethics. As I have emphasized throughout, what is dominant in one is likely to be subdominantly represented in the other.

## Core Elements

From the patterns revealed by the development of the ethics over time, Weber, Greeley, Novak, and I, among others, have extracted ideal-typical, or archetypal, cultural constructs. That is, each ethic has been found to have core properties. The general consensus is that the Protestant ethic is characterized by an individualistic, achievement-oriented perspective, with a work-wealth self at the center. In the Catholic ethic, sharing and acceptance are core elements. The ethic has a more communalistic orientation. Around these core properties in both Protestantism and Catholicism swirl the behaviors of individuals, organizations, churches, and sects, ebbing and flowing as other forces become involved as well.

## Central Properties

It is because the Protestant ethic developed in relationship to the Catholic ethic that I have been able to illustrate that the central pillars of the Protestant ethic and the Catholic ethic are the same—ideas about work, money, the person/family/community nexus, judgment and forgiveness, and this world as it connects to the next. Understanding the materials each ethic perceives these five pillars to be made of, the properties of each, is important to discerning each ethic's implications.

## Conceptual Details

In addition, around the core values and central properties of the ethics, a latticework of conceptual details can be constructed. It is here that we find derivative properties, like concern for the poor and the disadvantaged and support for communal capitalism, or support for the achiever and for individualistic capitalism.

Being achievement oriented, the Protestant ethic naturally allots to achievers the lion's share of the culture's rewards and attention. At the same time, the corollary concept is that those who have not achieved are suspect. One wonders why they are not achievers and if perhaps they are not working hard enough or lacking in motivation. Such suspicion is especially reserved for the poor. Individualistic capitalism (to use Thurow's term, 1992) is supported.

In the Catholic ethic, a sharing orientation places others more at the center of life. To call upon Thurow again, communalistic capitalism is more likely. Achievers are the ones who are somewhat suspect while those who have little receive attention and concern.

The work of other social researchers fits well into this view of the lattice surrounding the main ideas in the two ethics. In Chapter Eight, I mentioned that Lykes had identified the individualistic and the communal types of selves in doing gender research. McClelland's work on "learned needs" also finds these types. McClelland talks about the "need for achievement" (n-ACH) and the "need for affiliation" (n-AFF). N-ACH is defined as "behavior directed toward competition with a standard of excellence." N-AFF is "the desire to establish and maintain friendly and warm relations with other individuals" (Steers and Porter, 1991, pp. 39, 41; see also McClelland, 1965). The measures used capture and portray some of the values discussed here. The individuals tested were given some pictures and asked to make up stories interpreting or fantasizing what was happening in those pictures. "McClelland believed that analyzing these fantasies is the best way to measure the strength of [the respondents'] needs. Individuals with a high need for achievement write stories about people who are striving to accomplish a particular goal, and think about how to do it. On the other hand, individuals who write stories that center on social interactions and being with others have a high need for affiliation" (Steers and Porter, 1991, p. 39). Clearly, these two views of the self do exist in society.

Edward Banfield and James Q. Wilson, (1963) have developed an interesting juxtaposition between "private regarding" and "public regarding" politics that also fits into the lattice of supporting ideas. Private regarding politics assumes that government exists to meet personal needs. Of course, when your kid is picked up by the cops, the alderman will help; of course, coal should be provided by the city for the winter, and so on. Politics provides the basic needs; you work for what you want above that. A public regarding orientation, however, assumes that government provides only that which you could not possibly provide for yourself—a national park, a school system, and so on. You are responsible for meeting your own basic needs, and the government works above that. The Catholic ethic is well described by a public regarding orientation; the Protestant ethic by a private regarding one.

Finally, another piece of latticework involves our sense of identity. Do we perceive that we "discover" a sense of identity or do we think it is earned/created? Discovery is more the mode in the Protestant ethic. Finding out whether one has been given salvation is one instance of this discovery. A secular example is discovering one's intelligence. When people respond to the question about why someone gets good grades with the answer that he or she "is smart," they are looking at intellectual ability (as some look at character) as a gift rather than as a creation. Leadership and sports ability are often refereed to in this way as well. We hear of "natural" leaders and "natural" athletes. On the other hand, President Clinton's view, mentioned earlier, that character is a journey, not a destination, reflects the idea that identity is created and earned. The core concepts, central properties, and latticework of the Protestant and Catholic ethics are summarized in Figure 9.1.

But then comes the question, So what? Providing an organizational framework into which other research and a variety of perspectives fit is part of the response. But there are other elements that will be important in the future.

## So What?

One answer to the so what question is that the new conceptual framework formed by the Protestant ethic, the Catholic ethic, and their juxtaposition allows us to better understand our cultures and ourselves.

**Figure 9.1.  Summary of Core Concepts, Central Properties, and Latticework of the Protestant and Catholic Ethics.**

|  | Protestant Ethic | Catholic Ethic |
|---|---|---|
| Core concepts | Achievement<br>Individualism | Sharing<br>Communalism |
| Central properties | Work/wealth as self<br>Person focused<br>Judgment/exclusion<br>This world<br>Scarce resources | Work/wealth as resources<br>Family/community focused<br>Forgiveness/acceptance<br>Next world<br>Abundant resources |
| Latticework | Pro-achievers<br>Suspicion of poor<br>Individualistic capitalism<br>Need for achievement<br>Public regarding politics<br>Identity discovered<br>(Other features still to be<br>  found?) | Pro-poor<br>Suspicion of achievers<br>Communalistic capitalism<br>Need for affiliation<br>Private regarding politics<br>Identity earned/created<br>(Other features still to be<br>  found?) |

## The Catholic Ethic and the Spirit of Welfarism: Making Helping Easier

To paraphrase Weber's title, the Catholic ethic has a spirit of welfarism; it supports helping others and it supports the idea of the welfare state and the use of organized resources—be they church, state, or church and state together—to provide that help. I am continually tempted to say, "help for those in need" rather than help for others, and that would be true but only as a subtruth. The culture of sharing does not *start* by asking about those in need, implying a special "them." It begins simply with the concept of sharing to meet social need. Family allowances are an obvious form of help to supply, because families with children need assistance. Support for the elderly, for the sick, and for the unemployed is obviously necessary. Age, sickness, and lack of work are needs that everyone will experience eventually, and thus, the social structure should meet those needs. Such social provision is not a "safety net"; it is a playground, accessible to all. Whether you have a big yard or a small yard, you can still use the playground.

It is within this perspective that the Catholic ethic argues for a preferential option for the poor. It takes an interest in those at the bottom of the resource ladder. The option for the poor, though, is driven by the concern that it is difficult for you to enjoy your gains while others are suffering. It is irrelevant whether you "deserve" those gains or not; you should share.

This public regarding emphasis of the Catholic ethic supported the development of the welfare state in Europe (see Misner, 1991; Wilensky, 1981). Wilensky even explains, as I mentioned, how the Catholic ethic can function in officially Protestant countries.

In the United States, I believe we saw the Catholic ethic emphasis at work in the passage of the Social Security Act. Given, as I noted, that the United States government (the American people) had failed to extend and institutionalize two large-scale "welfare" programs earlier (the Freedman's Bureau and Civil War widows pensions), it required a very bad condition (the Depression) *and* a reconstituted set of demographics (many more Catholics and Jews) to make the Social Security Act possible. Certainly, not all Catholics and Jews supported social security and not all Protestants opposed it. But I suggest that the change in population demographics was parallel with a change in intellectual demographics, which in turn, allowed for a shift in what John Kingdon, my political science colleague at the University of Michigan, would call "a change in the agenda."

### The Protestant Ethic and the Spirit of Pauperism: Making Helping Harder

From the perspective of the Protestant ethic, helping is harder, both generalized helping (as in child allowances) and specialized helping of the very needy (as in welfare payments). *Pauperism*, as used here, refers to a belief matrix that raises questions about being in need and, even more, about accepting help for that need. The Protestant ethic's support for the achiever necessitates questions about those who do not achieve. As I have pointed out, we Americans have trouble providing aid for the poor, and even though we do so, we worry—worry that "they" will take advantage of "us," that "they" will flee work for welfare, and that "they" might even prefer welfare to work. Michael Lewis (1978), in his study of a metropolis he calls Middle City, reflects some of these attitudes and perspectives. One of his chapters is headed: "Those people! They're just no good; they live off the hard-working people; they don't care about their families; they're drunk; they're always causing trouble—they're getting away with murder" (p. 133). This theme of moral judgment is picked up by Handler and Hasenfeld (*The Moral Construction of Poverty* (1991) and by Michael B. Katz (1989) who studies the U.S. journey "From the War on Poverty to the War on Welfare."

Race is a factor in people's attitudes toward the poor, but poverty is the dominant condition.

> There are people in Middle City who never miss an opportunity to remark on the personal inadequacies of the poor, and particularly the black poor. . . . [Justice of the Peace] Arnold Stallings has been accused of discriminating against black defendants who appear before him. In point of fact he does not do so. He does, however, treat *poor* defendants—black and white—in a manner that can best be described as paternalistic. . . . Poor persons appearing before Justice of the Peace Stallings are very soon made to feel that their future depends not so much upon the impersonal and principled workings of the law as on Stallings' personal sense of rectitude [Lewis, 1978, pp. 145–146].

Needing help is problematic in the Protestant ethic tradition. Sometimes, though, accepting help is an even worse mark against character than needing it, because, so the reasoning goes, receiving help makes people *more* dependent. Lewis supplies another example.

Poor persons seeking help will have to contend with Miss Mary Cloud, the sixty-year-old welfare assistant, who, while sizing up the applicants, harbors the assumption that unless she guards against it, they will perpetrate frauds against the interests and taxes of the good hard-working people of Middle City. They will have to convince her that they are not only really in need, but also that they are worthy of any assistance—no mean task because Mary Cloud believes, as she puts it, that, "welfare has become a way of life for many people who come in here" [p. 156].

The perspective Lewis illustrates, the suspicion and hesitancy to help, is worth noting. In some sense, the culture of achievement creates a situation in which the poor threaten the nonpoor. Lewis speaks of the gap between achievement and aspiration among the Americans of Middle City as a corrosive to their very sense of self: "What do they do about these threats to their self-worth? What do these good Americans do about this sense that whatever they have achieved, they have achieved too little?" (p. 134). If achievement is everything, then lack of achievement must be something to look down upon, if only to reassure the viewer that she or he is still "okay." And when you feel that you have not achieved enough, that your position on the ladder of accomplishment is nowhere near what you had hoped, helping someone below you becomes an even tougher task than it is for the successful achiever.

While I am not investigating Weber's thesis that the Protestant ethic caused capitalism, it is possible to say that the Protestant ethic made it easier to take a pauperizing view and, thus, made accumulating profits easier, helping harder.

## Liberalism and Conservatism

Despite some similarities, the support of the Catholic ethic for a culture of sharing is not the same as a politically liberal posture, in 1990s parlance. "Liberal" today tends to be equated with supportive to encouraging views toward all oppressed groups, a hostility toward the oppression itself (which is associated with powerful organizations), and a willingness to use governmental power to counter oppression (except of course when that power *is* the oppressor). The Catholic ethic is not liberal in this sense. I have examined this question through research involving a multiyear analysis of national election studies for the years 1952 to 1978. Data were available to show whether being Catholic predicted either a liberal or conservative orientation. The question that had been asked was phrased as a "thermometer," asking how warmly or coldly the respondent felt toward a particular group. The four groups were Republicans, conservatives, Democrats, and liberals. Beta weights (measures of predictive strength) ranged from .00 (low) to .80 in a positive direction (very strong) and to −.80 in a negative direction (very strong). Catholics' beta weights were essentially zero, at .03, .04, .01, and −.02. respectively for the four groups. Being a Catholic did have power elsewhere, however; their beta weight was .28 for church attendance, as one would expect. This relationship suggests that the data are working in the right direction; thus, we can trust the other findings too (Tropman, 1987; Table 4, p. 156).

Sharing is not liberalism. Catholic family orientation, for example, may lead to support for marriages that liberals would think it was all right to dissolve and for pregnancies that liberals would think should be the mother's choice. The culture of sharing does not include all the points that might come under a liberal umbrella.

## Now What?

What might be some next steps that one could take with the material I have presented? Two paths come to mind. One has to do with policy analysis. These concepts should help us understand better some of the policy dilemmas that face us. A second is more scholarly. Further knowledge about these concepts can be pursued and future research designed.

## Policy Analysis

Policy analysis looks at ideas and programs that are existing or contemplated and tries to see how they are working, what parts are positive, and what parts need to be changed. All policy rests on assumptions of what the world is or is not like, how people behave, what motivates us and what does not. Almost always, the problems with policy analysis that occur do so because hidden assumptions were incomplete or wrong. The idea of the Catholic ethic provides a new set of assumptions from which to examine analysis and through which to examine ideas and programs already in place.

*Work- and Money-Oriented Behavior.* The two views of work contained in the Protestant and Catholic ethics—as meaning providing and resource providing—help us understand a number of conflicts that repeatedly occur around work. The concept of work as a provider of meaning supports the behavior of the workaholic. As a "characteristic" American worker, the workaholic stands in contrast to his or her "characteristic" counterpart in other countries. The German worker, for example, often values leisure over work, generally has longer vacations, and often thinks Americans are "out of their minds" because of the way they work. "You didn't get a thirteenth month's salary this year? You probably did not get the 39 paid holidays and vacation days that Germans get either" (Whitney, 1995, p. E5). Understanding the ethics also helps us to understand the sometimes judgmental attitude toward the nine-to-fiver. If one thinks that nine to five is only the beginning of the workday, then the character of someone who actually stops at five is suspect.

The different attitudes surrounding the ethics help us understand different attitudes toward the work/welfare dilemma. Some part of American policy thinking is always linking work to aid; in the example given earlier of the Nichlos plan, the hungry were not even eligible for slops (that uneaten food from restaurant plates scraped into five-gallon tins) without chopping wood. Nichlos worried that the "undeserving" would queue up! Another stream of thought, though, emphasizes the provision of aid without a "work test."

One practical application of our new knowledge might be to look at work orientation—if there are different attitudes toward work, then different motivational systems will be useful. If people value work as instrumental rather than transcendental, then their willingness to invest extra time in work for future rewards is lower. Managers might need to take that into account. We would need to know about these orientations in some detail before we could design effective motivational systems, but it would be a step along the road to a better satisfied workforce.

Money-related behavior and money-related views can be illuminated by the Catholic ethic–Protestant ethic contrast. If "it appears that *who we are* has been defined more and more through *what we have* as individuals; [that] material possessions have become symbols of personal and social identity" (Dittmar, 1992, p. 13), then it is not surprising to hear phrases like "Money talks; bullshit walks." And we can also better understand concepts like "affluence guilt," which exist side by side with acquisitive desire. We all know people who never seem to have enough; we also know people who seem satisfied if somewhat minimal needs are met.

*Individual Versus Family and Community.*  We can add to our knowledge of conflicts between an individualistic orientation and a family and community orientation by seeing the tensions between the two ethics within these conflicts. The individualism of the Protestant ethic pulls against the ligatures of family and community while also producing a longing for what it is not, for family and community. The communal orientation of the Catholic ethic puts tensions on individuals seeking to achieve outside of the communal circle while producing a longing for permission for just such achievement. Bellah and his colleagues (1986) worry about the problem of lack of community, as does Robert Wuthnow. In reviewing Wuthnow's *Christianity in the 21st Century*, John Wilson (1994) of Duke University asks: "What are the possibilities of genuine community in an age of high mobility? How can we prevent the search for identity from becoming a retreat into privatism and the cult of the individual? How can trust, altruism and compassion survive in an increasingly materialistic and calculating society?" (p. 440). Wuthnow says that the Christian church is part of the answer to these questions. And he is right. While the Protestant ethic might be individualistically oriented, Protestant churches may be a countervailing source of community and compassion for Protestant individuals.

But another answer is that there is a Catholic ethic, which tilts away from individualism and which can help a balance to be achieved. This can be true even though *individual* Catholics are at the same time seeking achievement goals.

**Mercy.**   American society is a harsh society in many ways. The market economy does what it does, and we take the heat (or reap the benefits.) Newman's image (1988) of unemployment and the consequent downward mobility as "falling from grace" captures this idea exactly. A friend of mine once described American society as being like the "Gong Show": "We are out there, doing our stuff, and maybe we keep on, or maybe we get gonged!" He was conveying, most of all, the anxious uncertainty that he felt he lived with at all times.

Understanding the Protestant ethic allows us to place this kind of view in a larger perspective, one in which people are often judged as falling short and often judge themselves in the same corrosive way as Lewis (1978) has suggested.

As I have outlined, our criminal justice system is driven by this judgmental orientation as well. Our sense that crime should be some*one's* fault, an individual's fault, and that that person should pay the price is going to be hard to change. Alternative views do exist though that take a more communitywide view of cause and that at least include community conditions in the understanding of predisposing cause if not precipitating cause. Seeing a need to redeem oneself as opposed to an obligation to "pay the price" is a way to understand the difference between these two orientations to criminal justice.

*This World and the Next: The Heavenly Calculus.*   Perceptions of scarcity or abundance of material goods link to perceived scarcity and abundance of other goods in the Protestant and Catholic ethics. The Protestant ethic sees goods as scarce ("A penny saved is a penny earned") but opportunities for career advancement, through hard work, everywhere ("Anyone can get ahead"). Certainly, one of the major obstacles to developing adequate responses to unemployment, homelessness, and poverty has been the perception of abundance of opportunity combined with the perceived scarcity of resources for helping. More awareness of the competing view that opportunities are limited and help should be available and generous might encourage us to respond more situationally to people's needs.

## Scholarly Analysis

This excursion into the Catholic ethic suggests a number of questions and concerns for us to consider in the future: Can the concept of the Catholic ethic be tested empirically? If so, are the properties of work, money, the self juxtaposed to family and community, judgment juxtaposed to forgiveness, and this world juxtaposed to the next truly the central concepts? Are there others? Are there central concepts of the Catholic ethic beyond sharing and a sharing culture? Related to the matter of testing is the idea of even more basic value orientations than the ethics themselves (that is, value systems like the Alpha and Omega attitudes). Can these basic cultural orientations be shown to exist, and if so, are the properties suggested here the correct or the only ones? And what of the heavenly calculus? Can we find some way to examine its formulas more thoroughly? Finally, what are the practical implications of whatever testing we may do?

Other ethics could be analyzed and illuminated as well. The likelihood of a Jewish ethic has already been mentioned. Some exploration of this point is already underway. The Jewish Ethic Research Group is exploring ideas about helping and providing for people's needs within historical and contemporary Jewish culture(s). As one example, the medieval Jewish philosopher Maimonides (1135–1204) described eight levels of charity (this list was provided by Armand Lauffer, director of Project STAR, University of Michigan):

8. Providing a loan, providing means for employment of the recipient, or even involving the recipient in a partnership arrangement, leading to self-sufficiency

7. Giving alms to the needy such that the recipient does not know from whom the gift comes, and the donor does not know to whom it goes

6. Dropping money into a charity box, so long as the treasurer is honest

5. Giving to the recipient, and knowing who the recipient is, so long as the recipient is unaware of the donor

4. Giving with one's own hand (i.e., directly) before being asked

3. Giving with one's own hand, but after being asked

2. Giving less than is fitting, but graciously

1. Giving grudgingly, but morosely

One wonders where U.S. society would rank on this list.

Muslim, Mormon, Amish, and other religions and religious sects represent important areas for investigation as well, in terms of core values, central properties, and latticework.

***Tests of the Catholic Ethic Properties and Derivatives.*** Testing out the Catholic ethic concept could involve a number of approaches. One well-accepted approach is detailed historical analysis. In this case, one could look at a broad range of data from historical documents to traditional practices and to the daily lives and activities of Protestants and Catholics. Different settings and centers (including urban and rural ones) would need to be included as would different time periods from the early years of Christianity through the intervening centuries to contemporary manifestations worldwide. It would be a massive undertaking, something like Mollat's work in *The Poor in the Middle Ages* (1986) and Misner's achievement in his *Social Catholicism in Europe* (1991).

A second kind of assay would review policy documents. The encyclicals are one handy source, but there are others, as Schwab (1991) has pointed out, such as Gremillion's *The Gospel of Peace and Justice*.

Adopting the public opinion perspective, one could use survey research to look specifically at religious identification as a variable or factor. Hofstede's *Culture's Consequences* (1980) is one example of such research. Hofstede finds that religion continues to be an important variable worldwide, but now that I have examined religious culture more closely, I find I am less sure what he means by the designations Catholic and Protestant because I am less sure what his respondents may have meant.

Among examples of relevant research is Falter's study of Hitler (1991), which found that Protestants were twice as likely to support the Nazis as were Catholics (reported by Hamilton, 1993). Varenne (1993) reports Lamont's finding that "the French, in general, are clearly less money oriented than Americans" (p. 601). But we now must look further. Rokeach (1969a, 1969b) finds those with "religious values" to be lacking in social compassion (p. 35) but defines religion through church attendance, hardly an encompassing, culturally sensitive definition.

There are thus pieces of information that seem to indicate religious ethic differences, but those pieces need to be put together in two ways. One has to do with the five levels of religious identification listed earlier, running from a base of essences to compliance with outward forms and requirements.

As discussed, an individual may ascribe to all of these levels, a couple of them, or only one. However, regardless of what package of identification the individual uses, he or she may still call himself or herself Protestant or Catholic (or whatever religion the list might be expanded to include). In short, today, religious identification may be intense or it may be nominal or it may take place at any level in between these two extremes. We currently lack substantive knowledge about which behavioral and cultural packages individuals signify when they use the names Catholic and Protestant.

Whatever system we use to reflect any one person's combination of commitments, it illustrates our need to distinguish levels of religious identification, all of which now go by the same religious name. One benefit of this multilevel approach might be to help us understand the current culture wars and their possible links to religion. Hunter (1991) points out that "the divisions of political consequence today are not theological and ecclesiastical in character but the result of differing world views. That is to say they no longer revolve around specific doctrinal issues and styles of religious practice and observation but around our most fundamental and cherished assumptions about how to live our lives" (cited in Hammond, Shibley, and Solow, 1994, p. 289). From the perspective I have presented, such cherished assumptions are likely to reflect elements like the Alpha or Omega attitude or the Protestant or Catholic ethic rather then simple religious identification.

A related task would develop the measures that would allow us to identify the appropriate levels in respondents. I have mentioned five levels—but we might find six or seven useful, or perhaps three would do. There are probably an infinite number of colors and shades. With a little selective perception, we can always convince ourselves that the levels we seek to measure are the dominant ones. And for our little time and place in the world our perception could be "true." But one can always go deeper. Primary colors are the base for other colors. In this metaphor, if the Alpha and Omega attitudes are primary colors, the religions might be hues. Since primary colors are never solitary ones, the task of organizing the religious palette will be an exciting one.

But this kind of approach, while it may ultimately link to Catholic ethic and Protestant ethic (and Jewish and other ethic) activities does not really ask about the Catholic ethic itself. We need to begin to develop a Catholic "scale," much like Greeley's GRACE scale (1990). We would want to know how respondents felt and, if possible, what they thought others thought. Thus, they could be informants as well as respondents.

***Other Typologies.***    The approach of the ethic rooted in religion is not the only typological work currently underway. Others are seeking to discover sources of our values in other ways. One who has looked at the question of value packages in relation to economic justice is Stephen Hart, in his book *What Does the Lord Require?* (1992; for reviews, see Johnson, 1993, and Steidlmeier, 1994). Hart looks at "Christians" and does not seek to distinguish Protestants from Catholics, although he has both in his data. He does not see that distinction as a crucial one. He does comment, however, that "the basic themes used by both kinds of Christians are similar, but Catholics do tend to relate faith to economic issues in a somewhat more liberal way than Protestants" (p. 5). This conclusion is consistent with what I have seen as long as one distinguishes between white and black Protestants, as black Protestants seem to be more "liberal" than Catholics.

Hart defines "liberal" and "conservative" through discussing two questions: "The first is [about] the debate over equality and inequality. . . . [W]hat kinds of inequality are justifiable? To what extent should we make sure that every person has access to decent food, housing, education and other important resources for life, versus relying on self-help, possibly supplemented by private charity? The second basic question is about private enterprise and the degree to which it should be constrained or abolished. To what extent do private owners have the right to make unimpeded decisions about how to use productive resources? To what extent should these be constrained by workers, communities or the government?" (p. 83). Thus, "liberal" refers to views that come down on the side of "equality" and "constraint" of private enterprise. "Conservative" refers to views that come down on the side of "inequality" and "unimpeded" private enterprise.

Hart's report of results from the General Social Survey, a poll taken regularly by the National Opinion Research Center at the University of Chicago, shows African American Protestants as 57 percent liberal; Catholics, 46 percent liberal; traditional Protestants, 46 percent liberal; moderate Protestants, 43 percent liberal; and modernist Protestants, 40+ percent liberal (based on an average response to thirty-nine questions) (Table 7–1, p. 158).

This approach to issues of economic justice seems to be one right out of the Protestant ethic tradition. The basic questions start from the premise that distinctions have to be made and justifications offered. Hart's concept of economic justice differs from the concept in the Catholic ethic, which has the different starting point of being more communal and more oriented toward sharing with a preferential option for the poor on top of that.

Hart comes close, though, very close, to an approach like that I have offered here. Consider his typology, presented in Table 9.1. I have added the Catholic ethic and Protestant ethic distinctions.

It seems appropriate to suggest that the first two horizontal rows are versions of the Catholic ethic orientation, while the second two are versions of the Protestant ethic orientation. Hart even uses some of the same language I have found appropriate ("sharing" and

Table 9.1. Languages Linking Faith to Economic Issues: Hart's Typology and the Catholic and Protestant Ethics.

| Language | Political Stand | Basic Values | Main Building Blocks Used |
|---|---|---|---|
| *Catholic Ethic* | | | |
| Corporatism | Mixed | Communal | Christian love |
| Sharing and caring | Moderately liberal | Communal | Christian love |
| *Protestest Ethic* | | | |
| Equality and rights | Strongly liberal | Mixed | Love, universalism, voluntarism |
| Economic freedom | Conservative | Individualistic | Universalism, voluntarism |

*Source:* Adapted from Hart, 1992, Table 5–1, p. 124.

"communalism"). While not a perfect fit, his thinking and mine are close enough to be mutually supportive. Operating from a different set of premises, looking at the world somewhat differently, and using different methodology (in-depth interviews done in 1976) he, like Greeley with his concept of a Catholic myth, comes very near to a Protestant ethic–Catholic ethic fulcrum for cultural values.

Hart's work contains some other important points that I, too, have found important to stress. One is that the four orientations come from different emphases around core values and central properties, not different values. It is the mix that matters, the properties that predominate. (Hart's properties are a set of five key "building blocks" of the Christian faith: voluntarism, universalism, love, this-worldliness, and otherworldliness, p. 43ff.)

Hart also emphasizes, as I have, the actual mix of motives within the ethics and, even more particularly, within people. Since the Protestant ethic turned the Catholic ethic inside out, one would expect exactly this result. What Hart calls "equality and rights" could encompass the social gospel movement, the Quakers, the Salvation Army, and other Protestant groups stimulated by that subdominant portion of the Protestant ethic. There is a mixed picture when one looks for expressions of the Catholic ethic as well. Hart,

too, has found that a single ethic can result in very different interpretations and actions. One can only say, of course. However, his
explanation of the differences is that individuals have different
interpretations of "what the Lord requires." He does not explore the
possibility that within in the traditions themselves are conflicting
priorities requiring choices and alignments. When Hart's typologies
are labeled as Catholic or Protestant ethics, the idea of varieties of
viewpoint within the Protestant ethic and the Catholic ethic comes
crisply to the fore.

E. Digby Baltzell (1979), in his treatment of the early religious
influence on the cultures of Boston and Philadelphia (*Puritan
Boston and Quaker Philadelphia: Two Protestant Ethics and the Spirit of
Class Authority and Leadership*) addresses the same issue. In many
ways, the structure of his work also has parallels to the structure
used here. Baltzell is interested in religious culture as an independent variable, and he has a dependent variable in mind. He creates two cultural plates, two expressions of the Protestant
ethic—Puritanism and Quakerism—and looks at the extent to
which and the ways in which those different cultures produced
"leaders" and politically prominent individuals. Baltzell feels the
difference, at its core, lies in the "Quaker ethic of privacy and success, on the one hand, and the Puritan inclination toward public
authority, leadership and fame, on the other" (p. 10). As he points
out, "Christians have always disagreed on which [elements of faith]
should be emphasized at any time and place" (p. 93); and he seeks
to capture the essential features of the Puritan and Quaker "Protestant ethics" (see Table 9.2).

*Ideas and People.* Two questions in the area of scholarly analysis
deserve further research attention. One has to do with the kinds of
data one might use to look at the relationship between ideas/val-
ues/attitudes/beliefs and the people who have them. This point has
already been discussed above. The next question has to do with the
relationship between what people believe (the level of belief, the
intensity, and so on) and what they do. There are obviously many

Table 9.2. The Two Plates: Puritan and
Quaker Ethics and Their Cultural Consequences.

| Puritan Ethic | Quaker Ethic |
|---|---|
| *Religious Patterns* | |
| 1. Old Testament | 1. New Testament |
| 2. God transcendent | 2. God immanent |
| 3. Predestination and election | 3. God in every person |
| 4. Particular calling | 4. General calling |
| 5. Source of evil: sinful man | 5. Source of evil: the world |
| *Cultural Consequences* | |
| 6. Hierarchical communalism | 6. Egalitarian individualism |
| 7. Aristocratic-patrician | 7. Democratic-plutocratic |
| 8. Ethnocentrism | 8. Xenophilia |

*Source:* Adapted from Baltzell, 1979, p. 94.

forces—religious values, other values, aspects of the social structure—that impact how people actually behave. The illustration in Chapter One of the found wallet pointed that out. Hence, charitable or sharing *behavior* might be determined by a mix of contradictory factors.

Survey data about such behavior (the Independent Sector used the Gallup organization to perform a poll-based assessment), reveal contradictory messages when religious identification (Catholic and Protestant) is used as a control. Protestants reported giving more to charities (Independent Sector, p. 333). On the other hand, fewer Catholics than Protestants felt they were doing enough in the area of helping others (p. 902).

Differences between Protestants and Catholics on policy opinion questions (what should be done in various areas such as helping the poor, health care, and so on) are small, though according to Kellstedt and others (1994), they are greater between Catholics and evangelical Protestants than between Catholics and mainline Protestants. And leaving religious identification aside, a structural variable—frequent church attendance—seems to be a key predictor.

Clearly, more detailed analysis is needed. Approaches that take the *kind* of religious background respondents have into account (using some of the religious typologies developed, for example, by Hart) are essential. There is much to do here, and comparison is essential.

## Conclusion

This book has been about religion and culture, about their interrelationship and about the different orientations religion-based cultures have toward the disadvantaged. I have made an argument for the existence and importance of a Catholic ethic, parallel to the more famous Protestant ethic. Since it makes good sense that there is a Catholic ethic, the question why the concept is not popular in social scientific thinking had to be addressed. Concern for the disadvantaged has often been called charity, at least in the United States. That term has an air of disdain attached to it. In naming the Catholic concern for the poor a culture of sharing, I wanted to convey the Catholic belief that the disadvantaged have some claim on our resources; sharing implies that there is *a community* involved in the procuring and development of resources and that all are entitled to enjoy them, though perhaps not in equal amounts. Thus, the Catholic ethic is a sharing ethic, supporting a culture of sharing throughout the population that it touches.

# References

Adie, D. "Madame Bountiful Supplanted by Organized Social Work." *Buffalo Evening News*, Oct. 11, 1930, p. 14.

Ager, S. "Affluence Guilt." *Detroit Free Press*, Feb. 9, 1993, p. 3F.

Ager, S. "'Good' Often Seems to Mean 'Plenty.'" *Detroit Free Press*, July 14, 1994, p. 3A.

Associated Press. "Report on Who's Bound for Hell Bedevils Baptists." *Ann Arbor News*, Sept. 19, 1993, p. 1.

Auchincloss, L. *The Winthrop Covenant*. New York: Ballantine Books, 1976.

Baltzell, E. D. *Puritan Boston and Quaker Philadelphia: Two Protestant Ethics and the Spirit of Class Authority and Leadership*. New York: Free Press, 1979.

Banfield, E., and Wilson, J. Q. *City Politics*. New York: Vintage Books, 1963.

Bellah, R. N. *Tokugawa Religion: The Cultural Roots of Modern Japan*. New York: Free Press, 1957.

Bellah, R. N., and others. *Habits of the Heart: Individualism and Commitment in American Life*. New York: Perennial Library, 1986.

Bellah, R. N., and others. *The Good Society*. New York: Knopf, 1991.

Berkovitch, S. *The Puritan Origin of the American Self*. New Haven, Conn.: Yale University Press, 1975.

Billington, R. A. *The Protestant Crusade*. Chicago: Quadrangle Books, 1964. (Originally published 1938.)

Bray, H. "If the Suit Fits . . . Sue Them." *Detroit Free Press*, Nov. 15, 1993 p. 4F.

Calvez, J.-Y. "Economic Policy Issues in Roman Catholic Teaching." In J. Gannon, *The Catholic Challenge to the American Economy*. New York: Macmillan, 1987.

*The Catholic Encyclopedia*. New York: Nelson, 1987.

Charity Organization Society. *Fifty Years of Social Work, 1877–1927*. Buffalo, N.Y.: Charity Organization Society, 1927.

Coleman, J. A. *One Hundred Years of Catholic Social Thought: Celebration and Challenge*. Maryknoll, N.Y.: Orbis, 1991.

Cone, J. *A Black Theology of Liberation*. Maryknoll, N.Y.: Orbis, 1986.

DeParle, J. "The Clinton Welfare Bill Begins Trek in Congress." *New York Times*, July 15, 1994, p. A1.

Desan, P. "Thinking in Market Terms." *The University of Chicago Magazine*, Oct. 1993, pp. 8–9.

de Schweinitz, I. *England's Road to Social Security from the Statute of Laborers in 1349 to the Beveridge Report of 1942*. Philadelphia: University of Pennsylvania Press, 1943.

DeSmet, K. "The Private Penance of Tom Monaghan." *Detroit Free Press*, Nov. 17, 1991, p. 1.

DeSmet, K. "City Merchants' Anti-Panhandling Campaign Raises an Issue of Morality." *Detroit News*, July 10, 1992, p. 12A.

Deveny, K. "Immigrants: Still Believers After All These Years." *Wall Street Journal*, July 12, 1994, p. B1.

Dittmar, H. *The Social Psychology of Material Possessions*. New York: St. Martins Press, 1992.

Dudar, H. "Art That 'Can Make People Laugh and Frighten Them, Too.'" *Smithsonian*, 1993, 24(3), 70–86.

Durkheim, E. *The Division of Labor in Society*. (K. Lang, trans.) New York: Free Press, 1960a.

Durkheim, E. "The Dualism of Human Nature and Its Social Conditions." (C. Blend, trans.) In K. H. Wolff (ed.), *Emile Durkheim, 1858–1917: A Collection of Essays*. Columbus: Ohio State University Press, 1960b.

Edwards, R. *The Encyclopedia of Social Work*. Silver Spring, Md.: National Association of Social Workers, 1995.

Ellis, J. T. *American Catholicism*. Chicago: University of Chicago Press, 1969.

Erikson, E. *Childhood and Society* New York: W.W. Norton, 1950.

Erikson, K. *Everything in Its Path: Destruction of Community in the Buffalo Creek Flood*. New York: Simon & Schuster, 1976.

Falter, J. *Hitler's Wahler*. Munich, Germany: C.H. Beck, 1991.

Fanfani, A. *Catholicism, Protestantism, and Capitalism*. New York: Sheed & Ward, 1936.

Finn, J. (ed.). *Private Virtue and Public Policy*. New Brunswick, N.J.: Transaction, 1990.

Frost, R. *The Road Not Taken*. Troy, Mo.: Holt, Rinehart & Winston, 1971.

Gallagher, J. "A Stranger in Paradise." *Detroit Free Press*, Nov. 15, 1993, p. 6F.

Gannon, T. M. (ed.). *The Catholic Challenge to the American Economy*. New York: Macmillan, 1987.

Ganster, D. C. "Protestant Ethic and Performance: A Reexamination." *Psychological Reports*, 1981, 48(1), 335–338.

Gerber, D. A. "Ambivalent Anti-Catholicism: Buffalo's American Protestant Elite Faces the Challenge of the Catholic Church, 1850–1860." *Civil War History*, June 1984, pp. 119–143.

Gilligan, C. *In a Different Voice*. Cambridge, Mass.: Harvard University Press, 1982.

Glazer, N., and Moynihan, D. P. *Beyond the Melting Pot: The Negroes, Puerto*

Ricans, Jews, Italians, and Irish of New York City. Cambridge, Mass.: MIT Press, 1963.

Glenn, N. D., and Hyland, R. "Religious Preference and Worldly Success: Some Evidence from National Surveys." *American Sociological Review*, 1967, *31*(1), 73–85.

Glenn, N. D., and Weaver, C. N. "Enjoyment of Work by Full-Time Workers in the U.S.: 1955 and 1980." *Public Opinion Quarterly*, 1982, *46*, 459–470.

Gordon, L. "How Welfare Became a Dirty Word." *The Chronicle of Higher Education*, July 20, 1994, pp. B1–B2.

Greeley, A. M. *The American Catholic*. New York: Basic Books, 1977.

Greeley, A. M. *The Catholic Myth: The Behavior and Beliefs of American Catholics*. New York: Charles Scribner's Sons, 1990.

Greeley, A. M. *The Cardinal Virtues*. New York: Warner Books, 1991.

Gremillion, J. *The Gospel of Peace and Justice*. Maryknoll, N.Y.: Orbis Books, 1976.

Gusfield, J. *Symbolic Crusade: Status Politics and the American Temperance Movement*. Urbana: University of Illinois Press, 1963.

Gustafson, J. M. *Protestant and Roman Catholic Ethics: Prospects for Rapprochement*. Chicago: University of Chicago Press, 1978.

Hamel, G. H. *Poverty and Charity in Roman Palestine, First Three Centuries C.E.* Vol. 23 of *Near Eastern Studies*. Berkeley: University of California Press, 1990.

Hamilton, S. "The Rise of the Nazis." Review of *Hitler's Wahler*, by J. Falter. *Contemporary Sociology*, 1993, *22*(4), 543–544.

Hammond, P., Shibley, M., and Solow, P. "Religion and Family Values in Presidential Voting." *Sociology of Religion*, 1994, *55*(3), 277–290.

Handler, J., and Hasenfeld, Y. *The Moral Construction of Poverty*. Newbury Park, Calif.: Sage, 1991.

Hart, S. *What Does the Lord Require?* New York: Oxford University Press, 1992.

Heaven, P. C. "The Protestant Ethic Scale in South Africa." *Psychological Reports*, 1980, *47*(2), 618.

Herberg, W. *Protestant, Catholic, Jew*. New York: Doubleday/Anchor, 1960.

Hirschman, A. O. *The Rhetoric of Reaction: Perversity, Futility, Jeopardy*. Cambridge, Mass.: Harvard University Press, 1991.

Hodgkinson, V., and Weitzman, M. *Giving and Volunteering in the United States*. Washington, D.C.: Independent Sector, 1992.

Hofstede, G. *Culture's Consequences: International Differences in Work-Related Values*. Newbury Park, Calif.: Sage, 1980.

Holland, J. *Toward a Theology of Work: The Modern Degradation of Work*. Winona, Minn.: St. Mary's Press, 1984–1985a.

Holland, J. *Toward a Theology of Work: Toward a Holy Economy*. Winona, Minn.: St. Mary's Press, 1984–1985b.

Holland, J. *Toward a Theology of Work: Work as Co-Creation*. Winona, Minn.: St. Mary's Press, 1984–1985c.

Holland, J., and Henriot, P. *Social Analysis: Linking Faith and Social Justice*. (Rev. ed.) Washington: Center of Concern, 1983.

Hudson, W. S. *American Protestantism*. Chicago: University of Chicago Press, 1961a.

Hudson, W. S. "The Weber Thesis Reexamined." *Church History*, 1961b, *30*, 88–99.

Hunter, J. *Culture Wars*. New York: Basic Books, 1991.

Independent Sector. *Detailed Tabulations, Volumes I and II*. Washington, D.C.: Independent Sector, 1990.

Ingrassia, P., and Stertz, B. A. "Mea Culpa: With Chrysler Ailing, Lee Iacocca Concedes Mistakes in Managing: . . . I'm Confessing My Sins Here." *Wall Street Journal*, Sept. 17, 1990. p. 1.

Jencks, C. *Inequality*. New York: Basic Books, 1982.

Johnson, B. Review of *What Does the Lord Require?* by S. Hart. *Contemporary Sociology*, 1993, *22*(5), 658.

Katz, M. B. *The Undeserving Poor: From the War on Poverty to the War on Welfare*. New York: Pantheon, 1989.

Kellstedt, L., Green, J., and Guth, J. "Religious Voting Blocks in the 1992 Election Year." *Sociology of Religion*, 1994, *55*(3), 307–326.

Kemelman, H. *Friday the Rabbi Slept Late*. New York: Crown, 1964.

Kennedy, R.J.R. "Single or Triple Melting Pot: Intermarriage Trends in New Haven, 1870–1940." *American Journal of Sociology*, 1944, *49*(4), 331–339.

Kersten, L. L., and Kersten, K. K. *The Love Exchange*. New York: Fell, 1981.

Killinger, B. *Workaholics: The Respectable Addiction*. New York: Simon & Schuster, 1992

Klein, J. "The Politics of Promiscuity. *Newsweek*, May 9, 1994a, pp. 16–20.

Klein, J. "Shepherds of the Inner City." *Newsweek*, Apr. 18, 1994b, p. 28.

Kosmin, B., and Lachman, S. P. *One Nation Under God: Religion in Contemporary American Society*. New York: Harmony, 1993.

Kristol, I. "The Tragic Error of Affirmative Action." *The Wall Street Journal*, Aug. 1, 1994, p. A18.

Kushner, H. S. *When Bad Things Happen to Good People*. New York: Avon, 1983.

Lamont, M. *Money, Morals and Manners: The Culture of the French and the American Upper Middle Class*. Chicago: University of Chicago Press, 1992.

Lang, K. "Alienation." In J. Gould and W. Kolb, (eds.), *A Dictionary of the Social Sciences*. New York: Free Press, 1964.

Lenski, G. *The Religious Factor*. New York: Doubleday/Anchor, 1963.

Lewin, T. "Appeals Court Overturns California's Welfare Cut." *The New York Times*, July 15, 1994, p. A7.

Lewis, M. *The Culture of Inequality*. Amherst: University of Massachusetts Press, 1978.

Liepman, K. *Journey to Work: Its Significance for Industrial and Community Life*. New York, Oxford University Press, 1944.

Lipset, S. M. *The First New Nation*. New York: Basic Books, 1963.

Lykes, M. B. "Gender in Individualistic Versus Collectivistic Bases for Notions About the Self." *Journal of Personality*, 1985, *53*(2), 356–383.

McCarthy, E., and McGaughey, W. *Nonfinancial Economics: The Case for Shorter Hours of Work*. New York: Praeger, 1989.

McClelland, D. C. "Toward a Theory of Motive Acquisition." *American Psychologist*, 1965, *20*, 321–333.

McGregor, D. *The Human Side of Enterprise*. New York: McGraw-Hill, 1960.

Mack, R., Murphy, R. J., and Yellin, S. "The Protestant Ethic, Level of Aspiration, and Occupational Mobility: An Empirical Test." *American Sociological Review*, June 1956, *21*, 295–300.

March, J. G., and Simon, H. *Organizations*. New York: Wiley, 1958.

Marshall, G. *In Search of the Spirit of Capitalism: An Essay on Max Weber's Protestant Ethic Thesis*. New York: Columbia University Press, 1982.

Martinson, O. B., and Wilkening, E. A. "Religion, Work Specialization, and Job Satisfaction: Interactive Effects." *Review of Religious Research*, 1983, *24*(4), 347–356.

Meeks, W. A. *The Moral World of the First Christians*. Philadelphia: Westminster Press, 1986.

Miller, W. D. *Dorothy Day*. New York: HarperCollins, 1982.

Misner, P. *Social Catholicism in Europe from the Onset of Industrialization to the First World War*. New York: Crossroads, 1991.

Mollat, M. *The Poor in the Middle Ages: An Essay in Social History*. (A. Golhammer, trans.) New Haven, Conn.: Yale University Press, 1986.

Morgan, E. *The Puritan Dilemma: The Story of John Winthrop*. Boston: Little, Brown, 1958.

Mueller, G. H. "The Protestant and the Catholic Ethics." *Annual Review of the Social Sciences of Religion*, 1978, *2*, 143–156.

Murphy, D. E. "Polish-German Relations Thaw." *Los Angeles Times*, Aug. 4, 1994, p. A11.

Murray, H. *Do Not Neglect Hospitality: The Catholic Worker and the Homeless*. Philadelphia: Temple University Press, 1990.

Myrdal, G. *An American Dilemma: The Negro Problem in Modern Democracy*. (2 vols., anniversary ed.) New York: HarperCollins, 1962.

Newman, K. S. *Falling from Grace: The Experience of Downward Mobility in the American Middle Class*. New York: Free Press, 1988.

Newman, K. S. Review of *Tell Them Who I Am: The Lives of Homeless Women*, by E. Liebow. *Contemporary Sociology*, 1994, *23*(1), 43–44.

Niebuhr, H. R. *The Kingdom of God in America*. Hamden, Conn.: Shoe String Press, 1956.

Niebuhr, R. *Moral Man in Immoral Society*. New York: Charles Scribner's Sons, 1932.

Novak, M. *The Catholic Ethic and the Spirit of Capitalism*. New York: Free Press, 1993.

Oates, J. C. *Them*. New York: Vanguard Press, 1969.

O'Brien, D. "The Economic Thought of the American Hierarchy." In J. Gannon, *The Catholic Challenge to the American Economy*. New York: Macmillan, 1987.

O'Neal, S. "The Real Shaquille." *USA Weekend*, Oct. 1–3, 1993, pp. 6–8.

*On Social Concern* (in English). Boston, Mass.: Daughters of St. Paul, 1988.

Ostling, R. N. "The Search for Mary: Handmaid or Feminist?" *Time*, Dec. 30, 1991, pp. 62–66.

Palmer, P. J. "Scarcity, Abundance, and the Gift of Community." *Community Renewal Press*, 1990, *1*(3), 2–6.

Parsons, T. "Anglo American Society." In D. L. Sills (ed.), *International Encyclopedia of the Social Sciences*. Vol. 2. New York: Macmillan/Free Press, 1968a.

Parsons, T. "Christianity." In D. L. Sills (ed.), *International Encyclopedia of the Social Sciences*. Vol. 2. New York: Macmillan/Free Press, 1968b.

Parsons, T., and Bales, R. F. *Family: Socialization and Interaction Process*. New York: Free Press, 1955.

Pascale, R. T., and Athos, A. G. *The Art of Japanese Management*. New York: Simon & Schuster, 1981.

Piercy, J. K. Introduction. In C. Mather, *Bonifacius*. Gainesville, Fla.: Scholars Facsimiles and Reprints, 1967.

Popcorn, F. *The Popcorn Report*. New York: Dell, 1991.

Potok, C. *The Chosen*. Greenwich, Conn.: Fawcett, 1967.

Pumphrey, R. E., and Pumphrey, M. W. (eds.). *The Heritage of American Social Work*. New York: Columbia University Press, 1961.

Quinn, R. E. *Beyond Rational Management: Mastering the Paradoxes and Competing Demands of High Performance*. San Francisco: Jossey-Bass, 1989.

Rauschenbusch, W. *Christianity and the Social Crisis*. New York: Macmillan, 1907.

Reisman, D., Glazer, N., and Denny, R. *The Lonely Crowd*. New Haven, Conn..: Yale University Press, 1961.

Rokeach, M. *Beliefs, Attitudes, and Values: A Theory of Organization and Change*. San Francisco: Jossey-Bass, 1968.

Rokeach, M. "Part 1: Value Systems and Religion." *Review of Religious Research*, Fall 1969a, *11*, 1–23.

Rokeach, M. "Part 2: Religious Values and Social Compassion." *Review of Religious Research*, Fall 1969b, *11*, 24–39.

Rorabaugh, W. J. *The Alcoholic Republic: An American Tradition*. New York: Oxford University Press, 1979.

Rotter, J. "Generalized Expectancies for Internal Versus External Control of Reinforcement." *Psychological Monographs*, 1966, 80 (entire issue 1).

Ryan, W. *Blaming the Victim*. New York: Vintage Books, 1971.

Ryan, W. *Equality*. New York: Pantheon Books, 1981.

Sampson, E. E. "The Decentralization of Identity: Toward a Revised Concept of Personal and Social Order." *American Psychologist*, 1985, *40*(11), 1203–1211.

Schaeffer, P. "Presbyterians Disagree over New Work Ethic." Commentary on the report *Vocation and Work*. *Religious News Service*, July 29, 1991, p. 8.

Schervish, P. "Just Compensation: Application and Implication of Catholic Social Teaching." *Social Thought*, 1991, *17*(4), 4–15.

Schlesinger, A. M., Jr. *The Crisis of the Old Order*. Boston: Houghton Mifflin, 1957.

Schrag, P. *The Decline of the Wasp*. New York: Simon & Schuster, 1970.

Schuman, H. "The Religious Factor in Detroit: Review, Replication and Reanalysis." *American Sociological Review*, 1971, *36*(1), 30–47.

Schwab, G. "Catholic Auspice of Human Service Organizations." Unpublished manuscript, Ann Arbor, Michigan, 1991.

Simon, W., and Novak, M. "Liberty and Justice for All." In J. Finn (ed.), *Private Virtue and Public Policy*. New Brunswick, N.J.: Transaction, 1990.

Sinclair, U. *The Jungle*. Cambridge, Mass.: R. Bentley, 1971.

Smetana, J. G. "Caring About Care." Review of *Who Cares?* by M. M. Brabeck. *Contemporary Psychology*, 1991, *36*(6), 493–494.

Spikard, J. Z. "Experiencing Religious Rituals." *Sociological Analysis*, 1991, *52*(2), 191–204.

Steers, R., and Porter, L. *Motivation and Work Behavior*. (5th ed.) New York: McGraw-Hill, 1991.

Steffens, L. *The Shame of the Cities*. New York: McClure, Phillips, 1905.

Steidlmeier, P. "Does Caring Equal a Concern for Social Justice?" Review of *What Does the Lord Require? How American Christians Think About Social Justice*, by S. Hart. *Nonprofit and Voluntary Sector Quarterly*, 1994, *23*(2), 182–187.

Stinchcomb, A. J. "Social Structure in Organizations." In J. G. March (ed.), *Handbook of Organizations*. Skokie, Ill.: Rand McNally, 1965.

Tannen, D. *You Just Don't Understand*. New York: Morrow, 1990.

Tawney, R. H. *The Acquisitive Society*. Orlando, Fla.: Harcourt Brace Jovanovich, 1948.

ter Voert, M. "The Effect of Religion on Work Attitudes in the Netherlands." Paper presented at the 21st International Conference for the Sociology of Religion, Aug. 1991, Maynooth, Ireland.

Thurow, L. *Head to Head*. New York: Morrow, 1992

Tönnies, F. *Community & Society (Gemeinschaft und Gesellschaft)*. (C. P. Loomis, ed. & trans.) (2nd ed.) East Lansing: Michigan State University Press, 1957. (Originally published 1887.)

Troeltsch, E. *The Social Teachings of the Christian Churches*. 2 vols. New York: HarperCollins, 1960. (Originally published 1911.)

Tropman, E. J., and Tropman, J. E. "Voluntary Agencies." In A. Minahan (ed.), *The Encyclopedia of Social Work*. Silver Spring, Md.: National Association of Social Workers, 1987.

Tropman, J. E. "The 'Catholic Ethic' Versus the 'Protestant Ethic': Catholic Social Service and the Welfare State." *Social Thought*, 1986, *12*(1), 13–22.

Tropman, J. E. *Public Policy Opinion and the Elderly*. Westport, Conn.: Greenwood Press, 1987.

Tropman, J. E. *American Values and Social Welfare: Cultural Contradictions in the Welfare State*. Englewood Cliffs, N.J.: Prentice Hall, 1989.

Varenne, H. Review of *Money, Morals and Manners: The Culture of the French and the American Upper Middle Class*, by M. Lamont. *Contemporary Sociology*, 1993, *22*(4), 600.

Vidich, A., and Bensman, J. *Small Town in Mass Society*. (Rev. ed.) Princeton, N.J.: Princeton University Press, 1968.

Watson, S. "Feast and Famine Shade Marriage." *Detroit Free Press*, Aug. 9, 1991, p. C1.

Weber, M. *The Protestant Ethic and the Spirit of Capitalism*. (T. Parsons, trans.) New York: Charles Scribner's Sons, 1956. (Originally published 1904–1905.)

Welch, C. *Protestant Thought in the Nineteenth Century: 1799–1870*. Vol. 1. New Haven, Conn.: Yale University Press, 1972.

Welch, W. "States Forging Ahead on Welfare Reform." *USA Today*, Aug. 13, 1993, p. 6A.

White, R., and Hopkins, C. H. *The Social Gospel: Religion and Reform in Changing America*. Philadelphia: Temple University Press, 1976.

Whitney, C. R. "In Europe, Touches of Leanness and Meanness." *New York Times*, Jan. 1, 1995, p. E5.

Wilensky, H. L. "Leftism, Catholicism, and Democratic Corporatism: The Role of Political Parties in Recent Welfare State Development." In P. Flora and A. J. Heidenheimer (eds.), *The Development of Welfare States in Europe and America*. New Brunswick, N.J.: Transaction, 1981.

Williams, R. M., Jr. *American Society*. (2nd ed.) New York: Knopf, 1960.

Wilson, J. Review of *Christianity in the Twenty-First Century*, by R. Wuthnow. *Contemporary Sociology*, 1994, *23*(3) 439–441.

Wolff, K. (ed. and trans.). *The Sociology of Georg Simmel*. New York: Free Press, 1950.

Wollack, S., Goodale, J., Wijting, J., and Smith, P. "Development of the Survey of Work Values." *Journal of Applied Psychology*, 1971, *53*(4), 331–338.

Woodward, K. L. Review of *Encountering Mary*, by S. L. Zimdars-Swartz. *New York Times Book Review*, Aug. 11, 1991, p. 1ff.

Wortman, C. "Causal Attributions and Personal Control." In J. Harvey and W. J.

Ickes, *New Directions in Attribution Research*. Vol. 1. Hillsdale, N.J.: Erlbaum, 1976.

Yankelovich, D. *New Rules*. New York: Random House, 1981.

Yankelovich, D., and Immerwahr, J. "Putting the Work Ethic to Work. *Society*, Jan./Feb. 1984, *21*, 58–76.

Zangwill, I. *The Melting Pot*. New York: Macmillan, 1922.

Zehnder, R. "Religious Opinion." *Independent Times* (Ann Arbor), 1994, *5*(3), p. 4.

# Suggested Readings

Baltzell, E. D. *The Protestant Establishment: Aristocracy and Caste in America*. New York: Random House, 1964

Bellah, R., and Hammond, P. *Varieties of Civil Religion*. San Francisco: HarperSanFrancisco, 1980.

Bem, D. *Beliefs, Attitudes, and Human Affairs*. Pacific Grove, Calif.: Brooks/Cole, 1970.

Beveridge, W. *Social Insurance and Allied Services*. New York: Macmillan, 1942.

Bishop, K. "Vouchers Place Money in the Hands of the Needy, Instead of the Greedy." *The New York Times*, July 26, 1991, p. 2.

Duncan, G., and Hill, M. "Attitudes, Behaviors, and Economic Outcomes." In G. Duncan and J. Morgan (eds.), *Five Thousand American Families*. Vol. 3. Ann Arbor, Mich.: Institute of Social Research, 1975.

Durkheim, E. *Suicide*. (J. A. Spaulding and G. Simpson, trans.) New York: Free Press, 1951.

Fanfani, A. "Catholicism, Protestantism, and Capitalism." In R. Green, *Protestantism and Capitalism: The Weber Theses and Its Critics*. Lexington, Mass.: Heath, 1959.

Fanfani, A. *Catholicism, Protestantism, and Capitalism*. Reappraisal and introductions by M. Novak and C. K. Wilbur. Notre Dame, Ind.: University of Notre Dame Press, 1984.

Furnham, A. "The Protestant Work Ethic: A Review of the Psychological Literature." *European Journal of Social Psychology*, 1984, *14*, 87–104.

Gallup, G., Jr. and Castelli, J. *The People's Religion*. New York: Macmillan, 1989.

Gallup, G., Jr. and Jones, S. *100 Questions & Answers: Religion in America*. Princeton, N.J.: Hermitage Press, 1989.

Garvin, C., and Tropman, J. E. *Social Work: An Introduction*. Englewood Cliffs, N.J.: Prentice Hall, forthcoming.

Gilbert, N. *Capitalism and the Welfare State: Dilemmas of Benevolence*. New Haven, Conn.: Yale University Press, 1983.

Gilder, G. *Wealth and Poverty*. New York: Basic Books, 1981.

Ginzberg, L. *Women and the Work of Benevolence: Morality, Politics and Class in the 19th Century United States*. New Haven, Conn.: Yale University Press, 1990.

Girvetz, H. "Welfare State." In D. L. Sills (ed.), *International Encyclopedia of the Social Sciences*. Vol. 16. New York: Macmillan/Free Press, 1968.

Glazer, N. *American Judaism*. (2nd ed.) Chicago: University of Chicago Press, 1972.

Glock, C. Y., and Stark, R. *Christian Beliefs and Anti-Semitism*. New York: Harper-Collins, 1966.

Gonsalves, S., and Goowin, B. "The Protestant Ethic and Conservatism Scales." *High School Journal*, 1984, 68(4), 247–253.

Gorrell, D. K. *The Age of Social Responsibility: The Social Gospel in the Progressive Era, 1900–1920*. Macon, Ga.: Mercer University Press, 1988.

Greeley, A. M. *The American Catholic*. New York: Basic Books, 1977.

Greeley, A. M. "Quadragesimo Anno After Fifty Years." *America*, Aug. 1–8, 1981, pp. 46–49.

Greeley, A. M. *Happy Are Those Who Thirst for Justice*. New York: Warner, 1987.

Greeley, A. M. "Evidence That a Maternal Image of God Correlates With Liberal Politics." *Sociology and Social Research*, 1988, 72(3), 150–154.

Greeley, A. M. "Protestant and Catholic: Is the Analogical Imagination Extinct?" *American Sociological Review*, 1989, 36(4), 485–502.

Greeley, A. M. *Religious Change in America*. Cambridge, Mass.: Harvard University Press, 1989.

Greeley, A. M. "Who Are the Catholic 'Conservatives'?" *America*, 1991, Sept. 21, pp. 158–162.

Greeley, A. M. "With God on Their Sides." Review of *Culture Wars*, by J. D. Hunter. *New York Times Book Review*, Nov. 24, 1991, pp. 13–14.

Greeley, A. M. "The Protestant Ethic: Time for a Moratorium." *Sociological Analysis*, Spring 1994, 24, 20–33.

Greenberg, J. "The Protestant Ethic and Reactions to the Negative Performance Evaluations on a Laboratory Task." *Journal of Applied Psychology*, 1977, 62(6), 682–690.

Greenberg, J. "Protestant Ethic Endorsement and Attitudes Toward Commuting to Work Among Mass Transit Riders." *Journal of Applied Psychology*, 1978, 63(6), 755–758.

Greenberg, J. "Protestant Ethic Endorsement and the Fairness of Equity Inputs." *Journal of Research in Personality* 1979, 13(1), 81–90.

Gronbjerg, K. A. *Mass Society and the Extension of Welfare, 1960–1970*. Chicago: University of Chicago Press, 1977.

Hadden, J. *The Gathering Storm in the Churches*. New York: Doubleday, 1969.

Hammond, P., and Williams, K. "The Protestant Ethic Thesis: A Social Psychological Assessment." *Social Forces*, 1976, 54(3), 579–589.

Handler, J., and Hasenfeld, Y. *The Moral Construction of Poverty*. Newbury Park, Calif.: Sage, 1991.

Hartz, L. *The Liberal Tradition in America: An Interpretation of American Political Thought Since the Revolution.* Orlando, Fla.: Harcourt Brace Jovanovich, 1955.

Hasenfeld, Y. Review of *The New Politics of Poverty,* by L. Mead. *Contemporary Sociology,* 1993, *22*(3), 376–377.

Heilbroner, R. L. "Benign Neglect in the United States." *Transaction,* 1970, 7(12), 15–22.

Hennesey, J. *American Catholics: The History of the Roman Catholic Community in the United States.* New York: Oxford University Press, 1981.

Henriot, P. J., DeBerri, E. P., and Schultheis, M. J. *Catholic Social Teaching: Our Best Kept Secret.* Maryknoll, N.Y.: Orbis, 1990.

Heppenheimer, T. A. "The Man Who Made Los Angles Possible." *Invention and Technology,* 1991, 7(1) 11–18.

Himmelfarb, G. *The Idea of Poverty.* New York: Knopf, 1984.

Himmelfarb, G. *Poverty and Compassion.* New York: Knopf, 1991.

Hirschman, A. O. *Exit, Voice, and Loyalty: Responses to Decline in Firms, Organizations, and States.* Cambridge, Mass.: Harvard University Press, 1970.

Hirschman, A. O. *Shifting Involvements: Private Interests and Public Action.* Princeton, N.J.: Princeton University Press, 1982.

Hobgood, M. *Catholic Social Teaching and Economic Theory: Paradigms in Conflict.* Philadelphia: Temple University Press, 1991.

Hochschild, A. R. *The Managed Heart.* Berkeley: University of California Press, 1983.

Hoff, M. "Response to the Catholic Bishop's Letter on the Economy." *Social Thought.* Winter 1989, pp. 41–52.

Hofstader, R. *The Age of Reform.* New York: Vintage Books, 1955.

Hollenbach, D. *Claims in Conflict.* New York: Paulist Press, 1979.

Holt, A. E. *Social Work in the Churches: A Study in the Practice of Fellowship.* Boston: Pilgrim Press, 1922.

Hoover, A. J. "Religion and National Stereotypes: A German Protestant Example." *History of European Ideas,* 1987, 8(3), 297–308.

Inglehart, R. *Culture Shift.* Princeton, N.J.: Princeton University Press, 1990.

Janowitz, M. *The Last Half Century: Societal Change in Politics in America.* Chicago: University of Chicago Press, 1978.

Jansson, B. *The Reluctant Welfare State.* Belmont, Calif.: Wadsworth, 1988.

John Paul II. *On Human Work.* Washington, D. C.: United States Catholic Conference, 1981.

Kahn, A. J. (ed.). *Issues in American Social Work.* New York: Columbia University Press, 1959.

Kammer, F. *Doing Faith Justice: An Introduction to Catholic Social Thought.* New York: Paulist Press, 1991.

Kersten, L. L. *The Lutheran Ethic: The Impact of Religion on Laymen and Clergy.* Detroit: Wayne State University Press, 1970.

Kirschner, D. S. *The Paradox of Professionalism: Reform and Public Service in Urban America, 1900–1940.* Westport, Conn.: Greenwood Press, 1986.

Klebaner, B. "Poverty and Its Relief in American Thought, 1815–61." *Social Service Review,* 1964, 38(4), 382–399.

Knadler, A. "Help Seeking as a Cultural Phenomenon: Differences Between City and Kibbutz Dwellers." *Journal of Personality and Social Psychology,* 1986, 51(5), 976–982.

Knudsen, D., Earle, J., and Schriver, D., Jr. "The Conception of Sectarian Religion: An Effort at Clarification." *Review of Religious Research,* 1978, 20, 44–60.

Kohn, A. *No Contest.* Boston: Houghton Mifflin, 1986.

Ladd, E. C. "Americans at Work." *Public Opinion,* Aug./Sept. 1981, 4, 21–40.

Lawrence, W. "The Relation of Wealth to Morals." In G. Kennedy (ed.), *Democracy and the Gospel of Wealth.* Lexington, Mass.: Heath, 1948.

Lay Commission on Catholic Social Teaching and the U.S. Economy. *Toward the Future: Catholic Social Thought and the U.S. Economy.* New York: American Catholic Committee, 1984.

Leege, D. "Parish Organizations: People's Needs, Parish Services, And Leadership." In *Notre Dame Study of Catholic Parish Life.* Report 8. Notre Dame, Ind.: University of Notre Dame, 1986.

Leege, D. "Parish As Community." In *Notre Dame Study of Catholic Parish Life.* Report 10. Notre Dame, Ind.: University of Notre Dame, 1987.

Leiby, J. "Moral Foundations of Social Welfare and Social Work: A Historical View." *Social Work,* 1985, 30(4), 323–330.

Lenski, G. "The Religious Factor in Detroit: Revisited." *American Sociological Review,* 1971, 36(1), 48–50.

Lerner, R. L. "A Case of Religious Counter-Culture: The German Waldensians." *American Scholar,* 1986, 55(2), 234–247.

Levi, W. *From Alms to Liberation: The Catholic Church, the Theologians, Poverty, and Politics.* New York: Praeger, 1989.

Liebman, R. C., Sutton, J. R., and Wuthnow, R. "Exploring the Social Sources of Denominationalism." *American Sociological Review,* 1988, 53(3), 343–352.

Liebman, R. C., and Wuthnow, R. *The New Christian Right.* New York: Aldine, 1983.

Liebow, E. *Tell Them Who I Am: The Lives of Homeless Women.* New York, Free Press, 1993.

Linder, R. *The Fifty-Minute Hour: A Collection of Psychoanalytic Tales.* Troy, Mo.: Holt, Rinehart & Winston, 1954.

Lipset, S. M., and Bendix, R. *Social Mobility in Industrial Society.* Berkeley: University of California Press, 1959.

Little, K. *Maria M. Love: The Life and Legacy of a Social Work Pioneer.* New York: Western New York Heritage Institute, 1994.

McIntosh, W. A., and Alston, J. P. "Lenski Revisited: The Linkage Role of Religion in Primary and Secondary Groups." *American Journal of Sociology,* 1982, *87,* 852–882.

MacIntyre, A. *After Virtue.* Notre Dame, Ind.: University of Notre Dame Press, 1981.

McJimsey, G. *Harry Hopkins: Ally of the Poor and Defender of Democracy.* Cambridge, Mass.: Harvard University Press, 1987.

Malinowsky, B. *Magic, Science and Religion and Other Essays.* (Selected by and with an introduction by R. Redfield.) Boston: Beacon Press, 1948.

Marciniac, E. "Toward a Catholic Work Ethic." *Origins,* Feb. 25, 1988, pp. 631–637.

Marshall, G. *Presbyteries and Profits: Calvinism and the Development of Capitalism in Scotland: 1560 to 1707.* New York: Oxford University Press/Clarendon Press, 1980.

Martin, R. K. *Social Theory and Social Structure.* (Rev. ed.) New York: Free Press, 1957.

May, H. F. *The Enlightenment in America.* New York: Oxford University Press, 1976.

Mead, L. *The New Politics of Poverty.* New York: Basic Books, 1992.

Merrens, M., and Garrett, J. B. "The Protestant Ethic Scale as a Predictor of Repetitive Work Performance." *Journal of Applied Psychology,* 1975, *60*(1), 125–127.

Merton, R. *Social Theory and Social Structure.* (Rev. ed.) New York: Free Press, 1957.

Miller, W. B. "Implications of Urban Lower-Class Culture for Social Work." *Social Service Review,* 1959, *33*(3), 219–236.

Miller, W. C. *A Handbook of American Minorities* New York: New York University Press, 1976.

Mills, C. W. *The Power Elite.* New York: Oxford University Press, 1956.

Mirels, H. L., and Darland, D. M. "The Protestant Ethic and Self Characterization." *Personality and Individual Differences,* 1990, *11*(9), 895–898.

Mirels, H. L., and Garret, J. "The Protestant Ethic as a Personality Variable." *Journal of Consulting & Clinical Psychology,* 1971, *36*(1), 40–44.

Montgomery, J. D. "Programs and Poverty: Federal Aid in the Domestic and International Systems." *Public Policy,* 1970, *18*(4), 517–537. Reprinted in J. E. Tropman and others (eds.), *Strategic Perspectives on Social Policy.* New York: Pergamon Press, 1976.

Mooney, C. F. *Public Virtue: Law and the Social Character of Religion.* Notre Dame, Ind.: University of Notre Dame Press, 1986.

Mosqueda, L. *Chicanos, Catholicism, and Political Ideology.* Lanham, Md.: University Press of America, 1986.

Mullin, R. B. *Episcopal Vision/American Reality.* New Haven, Conn.: Yale University Press, 1986.

Murray, C. *Losing Ground: American Social Policy, 1950–1980.* New York: Basic Books, 1984.

Nadler, A. "Help Seeking As a Cultural Phenomenon." *American Psychologist,* 1986 52(5), 976–982.

Nash, R. H. *Poverty and Wealth: The Christian Debate Over Capitalism.* Westchester, Ill.: Good News/Crossway, 1986.

National Conference of Catholic Charities. *A Code of Ethics.* Washington, D.C.: National Conference of Catholic Charities, 1983.

Newman, J. "Jews Against Catholics?" *Mainstream,* Jan. 1986, pp. 44–51.

Niebuhr, H. R. *The Social Sources of Denominationalism.* Cleveland, Ohio: World Publishing Company/Meridian Books, 1959. (Originally published 1929.)

Niebuhr, R. *Beyond Tragedy: Essays on the Christian Interpretation of History.* New York: Charles Scribner's Sons, 1937.

Nussbaum, M. "Recoiling from Reason." *The New York Review,* Dec. 7, 1989, pp. 36–41.

Odendahl, T. *Charity Begins at Home: Generosity and Self-Interest Among the Philanthropic Elite.* New York: Basic Books, 1990.

Offe, C. *Contradictions of the Welfare State.* (J. Keane, ed.) Cambridge, Mass.: MIT Press, 1984.

O'Grady, J. *Catholic Charities in the United States.* Washington, D.C.: National Conference of Catholic Charities, 1930.

Organization for Economic Cooperation and Development, *The Welfare State in Crisis.* Paris: Organization for Economic Cooperation and Development, 1981.

Orloff, A. S., and Skocpol, T. "Why Not Equal Protection? Explaining the Politics of Public Social Spending." *American Sociological Review,* 1984, 49(6), 726–750.

Ouchi, W. *Theory Z.* New York: Bantam, 1981.

Paglia, C. "The Joy of Presbyterian Sex." *The New Republic,* December 2, 1991, pp. 24–27.

Palmer, P. J. *To Know as We Are Known.* San Francisco: HarperCollins, 1983.

Palmer, P. J. *The Active Life.* San Francisco: HarperCollins, 1990.

Paz, O. *The Labyrinth of Solitude.* New York: Garwood Press, 1985.

Philbrick, J. L. "The Protestant Ethic in East Africa." *Psychologica Africana,* 1976, 16(3), 173–175.

Pieper, J. *Belief and Faith.* New York: Pantheon Books, 1963.

Pines, A., and Kafry, D. "Tedium in the Life and Work of Professional Women as Compared with Men." *Sex Roles,* 1981, 7(10), 963–977.

Piven, F., and Cloward, R. *Regulating the Poor: The Function of Public Welfare.* New York: Pantheon, 1971

Pope, L. *Millhands and Preachers* New Haven, Conn.: Yale University Press, 1942.

Quadagno, J. S. "Welfare Capitalism and the Social Security Act of 1935." *American Sociological Review*, 1984, 49(5), 445–446.

Quatrochocchi, S. "Fringe Benefits as Private Social Policy." In J. E. Tropman, M. Dluhy, and R. Lind (eds.), *New Strategic Perspectives on Social Policy*. Elmsford, N.Y.: Pergamon Press, 1984.

Ray, J. J. "The Protestant Ethic in Australia." *Journal of Social Psychology*, 1982, 116(1), 127–138.

Reich, R. *The Next American Frontier*. New York: Times Books, 1983.

Rischin, M. *The American Gospel of Success: Individualism and Beyond*. Chicago: Quadrangle Books, 1965.

Roberts, J. D. *Black Theology Today*. New York: Mellen, 1983.

Roberts, K. *Religion in Sociological Perspective*. (2nd ed.) Belmont, Calif.: Wadsworth, 1990.

Rojak, D. C. "The Protestant Ethic and Political Preference." *Social Forces*, 1973, 52(2), 168–177.

Roof, W., and McKinney, W. *American Mainline Religion: Its Changing Shape and Future*. New Brunswick, N.J.: Rutgers University Press, 1987.

Root, L. "Employee Benefits and Income Security: Private Social Policy and the Public Interest." In J. E. Tropman, M. Dluhy, and R. Lind (eds.), *New Strategic Perspectives on Social Policy*. Elmsford, N.Y.: Pergamon Press, 1984.

Rose, R. L. "Milwaukee Prelate Irks Conservative Catholics with Abortion Stance." *The Wall Street Journal*, July 11, 1991, p. 1.

Rotenberg, M. "The Protestant Ethic Against the Spirit of Psychiatry: The Other Side of Weber's Thesis." *British Journal of Sociology*, 1975, 26(1), 52–65.

Rothman, D. J., and Wheeler, S. (eds.), *Social History and Social Policy*. San Diego, Calif.: Academic Press, 1981.

Russell, J. R. *The Devil: Perceptions of Evil from Antiquity to Primitive Christianity*. Ithaca, N.Y.: Cornell University Press, 1977.

Ryle, E. J. "Catholic Social Thought and the New Federalism." *Center Journal*, Summer, 1983, pp. 9–36.

Ryle, E. J. "Attitudes Toward the Poor and Public Policy Development." In M. J. Kelly (ed.), *Justice and Health Care*. St. Louis, Mo.: Catholic Health Care Association of the U.S., 1985.

Ryle, E. J. "Option for the Poor in Catholic Charities: Policy and the Social Teaching of John Paul II." *Social Thought*, Spring/Summer 1987, pp. 139–149.

Sachar, H. M. *The Course of Modern Jewish History*. (Rev. ed.) New York: Vintage Books, 1990.

Sandeen, E. R. (ed.). *The Bible and Social Reform*. Philadelphia: Fortress Press, 1982.

Santayana, G. *Persons and Places: The Background of My Life*. New York: Charles Scribner's Sons, 1944.

Saveth, E. "Patrician Philanthropy in America: The Late Nineteenth and Early Twentieth Centuries." *Social Service Review*, 1980, *54*(1), 76–91.

Schaeffer, F. *A Christian Manifesto*. Westchester, Ill.: Crossway Books, 1981.

Schiller, B. R. "Relative Earnings Mobility in the United States." *American Economic Review*, 1977, *67*(5), 926–941.

Schuman, H., and Johnson, M. "Attitudes and Behavior." In *Annual Review of Sociology*. Vol. 2. San Francisco: Annual Reviews, 1976.

Segalman, R. "The Protestant Ethic in Social Welfare." *Journal of Social Issues*, 1968, *24*(1), 125–141.

Sen, A. "Individual Freedom as a Social Commitment." *The New York Review*. June 14, 1990, pp. 49–54.

Shapiro, H. "Philanthropy: Tradition and Change." In H. Shapiro (ed.), *Tradition and Change*. Ann Arbor: University of Michigan Press, 1987.

Shelton, C. M. *In His Steps*. Springdale, Pa.: Whitaker House, n.d. (Originally published 1897.)

Sherrill, R. A. (ed.). *Religion in the Life of the Nation: American Recoveries*. Urbana: University of Illinois Press, 1990.

Shils, E., and Young, M. "The Meaning of the Coronation." In E. Shils, *Center and Periphery: Essays in Macro-Sociology*. Chicago: University of Chicago Press, 1975.

Siegelman, E. *Prejudice USA*. New York: Praeger, 1969.

Skinner, B. F. *Beyond Freedom and Dignity*. New York: Bantam, 1971.

Slater, P. E. *The Pursuit of Loneliness: American Culture at the Breaking Point*. Boston: Beacon Press, 1970.

Smith, H. *The Religions of Man*. New York: HarperCollins/Perennial Library, 1986.

Smith, T. L. *Revivalism and Social Reform*. New York: Abington Press, 1957.

Sombart, W. *The Jews and Modern Capitalism*. London: Unwin, 1913.

Sonnenfeld, J. "Commentary: Academic Learning, Worker Learning, and the Hawthorne Studies." *Commentary*, 1983, *61*(3), 904–909.

Stark, R. "Rokeach, Religion, and Reviewers: Keeping an Open Mind." *Review of Religious Research*, Winter 1970, *11*, 151–154.

Stark, R., and Glock, C. *American Piety: The Nature of Religious Commitment*. Berkeley: The University of California Press, 1968.

Stead, W. *If Christ Came to Chicago*. New York: Living Books, 1964.

Stein, J. *Fiddler on the Roof*. New York: Washington Square Press, 1964.

Stephens, R., Metz, L., and Craig, J. "The Protestant Ethic Effect in a Multi-choice Environment." *Bulletin of the Psychonomic Society* 1975, *6*(2), 137–139.

Stokes, R. G. "Afrikaner Calvinism and Economic Action: The Weberian Thesis in South Africa." *American Journal of Sociology*, 1975, *81*(1), 62–81.

Susman, W. *Culture as History: The Transformation of American Society in the Twentieth Century*. New York: Pantheon, 1984.

Swatos, W. H., Jr. (ed.). *Religious Sociology: Interfaces and Boundaries*. Westport, Conn.: Greenwood Press, 1987.

Swedenborg, E. *Heavenly Secrets*. New York: Swedenborg Foundation, 1985.

Tamney, J., Burton, R., and Johnson, S. "Christianity, Social Class, and the Catholic Bishop's Economic Policy." *Sociological Analysis*, Spring 1988, *49*, 78–96.

Tawney, R. H. *Religion and the Rise of Capitalism*. London: Murray, 1926.

Taylor, G. R. *Sex in History*. New York: Vanguard, 1954.

Tichy, N., and Devanna, M. A. *The Transformational Leader*. New York: Wiley, 1986.

Tiryakian, E. A. "Puritan America in the Modern World: Mission Impossible." *Sociological Analysis*, 1982, *43*(4), 351–368.

Tönnies, F. *On Sociology: Pure, Applied, and Empirical*. Chicago: University of Chicago Press, 1971.

Tracy, D. *The Analogical Imagination*. New York: Crossroads, 1989.

Trevor-Roper, H. *Catholics, Anglicans, and Puritans*. Chicago: University of Chicago Press, 1988.

Tropman, J. E. "The Constant Crisis." *California Sociologist*, 1978, *1*(1), 1978.

Tropman, J. E. "Copping Out or Chipping In." *The Humanist*, 1981, *41*(2), 43–46.

Tropman, J. E., and Morningstar, G. *Entrepreneurial Systems for the 1990s*. Westport, Conn.: Quorum, 1989.

Underhill, E. *Worship*. New York: HarperCollins, 1936.

Vaill, P. B. *Managing as a Performing Art: New Ideas for a World of Chaotic Change*. San Francisco: Jossey-Bass, 1989.

Vande Kemp, H. *Psychology and Theology in Western Thought: 1672–1965*. Millwood, N.Y.: Kraus, 1984.

Vandewiele, M., and Philbrick, J. "The Protestant Ethic in West Africa." *Psychological Reports*, 1986, *58*(3), 946.

Wald, K. *Religion and Politics in the United States*. New York: St. Martin's Press, 1987.

Wallace, R. "The Secular Ethic and the Spirit of Patriotism." *Sociological Analysis*, 1973, *34*(1), 3–11.

Walsh, T. J. *Nano Nagle and the Presentation Sisters*. County Kildare, Ireland: Presentation Generalate, Monasterevan: 1980. (Originally published 1959.)

Waterman, A. S. "Individualism and Interdependence." *The American Psychologist*, 1981, *36*(7), 762–773.

Waters, L. K., Batlis, N., and Waters, C. "Protestant Ethic Attitudes Among College Students." *Educational and Psychological Measurement* 1975, *35*(2), 447–450.

Weber, M. *From Max Weber*. (H. Gearth and C. W. Mills, trans.) New York: Oxford University Press, 1946.

Weber, M. *The Sociology of Religion*. (E. Fischoff, trans.) New York: Beacon, 1963.

Weigel, G., and Royal, R. *A Century of Catholic Social Thought*. Washington, D.C.: Ethics and Public Policy Center, 1991.

Welch, C. *Protestant Thought in the Nineteenth Century: 1799–1870*. Vol. 2. New Haven, Conn.: Yale University Press, 1972.

Wiesel, E. *Souls on Fire: Portraits and Legends of Hasidic Masters*. New York: Random House, 1972.

Wilbur, K. *A Sociable God*. New York: New Press/McGraw Hill, 1983.

Wilkes, P. "The Education of an Archbishop: 1." *The New Yorker*, July 15, 1991, pp. 37–59.

Wilkes, P. "The Education of an Archbishop: 2." *The New Yorker*, July 22, 1991, pp. 46–65.

Will, G. "A Sterner Kind of Caring." *Newsweek*, Jan. 13, 1992, p. 68.

Williams, C. "The Work Ethic: Non-Work and Leisure in an Age of Automation." *The Australian and New Zealand Journal of Sociology*, 1983, *19*(2), 216–237.

Wills, G. *Under God: Religion and Politics in America*. New York: Simon & Schuster, 1990.

Winslow, O. E. (ed.). *Jonathan Edwards: Basic Writings*. New York: New American Library, 1966.

Wolcott, R. T., and Bolger, D. F. (comp.). *Church and Social Action: A Critical Assessment and Bibliographical Survey*. Westport, Conn.: Greenwood Press, 1990.

Wolfensberger, W. *The Principles of Normalization in the Human Services*. Toronto: Leonard/Crawford/National Institute of Mental Retardation, 1972.

Wood, J. R. *Leadership in Voluntary Organizations: The Controversy over Social Action in Protestant Churches*. New Brunswick, N.J.: Rutgers University Press, 1981.

Wuthnow, R. *Communities of Discourse*. Cambridge, Mass.: Harvard University Press, 1989.

Wuthnow, R. *Acts of Compassion*. Princeton, N.J.: Princeton University Press, 1991.

Wuthnow, R., Hodgkinson, V. A., and Associates, *Faith and Philanthropy in America: Exploring the Role of Religion in America's Voluntary Sector*. San Francisco: Jossey-Bass, 1990.

Zaret, D. *The Heavenly Contract*. Chicago: University of Chicago Press, 1985.

# Index